WITH FREEDOM TO SINGAPORE

By

OSWALD W. GILMOUR

DEDICATION

To the memory of VIN to whom all men
were human and all things delightfully
absurd and to James and Balfour who with
the Author shared his comradeship in South
East Asia Command.

NOTE ON THE CURRENT TEXT

With Freedom to Singapore (1950) is a very different book to its predecessor, *Singapore to Freedom* (1943).

The earlier work, which detailed the author's flight before the Japanese troops invading Singapore in 1942, was promoted by the publisher as, "The vivid record of a great escape". It can still be enjoyed as a real-life adventure story to this day.

With Freedom to Singapore, released seven years later, is a very different genre of text, the publisher this time stressing its value to anyone seeking an understanding of the post-war situation in the rapidly diminishing British colonies:

> *Recent events show that the disturbing effects of the last war have been as serious in Malaya as in any country in the Far East. This book will prove of exceptional value to anyone who wishes to form an estimate of the present position in a country terrorised by bandits and torn by factions groping after some new political formula. It forms a backdrop to the day-to-day news from Singapore.*

> *But it may also be read for the story told here of a highly important task that faced the War Office after the fall of Singapore. The author carries his account from the early stages of the backroom planning to the last days of the Japanese occupation. He describes the*

Malayan scene following the arrival of the Allies; he tells us of the British effort to set the country on its feet again; and he weighs up the uncertainties of the future in the light of his twenty years' experience in the crossroads of South-East Asia.

With Freedom to Singapore *will revive old memories among those who have served in the Far East, and it will help to clarify the social and administrative problems of those who are serving there today.*

Thus, at the time of its first publishing, *With Freedom to Singapore* might have been appropriately classified under the rubric of "Politics & Current Affairs" and today—seventy years on—will find its place as an invaluable source document for any serious student of Singapore's past from World War Two through to the beginning of the 1950s.

In reproducing the work, I have maintained the 1950 first-edition's text almost exactly as it was written. Thus, it includes some antiquated spellings as well as language and attitudes that will be offensive perhaps to some 21st Century sensibilities. All images were also scanned from that edition.

Patrick Gilmour
Brooklyn, NY
November 2020

Table of Contents

COMMENT

SINGAPORE surrendered to the Japanese on February 15th, 1942, and was reoccupied by British Forces on September 5th, 1945.

In words such as those, history books of the distant future may, perhaps, record the fall of Singapore and its return to the Empire. History is a subject which expands in length and breadth as time goes on and none of it is ever superseded so that it can be omitted. British history of, say, the 10th century can be told in relatively few words as only a comparatively small number of people and a handful of countries were involved, but British history of the 20th century involves hundreds of millions of people and countries all over the earth. The ordinary pupil a hundred years hence will be unable to read or assimilate more than the major events of the 20th century and the student who wishes to go deeper will be forced, more than ever before, to turn to countless volumes to obtain the background and the make-up of history, the thinking, the planning, the multitude of small events which culminated in the results set down for the normal reader. Some more pretentious histories may record that, after the reoccupation, Singapore was governed by a Military Administration for a period and that this was replaced by a Civil Government on April 1st, 1946. One cannot expect greater detail than that, and yet many things happened in the world subsequent to February 1942, some of which had a direct and some an indirect bearing on the reoccupation and on the government of the Colony immediately after.

Singapore seldom appeared in the war news between its fall and the surrender of Japan three and a half years later. When mention was made of it, it was usually in connection with the many prisoners-of-war and civil internees incarcerated there. Possibly the only belligerent incidents reported were the several air-raids made by the American Air Force which concentrated its bombs on the civilian dock area, shipping and the Naval Base. At least two minor attacks of a different nature did take place but, so far as I am aware, they were not made public until hostilities ceased.

One was a viking deed of great daring but unfortunately tragic in its indirect consequences. A party led by Major I. Lyon,[1] who had escaped from Singapore in February 1942, returned there in September 1943, having sailed a captured Japanese fishing boat all the way from West Australia. The fishing boat was taken to within twenty-one miles of Singapore and then the raiders—for such they were—took to rubber canoes and, entering the harbour, sank seven Japanese ships, totalling 37,000 tons, with limpet bombs. All of the party got back safely to Australia after doing the round trip of over 4,000 miles through enemy controlled waters in 48 days.

The Japanese chose to assume that the damage to their shipping had resulted from fifth-column activities by the civilian internees. They raided the civil internment camp and took away a number of persons for questioning and torture. Some of these subsequently died as a result of the treatment they were subjected to. This raid on the camp occurred on October 10th, 1943, and afterwards became

---

[1] Throughout this book, servicemen are given the rank they held at the time of the narrative, though later most of them attained higher ranks.

known as the double-tenth raid, the phrase being copied from the name the Chinese give to their celebration of the birth of the Chinese Republic, which takes place on October 10th each year, that is on the tenth day of the tenth month.

Major Lyon endeavoured to repeat the performance some time later and, taking with him some of his former colleagues and some new men, reached Singapore waters. There his luck failed and his whole party of twenty-three met death. Thirteen were killed in a running fight and the remainder executed in Singapore.

The other incident was an attack of a similar nature but more orthodox. A midget submarine from the Navy carrying two men penetrated the defences of the Singapore Naval Base in July 1945 and, with limpet bombs, attacked Japanese shipping there. The raid was a conspicuous success from the point of view of damage done and this heroic deed was recognised after the war when the men responsible were decorated with the Victoria Cross.

These attacks, together with guerilla activity, if there was any on the island, virtually covered the belligerent side of the war so far as Singapore was directly concerned after February 1942, but they tell nothing of the design for reoccupation or of the island and its rehabilitation afterwards.

In the years preceding the surrender of Japan, much thought was given to both the military operation, which it was expected would be necessary to take the town, and to questions of staffing, administration and equipment after recapture in order that Singapore might be spared disease and unrest and be enabled to take its place as a base for further war operations as well as an exporting centre for some badly needed raw materials.

In the Middle Ages when knights were bold, the surrender and retaking of a town left, in most cases, little trace on the town. Buildings still stood except where, occasionally, they were burnt down. The administration and the services were of such a simple nature that an enemy occupation scarcely affected them. In those halcyon days, wars were between armies or, at any rate, armies in the field, and national victory did not depend to anything like the same extent on the civilian rear, its co-operation, its manufacturing capacity, its vision and its reservoir of administrative and technical ability.

To-day it is different and more complex. The occupation or reoccupation of a city brings innumerable problems. A city or town is a place where a large number of people live in a comparatively small area. This crowded life can only be achieved if there is a skilled administration backed by experts in many kinds of engineering, health, police duties, finance and so on. Without those, there will be disaster. When such a place changes hands, the former administrators and experts may no longer be there, and the machinery, records and supplies by which they maintained the life, health, comfort and usefulness of the inhabitants may be gone. It is no easy matter to replace them but replaced they must be, and that quickly, or disease, famine and revolution will result which, even apart from any humanitarian considerations, are the last things any invading force wants as they apply a very effective brake to its further operations. Important as it is to maintain the life and amenities in an occupied enemy city, it is even more important, from a long term point of view, when the city is a friendly one. It was of special importance in the case of Singapore where a large percentage of the people had no allegiance by birth to the incoming British Forces but was required to continue to live on British territory and, if possible, retain or acquire British sympathies.

A conquering force to-day must bring along with its fighting personnel another army of almost equal importance, an army with the skill and experience necessary to administer occupied territories with complicated modern needs. It must also lay on supplies adequate, at least, to prevent disease and unrest in the occupied centres of population.

At first sight, the organisation and supplies necessary for such a task in the case of a town of, say, a million people stagger the imagination. No haphazard thinking, no impromptu effort will suffice. The scale of requirements varies with a number of factors, some of which are the percentage of destruction to the town, the ability and willingness of the local people to cooperate in running the town and its amenities, the amount of food which is, or can be grown, locally, the supply of raw materials and the local capacity for production of engineering supplies and textiles. The climate is also important as it governs the scale of water supplies, clothes and shelter necessary; the races of people determine the types of food and other supplies which should be provided, and the facilities for transporting, importing and distribution have a bearing on everything.

When the Japanese occupied Singapore in February 1942, the Island was well stocked with food and other necessities of life and comfort. The scorched-earth policy had not been applied to the utility services nor to anything necessary for the peacetime running of the town. The skilled civilian officers were mostly there too and the Japanese used them, so the invader had a relatively simple job in keeping things going, especially as he adopted ruthless methods to attain his ends. Eventually he replaced

British skilled executives with his own nationals and the change in government was effected with the minimum interruption and upset. The conditions left to the Japanese after the 'biggest military defeat in British history' were such as did not hold them up for a moment in what was, from the point of view of territory occupied and time taken, perhaps the most extensive and amazing campaign in history.

Doubtless the Jap thought he had come to stay and he had the inestimable advantage of occupying an enemy town with everything there to enable the inhabitants to look after themselves if they cared to do so. He saw to it, that where it affected him, they did. Beyond that, he cared little if they starved or lacked necessities.

Britain never contemplated, not even in the dark days of 1942, leaving the Jap in possession but the same easy conditions could not be expected on regaining the town, nor could the Japanese attitude be adopted. Singapore had to be retaken sometime, possibly with great destruction, but the people were our own charge and there was a very grave responsibility towards them. They had to be freed from Japanese domination and they had to be put on their feet again. They would look to the British to restore their former standards of health, food, clothing and amenities or to improve on them. We could not let them down, if any effort of ours could prevent it. There could be no question of leaving them to take care of themselves after years of suppression and deprivation, nor of using them solely as a stepping-stone to other things. Our responsibility had to be discharged.

To discharge that responsibility required careful thought, intensive planning and hard work long before the day of liberation could be foreseen. The personal story in this book narrates a little of that planning and how it worked out, but does not presume to be an historical record.

Three years, six months and twenty-one days after Singapore surrendered to the Japanese it was reoccupied by British Forces in circumstances different to what had been contemplated up to a very short time before, but the planning and forethought were not in vain.

In 1942, certain events and journeyings[2] had brought me from the last hours of the old Singapore and deposited me in England. As I had previously spent many years in Singapore, I had a modicum of local knowledge and this asset assured me a place in "Operation Singapore"—if I may borrow an Army method of description. Thus on September 5th, 1945, when 'Shonan'[3] again became Singapore, I was there.

---

[2] See *Singapore to Freedom*, by the author.

[3] Name given by the Japanese to Singapore.

IN EXILE

THE manner of my return to Singapore was very different from the manner of my leaving. I have no quarrel with that!

How that return came about will appear later but, before it was accomplished, there were the intervening years when, in common with many others, I was a Malayan in exile. It is relevant to this book to look briefly at the community which shared that exile.

The Malayan community exiled during the Japanese occupation was composed partly of people who had been absent from the country on business or normal tropical leave when Japan, without declaring war, suddenly attacked and who, during the brief campaign, had been unable to return, and partly of those who had left the country and reached other lands while hostilities were in progress or immediately after they ceased.

In the last days of 1941 and the first weeks of 1942, while the Japanese were speeding down the Malay Peninsular, many women, especially those with children, voluntarily left Singapore. Some went to Britain but others, in the hope that they would be able to return soon, sought nearer countries such as Australia, India, Ceylon and South Africa.

When Singapore itself was besieged great numbers, who had stuck to their jobs or their husbands as long as seemed possible, were pressed by their menfolk and others to leave and were able to get away to a variety of places under great difficulties. At the eleventh hour and even after the surrender a fair number of both men and women left the island or were sent away in all kinds of small craft, from little steamships to rowing boats, in the hope that they could slip through enemy controlled waters. Many lost their lives, others were captured elsewhere and only a few succeeded in arriving at friendly ports.

In that way, such of the Malayan community, who were at liberty in 1942, were scattered widely over the free world. That world was not, on the whole, very pleasant to them. Individuals were sympathetic and helpful but the public in general was quite the reverse. It was galling to Malayans to hear the widespread, inaccurate and bitter accusations which were being cast at the civilian peoples of Malaya for alleged despicable conduct during the war in their country. They found it difficult to keep their tempers and calmly tell the truth about the unstinted, and often gallant, efforts of almost all the inhabitants. They frequently wondered what had happened to the British sense of fairness for, while British hearts bled for foreigners from Europe who had lost their countries, it was easy to gain the impression that they cared little and knew less about the men and women who built the Colonial Empire and, in the case of Malayans, upon whom tragedy had fallen. Malayans almost despaired of ever getting the truth across for, even when Cabinet Ministers went out of their way to say that the biggest military defeat in British history was in fact a military defeat and nothing else, the public scarcely seemed to hear.

After the fall of their country, by which they had lost all their possessions and, in many cases, had members of their family or relatives killed, missing or imprisoned, those at liberty had awakened from the shock only to find that the Malayan peoples were being used as scapegoats to explain the Japanese successes and many scurrilous and untrue things were being said about them. This vendetta reached such proportions that a minister of the Crown found it necessary to say in the House of Lords, "Much of that criticism is misdirected. It is mainly voiced by those who have no personal experience of the Colonies. Our failure is not administrative but military. We have no need to stand in a white sheet over our administration of Malaya." In the House of Commons a member said, "There is not the slightest thread of evidence that the European community in Malaya behaved otherwise than they were expected to behave. The male population was mobilised up to the age of 60 and all the women did hospital or A.R.P. work. All the talk about whisky swilling planters and 'blimp' Civil Servants is among the most disgusting things I have ever heard."

The dog having been given a bad name, the false stories and vile accusations lessened or became less audible with time and in their place a great silence seemed to fall on affairs of the Far East. True, the government kept reminding the public of that war and of the hard-pressed, ill-equipped forces in those regions but it seemed an uphill task to keep the British public as a whole interested in anything so far away. There was too much going on at its doorstep.

In spite of all, Malayan communities in free countries never faltered. Malaya seemed to have instilled an extraordinary loyalty among those who had lived and worked there and looked on it as their country. A complete stranger, who had travelled widely, said to me once, "I have never been to Malaya but I particularly want to go there. There must be something special about it for, although I have met folk from almost every Colony, none seems so loyal to their country, none adopts the name of the country to describe themselves, except Malayans. The British in Fiji do not call themselves Fijians nor do the

British in Burma call themselves Burmese but people of many races, including British, from Malaya, do call themselves Malayans."

Malayans who had lost all their possessions, their houses, their jobs, and often a member of their family and were living in vastly reduced circumstances and, in the case of women, sometimes on charity, bound themselves into Associations in England, Scotland, Ireland, Australia, New Zealand, South Africa, India and Ceylon and possibly in other places and sadly but confidently consoled each other and worked towards the day when Malaya would again be free.

Little news came through about prisoners-of-war or civil internees and what there was was unreliable. The number of missing about whom there was no news at all was appalling. Those of us who were at liberty were besieged with questions but, as during the last days of Singapore, everyone was too busy to know about anyone other than immediate associates, most of the questions went unanswered. Some of those questions are still unanswered.

Malayans in exile constantly followed the war news closely searching anxiously for any event or sign which might indicate that an attempt to re-occupy Malaya could be expected. For a long time there was little to encourage such a hope. By the autumn of 1943 the victories of Stalingrad and El Alamein were a year old and Italy had been eliminated from the Axis side but, in the East, there was little to rejoice at. Japan was still at the gates of Australia and India and had yet to make her biggest threat to the latter. It is true she had yielded ground to the Americans in the Pacific and had suffered a number of reverses at sea but her conquests and her prospects were substantially unassailed. Indeed it did not seem likely that any major effort would be made against Japan until victory in Europe was in sight and this was far from being the case. The defeat of Italy appeared to make little difference to German powers of resistance and Malayans could, as yet, see no distant glimmer of events which might eventually bring them back to their country.

Though only a few knew of it, it was about that time— Autumn 1943—that planning for the reoccupation of Malaya began in earnest and a new organisation for the purpose took form.

The following June saw the invasion of Western Europe commence on the Normandy beaches and this brought to all the hope of an early end to the European war, which to many was what really mattered. To Malayans, however, and those particularly interested in the Far East, it did not bring the end of the war into sight; they looked at it in a rather different way. It had long been held among them that there was no prospect of a big effort being made by Britain to recapture Malaya until the war in Europe was finished, and, in consequence, before the invasion of Europe, any serious attack on Malaya appeared very remote. Once the battle was joined in France, progress in the Far East seemed immeasurably nearer, and this hopeful feeling was encouraged by the then obvious success of America's island-hopping policy in the Pacific and by the check to Japan's big push on the Indian border.

Something to brighten the lives and hopes of Malayans, especially those with relatives or friends in Japanese hands, was, in 1944, long overdue. Since Japan's fateful attack, there had been little they could look on with pleasure or relief. Malayans had been kept in constant anxiety about relatives and friends in enemy hands or assumed to be so. The Japanese were so slow and so inaccurate in reporting prisoners-of-war and internees that many relatives were kept extremely long periods in suspense. It was also believed that deaths were frequently not reported, and, even after many months when letters or postcards had arrived, they had sometimes added to the uncertainty. John Smith, for example, had mentioned the death of his friend Tom Brown, but Tom Brown's relatives had heard nothing about it. Anxiety and horror were enhanced when reports of Japanese cruelties began to be published and one could read headlines such as "Jap cruelties to Prisoners", "Japs make British work as coolies" and "Britons tortured and starved". On February 28th, 1944, the Foreign Secretary in the House of Commons confirmed these anxieties. "I fear I have grave news to give the House", he said, and proceeded to disclose that the cheerful messages, contained in the large number of letters and postcards which had recently been received, were, in some cases at any rate, in terms dictated by the Japanese authorities. He said that the Japanese had hitherto withheld permission for neutral inspection of camps and neither the numbers of prisoners nor the names had been indicated. His Majesty's Government were satisfied that in Siam there were many thousands of prisoners from the British Commonwealth who were being compelled by the Japanese military to live under tropical jungle conditions, without adequate shelter, clothing, food or medical attention. Health was deteriorating, a high percentage was seriously ill and there had been some thousands of deaths.[4] The number of such deaths reported by the Japanese was just over a hundred. The Foreign Secretary also related a number of brutal outrages by the Japanese on prisoners in many parts of Asia, and indicated the deplorable condition of all Allied persons in their hands.

---

[4] The deaths eventually amounted to scores of thousands.

Towards the end of his speech he said, "Let the Japanese Government reflect in time to come that the record of their military authorities in this war will not be forgotten."

Those with their hearts in the Far East had indeed a heavy and unrelieved burden to bear. Unrelieved because there was no sign of anything happening which might bring an end to it and, also, because there did not seem to be much interest taken in the position. The British Army, nearest to Malaya, was nicknamed "the forgotten Army" and indeed, by the ordinary man in the street, it was forgotten. Not only the Forces, and the long road before them, were forgotten, Malaya itself seemed to have passed out of conversation and of peoples' minds. When in June 1944, Parliament met for a debate on the Colonies, only 50 members attended to consider the affairs of 60 million colonial people, and so another debate was held in July. It is little wonder that the thought uppermost in the minds of Malayans, on invasion day, was, "perhaps when Germany is finished something will be done about Japan". No matter how much they approved the strategy of the war generally, they could not help thinking that.

In the midst of the general hopefulness, stimulated by events in Europe in 1944 and early 1945, Malayans were not yet sanguine of a speedy recovery of Malaya, though every victory in Europe might bring victory in the East nearer. On September 27th, 1944, a "Service of Remembrance and Dedication" was held in St. Paul's Cathedral "on behalf of the Dioceses of Rangoon, Singapore, Labuan and Sarawak, Hong Kong and the Philippine Islands". The cathedral was packed and the Dean addressed the congregation at the start of the service in these words:

"Brethren, we are drawn together in this hallowed place on a rising tide of victory and hope to unite in commending to the care and mercy of Almighty God our fellow-countrymen and all other victims of aggression in the Far East, and in praying for their speedy deliverance and relief... we pledge ourselves to the offering of such services and sacrifices as may be required for the fulfilment of God's purpose and for the recovery of our brethren in His family..."

The main address was to have been given by the Archbishop of Canterbury, but, on account of his illness, the address which he had intended to give was delivered for him by the Bishop of London.

The service drew a large crowd to the great cathedral and most of it was composed of Malayans in exile, for London was their focal point. London is the only city in the British Isles with a real outward view. Other places have interests in the world outside, the large ports through their shipping, the manufacturing towns through their exports, but those interests are immediate and material and are usually concentrated on specific localities in certain parts of the world. London is interested in the whole earth materially, politically and culturally and it is, in the vast majority of cases, to London that people from abroad must come to settle their affairs or, when necessary, to get an understanding hearing.

Thus it was to London that most Malayans came. They came to get information, advice, help from the Colonial Office, the Association of British Malaya or other sympathetic bodies with Malayan connections. As the long three and a half years of their exile wore on they came in increasing numbers, especially women because, they argued, the time of liberation of their husbands or their families must be getting nearer and it seemed logical that London would be the place to which the freed would first be brought and in which information about them would be available. They wished to be on the spot when the day arrived.

Long before there was any chance of the exiled and the interned being united, indeed ever since the grim summer of 1942, I had, in common with many others, wondered, from time to time, what the Government was doing about the problem of the return of the British to Malaya. I recognised it as a problem, that is a problem of resettlement, apart from the other problem of the recapture of the country, although I was a long way from understanding its full implications. I had no means of finding out what was going on in Whitehall, but I have never subscribed to the popular view that Whitehall is a kind of mosque where you leave your brains (instead of your shoes) outside before you enter, and I waited confidently.

Then one day, in the autumn of 1943, a letter descended upon me from the Colonial Office.

THE MALAYAN PLANNING UNIT

A SENIOR Malayan Civil Servant said to me on one occasion, "Singapore fell on February 15th at 8 p.m. In my opinion we should have opened an office and started planning to go back at 9 a.m. on February 16th." I don't believe anything started quite so quickly as that but no doubt somebody, somewhere, was thinking hard from an early date. It was, however, almost eighteen months after the surrender before anything concrete began to take shape and my letter from the Colonial Office was the first inkling I had of it. The letter asked me to call, and, shortly afterwards, I did.

By far the greater part of the British Colonial Empire lies in the tropics. It is a broad girdle round the earth of sun-drenched lands of great variety and exquisite colour. The administrative heart and the focus of this group of associated lands is the Colonial Office, London, which was, in 1943, situated at the junction of Downing Street with Whitehall. The address was Downing Street and that sounded quite satisfactory, in spite of being a side street and a cul-de-sac. The external appearance of the building fitted in with its surroundings and, of course, it belonged to the privileged class of edifice, which displays its name on the smallest and least conspicuous notice possible.

Behind the somewhat gloomy but excusable exterior there were, as with most public buildings, offices and corridors, men and women. Even in the heart of the

19

Colonial Empire it would perhaps be asking too much to require the Civil Servants to display in their outward appearance any indication of their duties, but, if they ever do come to do such a thing, it will be instructive and not unpleasing to find each section dressed in the garb of the countries to whose interests they minister. It would certainly simplify the process of finding one's way about, if it were only necessary to follow a sarong and baju to the Far Eastern Section, a Nigerian head-dress to the West African Office and a Fijian skirt to the South Sea Islands stronghold.

However impracticable it may be to make Civil Servants more colourful, it should not be over difficult with public buildings. What did colonial peoples think of the interior of that building? There must have been many visitors from bright and lovely lands, who entered its unimposing doorway on isolated or periodical occasions. What kind of people did they think we were? Surely that was a building which ought to have been varied and distinctive, spacious and sun-catching, reflecting as far as possible the rainbow-coloured and sun-soaked lands over which it held sway.

Was it possible for officials hidden away in the building's gloomy depths to be in sympathy with the peoples of the Colonies, to understand their problems? Perhaps yes, but it was against odds. Anyhow, as I placated policemen, blast-walls and porters, filled in forms, traversed dusty corridors and stairs lit by low-powered yellow lights, passed through rooms cluttered up with Victorian furniture, and waited in draughty alcoves, I found it hard to think of palm tree and casuarina, green sea and blue sky, which were the things I wanted to think about the day I called.

I had gone there in response to the letter, and I was asked to join the Malayan Planning Unit. The Malayan Planning Unit, which had just been set up on July 5th, 1943, with an establishment of six posts, was a child of the War Office, but, most likely in its conception and certainly in its upbringing, the Colonial Office had a large part to play. The broad idea was that it should be a military unit, staffed by specially selected service personnel, and work under the directions of the War Office in consultation—up to a point at least—with the Colonial Office. In practice, it had a dual planning function, one being largely military and the other purely civil. The first involved planning for the governing and operation of Malaya under a Military Administration, for a period after recapture, and the second, for assisting the inauguration and the initial functioning of the Civil Government thereafter. Similar units were set up for Burma, Hong Kong and Borneo.

In the case of Malaya, the War Office had, I believe, authorised by September 1943, a War Establishment of twenty-five officers and had left to the Colonial Office the job of suggesting names to fill that Establishment. The latter naturally turned in the first place to Malayan Civil Servants and other Malayan Government employees, who were not incarcerated in the East. As, however, it was necessary to plan for other services besides those which, in the past, had been purely Government, certain persons from other public bodies and from the former commercial community were included.

Not least among the non-Government services which had to be covered were those of the former municipalities in the country, especially those of the Municipality of Singapore which were by far the largest and of utmost importance, not only to the inhabitants of the Island but to any proposals to use Singapore as a base for the further prosecution of the war. On that account I, as a former employee of the Singapore Municipal Commissioners, was called upon to join the new Unit.

During my interview at the Colonial Office I was asked to take up duties with the Unit as soon as possible and expect to be sent abroad in four or five months. In those few months I was to draw up plans for the rehabilitation of all the utility services, Government and Municipal, in the town and on the Island of Singapore.

"How you'll do it, I don't know," said my interviewer, "I expect you'll just sit and think for some time."

The Unit, which was accommodated in a block of flats at Hyde Park Gate, had been put in charge of Major-General H. R. Hone (later Sir Ralph Hone), who, before the war, had been in the Colonial Legal Service. He had never been to Malaya but had had experience in Military Government, as Chief Civil Affairs Officer, Mid-East. His deputy at the time was Lt.-Colonel P. A. B. McKerron[5] of the Malayan Civil Service. Others who had taken up duty before me or arrived about the same time included Lt.-Colonels J. O. Sanders, A. T. Newboult (later Sir Alex. Newboult), E. V. G. Day, and R. M. Williams, Majors A. Wallick and H. B. Langworthy and Captains A. L. McClure, C. Gifford, D. C. Watherston, and B. Clark, all Malayans. Each of them was dealing with some particular branch of the Unit's activities.

The Unit was eventually sub-divided into Sections, which covered, among other things, General Administration and Political, Legal and Judicial, Chinese Affairs, Public Health and Medical, Police Prisons and Fire-Brigade, Technical Services, Supplies, Rationing, Trade and Industry, Finance, Press and Publicity,

---

[5] Now Sir Patrick McKerron.

Custodian of Property, Agricultural, Veterinary and Forestry, Lands Mines and Surveys, Education and Labour and Personnel. There were many sub-sections to some of the main sections.

The question of staffing the various sections in a manner adequate to enable them to tackle the vast work of rehabilitation and at the same time carry on the functions of Government, Local Authorities and, to a certain extent, commerce, even for a limited time after reoccupation, was a tremendous problem. There was not nearly enough suitable Malayan personnel at liberty, and what there was, was scattered well over the globe. From about two thousand European Government officers in Malaya before the war, only some two hundred and thirty were free and about half of them were now in the fighting services, from which transfer was not easy. Most of the remainder had been seconded to other Colonies which were loath to part with them in their own difficult circumstances. Of Singapore Municipal officers, only about a dozen were at liberty out of well over a hundred. These latter had had their services terminated when Singapore fell and they had now found other posts or joined the Forces.

In the early stages of planning the shortage of staff was particularly acute and comparatively junior men were frequently striving with tasks which would have taxed the capacities of the most senior and experienced officials. Still, they attacked the job robustly, and stimulated by the thrill of again being engaged on Malayan affairs, did a tremendous amount of good work.

The lack of an adequate number of men with sufficient experience of the country and of the services which had to be rebuilt and run, while the great majority of those whose task it naturally was would be recuperating after a harsh internment, did not enable the Planning Unit to be as strong as might have been desired. Indeed, the Head of the Unit once described it as a 'second eleven'. This, however true the description, naturally enough did not please those who were doing their very best, feeling their way in a new kind of job and often, on account of the very novelty of the work and through nobody's fault, lacking what they considered adequate direction. Three years later, when all was over, I think any just verdict would have found the Unit worthy of its task.

There were many points connected with the staffing question. It was clear that, during early stages, the planning could be done with greatest efficiency and economy of effort by people who knew the conditions in the country and had actually worked on the services to be rehabilitated. When it came to operating those services, it would also be desirable that the great majority knew the country, the language, the habits of the people and the former methods used, but such people would not be available in adequate numbers, it being assumed that all prisoners-of-war and internees would have to be got home to recuperate without delay. The best that could be done was to arrange to run the country during the period of the Military Administration, possibly for six months or a year, by a nucleus of Malayan Officers augmented by a large number of others. The question then arose as to where the others were to come from, and, quite rightly, it was decided that men in the Forces should have the first opportunity; though indeed, there was little possibility of getting them elsewhere. Army Council Instruction No. 1426 of 1944 and similar orders for the Navy and Air Force were issued giving the usual terms of Government employment in the country before the war, and asking men with the necessary qualifications to volunteer for

Military Administration work, with the chance of permanent employment in civil life later.

This procedure brought its own difficulties, because, although it was known roughly how many officers would be needed during the Military Administration, it was not known, nor could it be accurately foretold, how many vacancies there would be in the service after all the former officers had recovered and got back to work. News from the Far East told of starvation, great hardships and cruelties being inflicted on captives in Japanese hands, and it was assumed, with medical advice, that a percentage increasing with age groups would never be able to return and work in the country and that others would not wish to do so, after their gruelling experiences. Again, there might be many deaths which had not been reported. Everything taken into account, it was calculated that the number back in the country, say a year after its liberation, would be small. Fortunately this did not prove to be so, but, in planning, the contingency had to be covered and more vacancies were anticipated than, I believe, materialised.

That Malaya would have to be fought for and that there would ultimately be separate Governments in Singapore and on the Mainland were two over-riding assumptions which were made right at the start, and these affected all planning. Happily, the first proved incorrect, but the second turned out to be correct, whether happily or not is a question on which there are still differences of opinion.

In addition to those two, each officer had to make a multitude of other assumptions in the course of his work. There was no reliable information—and indeed, very little of any kind, reliable or otherwise—about the condition of Malaya or what was going on in the country. In 1944 when most of the Unit's planning was done, there was nothing, or virtually nothing, known about the state of the land or its people and it was almost hopeless to assess with any accuracy what that state would be at an unspecified time ahead, when the country would be liberated after—as we then thought a bitter campaign would have been fought for its recapture.

Nevertheless, to give planning a basis, it was necessary to assess or assume the probable position on reoccupation. I attempted an assessment for Singapore Island and spent considerable time in examining Japanese broadcasts which had been picked up, and, in studying scanty reports of a few Asiatics who had managed to leave Malaya and reach India or free China. There were also available one or two copies of Singapore newspapers which had somehow been slipped out, and that was about all. The Report which I produced as a result of my searching may not, in the light of subsequent knowledge, have been a brilliant forecast but it was interesting to re-read it in Singapore some eighteen months later, and note that, in parts, it was not so far wrong. If nothing else, the preparation of that 'Appreciation' showed how thick was the mantle which had been drawn over the Far East at the time.

With so little to go by, officers of the Planning Unit had many guesses to make in their efforts to ensure that, on reoccupation of the country, suitable organisation and proper supplies would be available at the right place and at the right time. Many things had a bearing on what these organisations and supplies should be. They depended, among other things, on the method by which the country would be re-taken, the extent to which it would have deteriorated and, perhaps most of all, on how 'bloody-minded' the Jap would be in employing the scorched earth technique. All these things were anybody's guess.

In the case of the Technical Services, it is probably true that more guessing had to be done than was necessary in other Sections of the Unit. Adequate water, electricity, communications and sewerage services had to be provided very quickly after reoccupation if disease and unrest were to be prevented and no one knew how much of the existing services, if any, would be left when we got there. Malaya is far from the sources of supply of the plant and equipment necessary to ensure these either by renewal or repair. All that might be necessary had to be brought in, and, in addition, a staff of competent men to guide and control in place of those who had once done it and who would need rest and recuperation, if they had survived.

It was my duty to plan for the utility services, both Government and Municipal, on Singapore Island, and my Sub-section was known as Works (Singapore). Alan McClure, a very capable engineer and a Malayan Public Works Department officer, was tackling the same task for the Mainland of Malaya. We put our heads together and tried to reduce the vague instruction 'to plan for the rehabilitation of the utility services' to something more concrete. Obviously, the first step was to set down with as much detail as possible the structures of the various engineering services as they had existed. In my case, this was done partly from personal knowledge and partly from any records in London or elsewhere, I was able to obtain access to. There were not many records of the large Municipal services, as the Municipality was a local body, self-contained in Singapore. Its Agents in London, Messrs. Peirce & Williams, were, however, invaluable and spared no efforts to assist.

When everything, known or found, about a service had been set down, the big guess was made. A percentage of destruction was assumed, varying from one hundred per cent in the case of vulnerable plant and machinery, to a very small percentage in the case of protected installations such as underground pipes. Thereafter, it was a case of listing and ordering replacements ranging from a whole electricity or gas generating plant to a diminutive screw nail with corresponding tools. By the time this had been done for every service, the indents ran to hundreds of pages and involved a cost reckoned in millions.

There were two distinct phases to provide for, the first being the period when military considerations in Singapore would be paramount and when the Forces and civilians alike would be expected to exist on minimum supplies and comforts, as an army (or, for that matter, a civilian population) in a fighting or front-line zone does. The second was the succeeding period, which it was hoped would come six months, or at most a year, after liberation, when British responsibility towards a British colony directed that the conditions of living and all the amenities should be brought back to normal as quickly as possible.

For the first of the two periods, it was intended that the listed supplies would be obtained from service resources, but those necessary for the second period were the responsibility of the Colonial Office. In the unexpected circumstances in which Singapore was eventually reoccupied, the periods were not very clearly separated.

In planning for the second period I was not satisfied with schemes to reinstate in Singapore the standards which it enjoyed in 1941. Not unnaturally I had some rosy visions of a post-war world in which, with other places, Singapore would enjoy greater material advantages. I planned—as I thought—for better services and at the request of the Unit, prepared a number of long-term schemes. Two of these in particular interested me; a scheme for civil aviation and a scheme for housing. Of the former I need say nothing except that after I had drawn it up, it passed into more competent hands to deal with in a more realistic manner, but, of the second, I heard a great deal more. It was taken up enthusiastically by the Unit and by the Colonial Office. Money was sanctioned for preliminary work and an officer specially appointed to deal with it. I visualised rapid construction of prefabricated houses of a type suitable to the climate in satellite communities around the island, and knew that the housing standards which could thus be obtained would be vastly superior to those enjoyed by tens of thousands in Singapore, and should relieve the unbelievable over-crowding of parts of the urban area. The fate of the scheme will appear later in this story.

Until late in 1944 I was working alone in my division except for two months when Alex MacDougall, a retired Municipal employee, was with me. This was due to the difficulty of getting any suitable former members of the Municipal staff. Just as the work was getting too much, I had a stroke of luck. W. K. Wallace, just the man for the job, turned up unexpectedly from Australia and before long he had got down to it. Together we completed our plans during long hours which we did not grudge, in a cause we both had so much at heart. We found that there were many hurdles to be got over in arranging for tens of thousands of items to be collected in selected order, packed for travel, protected against damage by tropical sea, rain and air, marked with suitable codes and delivered at the right place and time. When, many months later, I saw those packages in Singapore with the right identification marks, I felt rather like a child, who for the first time in a London Underground Station, puts his only sixpence in a tuppenny ticket machine and gets the ticket and the change correct.

The early months of 1945 were marked by the arrival of men from all over the world who were being brought into the Unit's fold. Old friends, whom I had not seen for years, would walk into the office for a word or two and then disappear to a training camp in England or a base camp in India. First of my own staff to arrive was James Beattie, who had been with the New Zealand Air Force in New Guinea; then Vin Kelly came from the 1st Army in Italy. Close on their heels, Sam Bryden arrived from Australia, E.G. Vaughton from the Sudan, R. A. Jensen and S. G. Duncan from war work in the north of England. I would have given much to have had them earlier but, as it was, they arrived in time to help with crossing the last 't's and dotting the last 'i's of the planning work and it was good to know that they, at least, would be available on the day.

Everyone will remember how, during the war, after the long blacked-out winter nights, he drew aside the curtain in the mornings with an intense feeling of relief and let in the first faint glimpse of daylight. I got something of the same feeling, when a corner of the curtain, which had for three years been drawn across Singapore, was lifted for me early in 1945. Sergeant H. Jones of the Royal Signals, paid a visit to Hyde Park Gate. Sgt. Jones was no ordinary visitor, for he had been captured in Singapore in 1942, later sent to Siam by the Japanese to work on the notorious railway and, still later, brought back to Singapore, where, this time, he was employed on various works around the Island, which gave him an opportunity to see much, and get a good general impression of the conditions prevailing. About mid-summer 1944, the Japanese put him on a ship for Japan. The ship was torpedoed by the Allies and Sgt. Jones, with others, was rescued from the sea. Here in London was a man (actually there were several with him), who had been in Singapore six months before and could lift a small corner of the curtain. His patience in answering innumerable questions and his modest and balanced replies were enormously appreciated.

The glimpse I got beyond the curtain was stimulating. It seemed to assist in focussing efforts and set me to work with renewed vigour. Certainly, the few months left at Hyde Park Gate were busier than ever before, and Singapore seemed nearer.

When I started work with the Malayan Planning Unit it was expected that we should go to India in the spring of 1944, but when that time arrived there was no move. Although we did not know it, the impending invasion of Europe had upset plans for a Far Eastern campaign. The invasion of Malaya was postponed and our stay at Hyde Park Gate prolonged. We were, however, working all along the line in close co-operation with Headquarters of the 11th Army Group in India and a number of our officers, including General Hone, spent periods in India co-ordinating our planning with the work of the operating Forces.

From July 1943 to mid-summer 1945, the Unit was entrenched at Hyde Park Gate. During those two years the various sections began, continued and completed their planning work and, as it subsequently proved, there were very few, if any, factors or possible situations which had not been considered. The Sections worked pretty much in water-tight compartments, although the Council, which met frequently, saw to it that, where the work of one Section infringed on that of another, there was co-ordination. Now and again, things of interest to everybody happened.

There was, for example, the 15th February each year, when all the Unit gathered in one room to remember the fall of Singapore. The first year, there was only about a dozen of us, and, after Colonel McKerron had said a few appropriate things, we stood a couple of minutes in silence with heads bowed in homage to those who had fallen with Malaya and those still in enemy hands. The following year, in February 1945, General Hone addressed a very much larger number, and made us feel that the time of the testing was getting close. Well, that was what we had been working for, that was what we had been hoping for. Working and hoping, working for two years almost, hoping for three. There was virtually no end to the preparations one could make for a task like this and, no matter how much time there might be, there would always be something to do at the last minute. We were confident we could do the job, and yet, when the test of years of work is imminent, there must always be some apprehension. Would it go according to plan? Was there any vital thing which had been forgotten? Was there anything more we could do besides what we had in mind? It was up to us to be as ready as it was humanly possible to be, but that was not the main consideration. Whether we were ready or not, the main thing, which we never forgot, was to get our fellow countrymen and the British peoples out of the hands of the enemy, and to see the flag again flying over Malaya.

The European war was obviously drawing to a close; a big effort in the East must quickly follow. We knew nothing of the plan of attack, or when or where it would begin, for the recovery of Malaya. There was friendly rivalry as to whether Singapore or the Mainland Officers would have to function first. On January 1st, 1945, the two embryo Governments had been definitely separated within the Unit, Colonel McKerron being in charge of the Singapore Administration and Colonel Willan[6] that of the

---

[6] Now Sir Harold Willan.

Mainland. Both were responsible to the General's Headquarter staff. Each of these Branches had a full complement of Sections though, of course, there were some pan Malayan Sections, such as Police, which, on account of the nature of their duties, it was desirable should be operated under one control in both territories.

During those two years, it was not all a question of using the knowledge one had, for there was also a great deal to be learned. For a Military Administration to be successful, its officers must have, in addition to their specialised knowledge, gained in peace-time pursuits as civilians, a fair knowledge of the Army, its organisation, its methods, its means, and have received the fundamental training of a soldier. They must also know something of the science of Military Administration itself and they should know the language of the country they are to work in. Among the officers of the Malayan Planning Unit, there were many who had had military training and knew something of the Army. Even a greater number knew the Malay language, at least to a passable standard but, to almost all, Military Administration was new. To cover all cases, facilities were afforded to attend one or all of three schools, the Officers' Training School at Kettering, the Military Administration School at Wimbledon and the School of Oriental Studies in London. Officers did attend courses at these schools as necessary, subject to the exigencies of their planning work.

I think it is important to appreciate that the liberation of Malaya was not delayed because it took so long to plan for the Military Administration and its rehabilitating functions. When planning began, and almost till it finished, there was no date. That depended entirely on Military Operations. What would have happened if liberation had come much sooner or much later, I do not know. The Administration would have been compelled to function in either case, in the first, with less matured plans, and, in the second, possibly with a more complete, more competent and better-trained staff, and with materials closer at hand. Two years may seem a long time for this preparatory work, and undoubtedly, when Whitehall set up the Unit, it expected Malaya would be recaptured much sooner. Be that as it may, seldom can a miscalculation (if such it was) have been put to better account or been met with a greater combination of enthusiasm and impatience.

With the opening of 1945 everyone anticipated the final surrender of Germany, but it dragged a bit and, when it did come, the celebrations on the official victory day, May 8th, seemed less spontaneous and less enthusiastic than might have been expected. It had been too long imminent, people were tired and emotionally worn out and—we Malayans hoped—very conscious of the task still to be completed.

After the two days holiday there was a 'flap' at Hyde Park Gate. In spite of many previous unfruitful 'flaps', this one was taken seriously. It was time we packed our bags. Outstanding affairs were wound up; final lines were added to MSS. and sent for typing, officers burnt the top-secret, secret, confidential and restricted papers for which they no longer had any use, and people kept running about asking each other how and why and when, and all, surprisingly enough, to some advantage.

Not long afterwards, my instructions came from Calcutta. I was to be there at a date which left me little time for anything more than packing and saying another of those awful 'good-byes' that men and women, who work in the Colonies, say so often in the course of a lifetime and which do not grow much easier with the years. Sometimes they grow more difficult.

INDIA AND BURMA

WAS it an accident, or was it due to some student of psychology, that Transport Command sent its passengers for India to one of the most English parts of England pending their departure? A few hours by train, a bus journey and I was at one of its hostels, a magnificent country house surrounded by hundreds of acres of park land, where, once upon a time, an earl had lived.

Everything was faultlessly arranged and comfortable and I had plenty of time to appreciate it, for the aircraft did not leave the next day as scheduled, but twenty-four hours later. As always happens on such occasions, the passengers were kept hanging about waiting for definite news of the time of departure, but it wasn't too bad and I was able, later, to see a bit of Wiltshire in June and register an impression of the English countryside, which, for all I knew, might have to last for a long time.

We got off at last on the morning of June 5th, and, as the machine gained height, that same countryside, which had been thoroughly drenched with rain just previously, presented a picture, which is probably not to be seen anywhere else in the world. I do not think it is necessarily the most beautiful and it is certainly not the grandest landscape, but it has a unique quality, which no doubt is tied up with one's loyalties. The mixture of vivid and melancholy greens, the grasses and the trees, the patches of mist and of yellow sunlight and the gloom and the sparkle of dampness combined to make it England. England, which quickly disappeared below cloud.

During the briefing, we had been told that there would be cloud over England, but, from the coast of France, we should have sunshine all the way to Malta. It turned out just like that. The briefing officer had been disarming and amusing. His was the job to make us feel comfortable, telling us what to do in any emergency, where doing anything was any good, and, at the same time, belittling any possible incident, where there was nothing one could do. I suppose they hold examinations for briefing officers, and only those with a good technique pass. Ours had one strong line. He told us at great length, and with much illustration, what to do when coming down in the sea, what things to put on, what doors to open and what levers to pull. He finished every earnest exhortation with a brief and breezy, "and in ten minutes the Sea-Air Rescue Service will arrive." By far the greater part of our journey was over land, but we heard not one word of what was to be done if we hit a mountain side, or if a wing came off. If anything like that happened, matters would undoubtedly be beyond our control, but the art of successfully pooh-poohing such a possibility must, surely, be the first qualification for a briefing officer.

France, bathed in sunshine showed, from the air, few signs of her five year struggle. Here and there a wrecked vehicle and, rarer still, a derelict house, but, of course, we passed over only a few of the main battlefields. Serene and peaceful she looked from our little windows, and we saw nothing to reflect her torn heart and upset economy. France left behind, we passed over blue sea, rugged Sardinia, then more blue sea and Malta was beneath us.

Our aircraft was a 'Liberator', fitted out with almost peace time comfort, and we were a happy party on board. There was one other member of the Malayan Planning Unit, Major Walkinshaw, two Lieutenant-Colonels

38

returning to India from leave, a War-correspondent and a little French officer, decorated with many exciting looking badges, and bound on some highly secret mission, of which we never gained any inkling. We all palled up nicely.

Malta, and our reception there, assisted not a little in making us bosom friends in the minimum of time. Most of us were put in the accommodation for, and treated as, V.I.P.'s (Very Important Persons) for the first time in our lives, and, in my case, doubtless for the last time. The R.A.F. officer in charge started us off well for the evening by lavish entertainment in his private cocktail lounge and then sending us to a club for dinner. Malta was certainly a place to call at, not only for the warmth of its reception, but also on account of its recent gallant history. Of that gallantry there is no question, but I had developed an exaggerated mental picture of what I expected to find on that much assaulted island. Damage there was, and plenty of it, but still there seemed to be a great deal of Malta standing intact. That was a relief.

The next leg of the flight, on the following day, was marked by Benghazi, much desert, Tobruk on its little spit of sand negligible in size, but immense in memory, and by the valley of the Nile, unbelievably green and fertile in contrast.

At the Cairo airfield, we rested and wrote letters during the afternoon amid great heat and much dust. Just before darkness that evening we were off again. The crew of the aircraft had changed, and this new bunch of fellows was determined to make up the time we had lost in England, and to arrive on schedule in Calcutta. All through the night we flew, coming down only once at Shaibal for a brief spell. Shaibal, in Iraq, was an isolated desert station for the R.A.F., and the heat, even at 2 a.m., was stifling.

As happened in those days at many airfields, we were bustled out as soon as the machine landed, piled into a truck and driven miles to a canteen. The truck ride at Shaibal seemed particularly long and particularly rough, but, at the canteen, we had an acceptable meal with unlimited eggs, and that was something England didn't then provide. When we left the canteen's dim interior, we were internally satisfied and this, combined with the heat, sent us to sleep before the aircraft had risen to cooler regions. We had all (except the Frenchman) changed into tropical outfits at Cairo, and, in the higher altitudes, these were apt to be chilly.

Mid-morning, we reached Karachi and came down at a dusty, dirty and depressing airfield and transit camp outside the town. After a filthy lunch in a low, dark, wooden canteen which had its window openings covered with anti-fly wire like a meat-safe, but which was still full of flies, we were let loose till midnight. We washed and tried to tidy ourselves under difficulties, and then stood with scores of others on the dusty road, endeavouring to hitch-hike a ride to Karachi, some ten miles away.

This was India, unmistakable as ever with its magnificence, its dirt and its teeming peoples. India, which contributed so much to the Allied war effort, India, which wanted to cut its ties with Britain, India, so vast, so divided, so varied that it was impossible to speak of it as a whole in any one connection. Few Malayans, outside the Indian community, ever saw much of India but they knew of its restless political atmosphere and contrasted it unfavourably with the non-politically minded Malaya of pre-war days in which men of many races lived together in harmony. Whether events of the future will bring about an unhappy political alliance between India and Malaya is a matter for speculation, but it is certainly a possibility.

Although India will continue to attract tourists and businessmen from the West and will remain entrenched for a long time in the hearts of many Britishers, who have at one time lived there, her eyes, apart from diversionary glances at Africa, will be turned mostly Eastwards and her development, or disintegration, in the next quarter century will be worth watching.

All night long we flew over this enigmatical land from shore to shore, and, in the morning, came to our journey's end with a three-point landing at Dum Dum Airfield, outside Calcutta. I was to become familiar with that airfield in the next few months, and with the horrible drive from its gates to the centre of Calcutta.

If you haven't been to Calcutta during the monsoon, or just before it breaks, don't go from curiosity, it isn't worth it. A more detestable season is hard to conceive. Unbearably hot and moist as a marsh, it is impossible to feel comfortable for a single moment in the twenty-four hours of any day. The dirt settles in layers on exposed skin and works through tropical clothes elsewhere, it is then mixed with the continually flowing perspiration and runs in muddy streams from the body, or sinks odoriferously into garments. No garment, once donned, remains dry for five minutes, and humanity goes about as a sticky mess from morning to night and then relaxes on sweat-soaked sheets and pillows—if it is the type of humanity which uses sheets and pillows. When it rains, no rational garment affords complete protection and the chances are that, in a few minutes, the streets and pavements will be inches deep in water and slime, while many buildings suffer the same inundation.

Other features of Calcutta which do not, so far as I know, change with the seasons are its ubiquitous heaps of filth, its peripatetic cows, its persistent hawkers, its pitiful rickshaw pullers, its perverse traffic, its pot-holed and perforated streets, its prosperous merchants, its pauperised millions and its putrefying corpses in the morning streets. It has some fine buildings.

The war brought to Calcutta other things, which were not normally there. It brought scores of thousands of fighting men, British, American, Indians, Burmese and Negro predominating. It brought W.R.N.S., A.T.S., W.A.A.F.S., and Women's Nursing Services. With them came thousands of military vehicles and machines, and mountains of Allied money. It must also have brought a considerable volume of trade and a not inconsiderable volume of disease.

After England, India was a land of plenty. All those things, which were difficult or impossible to obtain at home, were in the shops or along the pavements of Calcutta. Razor blades, toothbrushes, pipes, fountain pens, watches, suitcases and a thousand and one other things, including foods and sweets, for which people cajoled or stood in queues in England to obtain, were there in unlimited quantities, and shopkeepers still went out after purchasers. In spite of the heat Calcutta was very much alive day and night, a hive of endless activity. It was a holiday centre of the Forces and the headquarters for many legions, its trade was booming and its entertainments, numerous as they were, were over-taxed. There was no black-out, or, at most, a very meagre one, and other war-time restrictions, if there were any, were not noticeable.

At this metropolis of mixed blessings, we arrived on June 8th and went straight to the Grand Hotel, which had been taken over as a leave and transit hostel for commissioned ranks of the services. I hope that some knowledgeable person with a facile, humorous and sympathetic pen will write the story of the Grand Hotel, Chowringhee, Calcutta, during the time it functioned as a service hostel. Surely, the war-time experiences of few buildings are more worthy of a book, a book which gives not only incidents and doings, but, also, the thoughts and feelings of those who sojourned there for short or long periods.

The hostel accommodated a thousand officers and many hundreds of them changed every night. As a rule, there were three officers to a room and they came from the ends of the earth. Major Walkinshaw and I stayed together and there was one spare bed in our room. This was occupied by a different man almost every night, generally by someone coming from the Burmese front to stay a few hours in Calcutta, before going to Britain under some air-borne leave scheme. They came in all kinds of clothes and in all sorts of condition. They spent their few hours in Calcutta in transforming themselves into a different condition and one in which they felt it might be possible to mix with human society. They bought new clothes, shaved more often than necessary for the sheer joy of shaving, spent money recklessly on soap and toilet preparations and on presents which, optimistically, they aspired to include in the limited baggage air travel allowed. The jungle-maulled clothes, the trusty boots, the tropical medicines and the bags, bottles and containers, which had been so precious a few hours before, were cast aside in a corner of the room. These were frequently left untouched after their departure and the green heap grew and grew in size and diversity, as guest after guest added his contribution and departed. I should have made a list of those discarded articles, as a lesson in jungle equipment, but the green pile was not inviting. Here, the soldier was a slave to green, his uniform, his underclothes, his towel, blanket and mosquito net were green, and even the toilet paper he found among his packed breakfast rations was green.

Sometimes, our third man was never seen by us. He would arrive during the day, when we were out, then go out himself to sample the fleshpots of Calcutta, returning when we were asleep, and departing at 4 a.m. to the airfield. It was an interesting synthesis for us next morning to build up his type from the rags, bags and bottles he left behind him.

Calcutta was short of water before the monsoon broke properly and I think the water which was available was not very safe. Anyhow, for a while, the only water which came from the taps was just on boiling point. It was possible to shave with it, but not to bath, so expedients had to be resorted to. I put some of the near-boiling water in the bath before breakfast and was able to get into it, without scalding myself, before dinner at 7 p.m. The water was off altogether between 8.30 a.m. and 6 p.m., and, when it came on, it might be any one of many colours.

Now for a rat story. As I was going up in the lift one evening an officer on the same journey said quite solemnly to his friend, "How are you feeling now, have the rats been at your toes again?"

The people who ran that hostel deserve the greatest praise. Theirs was a gigantic task. To cater every day for a thousand of the world's dirtiest officers, when many of those officers were not at all in an accommodating mood, was no sinecure. To serve a thousand adequate meals cleanly three times a day, which they did, and keep hundreds of bedrooms and many public rooms reasonably habitable was, in the circumstances, a colossal job. Every way I saw it, their organisation was excellent, and it was never more obvious than during the night hours. It was impossible to sleep without a fan and if one's fan broke down in the night great discomfort resulted, but all it was necessary to do was to phone the office and a man was sent to fix it in a few minutes. With unfailing certainty, they would wake the right officer, out of three in a room, when that officer had to get up at 3 a.m. to start an air journey, they provided him with an excellent breakfast at 3.20 a.m., brought his baggage down at 3.45 a.m., passed him through the cashier, and all but lifted him into his transport. They would probably have done that, if needed, without blinking an eye.

From the bedroom windows, there was much to be seen. The front rooms looked over the Chowringhee (the wide street in front of the hotel) and the vast open space called the Maidan. The former was always crowded with servicemen, walking to and fro, seeking this and that, and, usually, presenting a somewhat sordid picture. The side and back rooms looked onto Indian strongholds, and one frequently saw that which would have been better unseen. The noisy bargaining, the noisier fights, which, in Asiatic fashion, consisted of a few hasty blows and a prolonged chase and hullabaloo, the homeless pavement sleepers, and the filth being evicted from houses to lodge in the street. From one room, which I occupied, the view was over a flat roof, evidently used by a dhoby for drying clothes. It was a large roof and always strewn with sheets, towels and varied household linen. One morning, after a night so hot that sleep was difficult, I got up at the first glimpse of daylight and went to the window. As the light grew stronger, I noticed something strange about the sheets on the flat roof, they all had humps in the middle. I was not particularly curious until these humps began to move, and then I watched a strange awakening of dozens of Indians, singly and in pairs, as they stretched below the completely enveloping sheets and gradually emerged there from, with all the gestures and all the nakedness of oriental slumber, while Calcutta's crows cawed a raucous reveille over head hoping, against experience, for some leavings from impending breakfasts.

Instructed in movement orders to report to Headquarters No. 2 Area on arrival, Walkinshaw and I had, in the first few hours, made enquiries as to its address. No one had heard of it, so we retired to the lounge to think the matter over surrounded by hundreds of perspiring persons. The French officer, who had been our travelling companion, was still in his thick blue uniform and looked as if he had been dipped in a bath, clothes on, and badly wrung out. He told us he was still unable to tell us what he was going to do, and furtively disappeared with a mysterious air. A few minutes later, our problem was solved by the arrival of Brigadier McKerron and Colonel Regester who informed us that No. 2 Area did not yet exist. It was the name being given to a branch of the Forces which was to plan for, and afterwards govern, Singapore from the Military angle, and to which we Civil Affairs Officers, who were concerned with Singapore only, would be attached. It was shortly to be established in separate quarters and, in the meantime, we would work at the Headquarters of A.L.F.S.E.A. (Allied Land Forces South East Asia), where the other members of the Malayan Planning Unit, now known as C.A.S.(M.) (Civil Affairs Services, Malaya), were stationed.

A.L.F.S.E.A. Headquarters was at Barrackpore, fifteen miles out along the old military road, and was reachable by means of a ferry service of 15 cwt. trucks, fitted with wooden benches, which operated between the Headquarters and the Grand Hotel hostel. The journey between the two places must have been the world's most appalling routine run. Indian military drivers, with few exceptions, were the worst drivers I have ever come across, and, when let loose in the streets of Calcutta, the result was nerve-wrecking. Passengers were saved from complete nervous breakdowns by the fact that the trucks were well enclosed with canvas roof and sides, so that few of the hair breadth escapes were actually seen. Many of them could be imagined, however, by the endless sudden swerves, the wild blasts of horn, the angry and excited language of drivers and near-victims and by the almost instantaneous stops, when speed was reduced from a crazy pace to zero in the winkling of an eye. These stops, and the subsequent restartings, created chaos within the truck. All, from generals to privates, seated on the plain wooden benches, were thrown in a heap on the floor, first to the front of the vehicle and then to the rear. Sometimes, the heap went to the port side of the vehicle, as it swerved off the paved roadway onto the dirt track alongside, which was usually deep mud and sometimes it hit the roof, as a wheel went into one of Calcutta's super-colossal pot-holes. Those of us, who lived in the hostel, endeavoured, against all the odds, to keep body and clothes reasonably clean, but, after a ride in the A.L.F.S.E.A. ferry, we almost despaired of ever being clean again. Oil doesn't easily come off!

At Barrackpore, I found those of my colleagues, who had arrived before me, sweltering at desks beneath fans and punkahs and gradually overcoming their modesty, as they reduced clothing to the standard outfit of the seasoned soldier in South East Asia, namely a pair of shoes, a pair of shorts and nothing else. There wasn't very much I could do at Barrackpore, except bring myself up to date with what was going on and what was proposed, and learn the language of S.E.A.C.

South East Asia Command, like other commands, had developed its own jargon and one was constantly assailed by phrases like, "I haven't a clue", "I couldn't care less", "How right you are", "I couldn't agree with you more", "Extract digit" and "Wot no beer", and these were freely interspersed with Urdu words, the more common of which one had to learn in order to understand one's co-linguists. Then, there were Army terms peculiar to the Command such as LIAP, PYTHON, SLICK, STIFF, ALFRO and ACSEA to be learnt and, of course, a forest of initials as dense as the Malayan jungle.

A.L.F.S.E.A. H.Q. was beginning to unearth the reports I had sent to them more than a year previously and was thinking about ordering the supplies the Army had agreed to obtain. It seemed late in the day, but up till then work had been concentrated on Burma. Whether the supplies would ever have been obtained in time, I do not know, but I think it fortunate that the turn of events lessened the need. Many of the supplies, were, of course, standard military stores, but others were not, and, as will appear later, these latter articles were not easy to get.

It was about this time that a proposal was brought forward by A.L.F.S.E.A. that the Engineering Services of the M.P.U. or C.A.S. (M.) should be taken away from Civil Affairs and integrated (as it was termed), with the Royal Engineers on the operational side. It was argued that, in order to obtain our engineering stores from the Engineering Depots, this integration was necessary. I opposed it on the grounds that the services, we were to operate, were pre-war Civil Government services, and all those, who would work on them, apart from a few of my senior officers, were pre-war employees of the Civil Authorities, and would be, in many respects, still tied up with the rules and regulations of those Authorities, which, on reoccupation, were to be administered by the Civil Affairs staff. To me, it seemed that the Civil Affairs side would be bound to infringe on our work from every angle and, if we were not subject to its command, there would be endless sources of friction, nor did there appear to be any force in the argument about stores, as, surely, it would be easy to issue the necessary orders to allow us to draw them in a predetermined order of priority. I was, however, one among many on both sides (A.L.F.S.E.A. and C.A.S. (M.)), who thought otherwise at the time and the Engineering Services, in theory, became detached from C.A.S. (M.), but, in practice, they were in a most confusing and unsatisfactory position, which was afterwards maintained only by the exercise of a hampering amount of 'tact'.

Before long, No. 2 Area was established in its own quarters, in a schoolhouse not far from the centre of Calcutta. It was under the command of Brigadier J. A. E. Ralston, a man with much drive and personality, as well as a vigorous mode of expression. Very friendly and helpful, Singapore owes a good deal to him, although, to-day, his name is probably not known by one in fifty thousand of its inhabitants. His A.A. and Q.M.G. was Lt.-Colonel P. U. Campbell, another pleasant Scotsman with any amount of work on his plate. Civil Affairs was allotted one room in this schoolhouse with two tables, two chairs and a packet of thorns to be used as pins. As there were four of us, McKerron, Regester, Walkinshaw and myself, it required some organisation to enable us all to carry out spells of desk work. As it happened, Regester got ill, which reduced the difficulties of the situation from the accommodation point of view, and, when one of us managed to be out, as frequently happened, the remaining two could sit down. However, it was recognised that we would soon be moving, and, indeed, before many days, we received instructions to go to Ceylon on July 1st, and complete planning there.

The Supreme Allied Commander had, some time previously, set up his Headquarters at Kandy in the Ceylon hills and now A.L.F.S.E.A. was to follow, and, of course, No. 2 Area. Brigadiers and above would go by air and the rest by train. Now, a six-day train journey in India is a thing to be avoided, especially if it is a troop movement. No one was looking forward to it much, and when it did come, I am told, it included all the horrors. The start was typical. No. 2 Area personnel was taken out to Barrackpore to entrain, where, after waiting some time, they did entrain, got off again, entrained again, and, by the next morning, had covered the whole fifteen miles between Barrackpore and the Howrah Station, Calcutta, a net distance of two miles in the wrong direction.

Fortunately, I got an interesting job to do before the end of June, which enabled me to avoid the train journey. Rangoon had been entered by British Forces six weeks previously, and, as it was the first town in the Empire to be liberated which was at all comparable with Singapore, it was rightly thought that the authorities there would be meeting problems which we might well have to face later. It would be to our advantage to see how they were being tackled, and with what success. I volunteered to go to Rangoon and make the study, and my offer was quickly accepted.

There was dense monsoon cloud at a few hundred feet above sea level all the way to the Arakan, and the Dakota flew below it. Mostly, we travelled along the coast, and, on that dark, rain-swept day, this formidable part of the earth looked unbelievably gloomy, abandoned and threatening. In hundreds of miles, no sign of life was seen, nothing but water, angry shore, flooded and forgotten land. Coming down at Akyab and Meiktila in monsoon conditions, imagination could not fail to be horrified at the climate and country over which the XIVth Army had triumphed, and marvel anew at the exploits of the Air Forces, which had fed and supplied that Army from hostile skies.

On account of the need for getting to Ceylon early, my departure from Calcutta had been hurried, and no one in Rangoon knew I was coming. Mingaladon Airfield, a dozen miles from Rangoon, was having its daily drenching of monsoon rain as we landed in the early afternoon. Neither my fellow passengers nor I seemed to know exactly what to do and no advice was offered, but, as an R.A.F. truck, obviously meant for passengers, was standing there, we piled into it and it set off. When still several miles from Rangoon, the truck stopped in the pouring rain and the Indian driver descended and entered an ordinary looking house. We thought that he had gone to deliver a message, and so we waited. After about 25 minutes, someone got exasperated and followed him, returning in a few seconds to report that this was the Air Booking Centre, and the truck didn't go any further. How long we could have sat there without direction is anybody's guess. I mention this because, then, and more forcibly later, I was impressed with what seemed to be the casualness with which people travelled about in South East Asia. No matter how urgent your journey, or how emphatic your movement order, it seemed—no doubt incorrectly—that you had to question, argue, cajole and look after yourself just as much as if—which was quite possible—you were "thumbing" a ride for pleasure.

From the Air Booking Centre, I "thumbed" a ride into Rangoon, and, by request, was dumped at the offices of the British Military Administration, Burma. Here, where men started work at 7 a.m. and finished when they went to

51

sleep, I was received as though I had been an expected and important guest. They gave liberally of their hospitality and their time, and displayed endless patience in answering my many questions, although intrusion on their work, at that time, cannot have been what they would have chosen. Colonel Rennick, the Deputy Chief Civil Affairs Officer, kindly arranged a room for me in the house, which he was using as living quarters and office. The Chief Civil Affairs Officer, Major-General Rance,[7] was temporarily accommodated in the same building and these two gentlemen smoothed my path in all directions, so that I had an intensely instructive and interesting visit.

Rangoon was in a dreadful mess. The Railway Station had been entirely wiped out and most of the buildings, which still stood in the centre of the town, were little more than shells. Vacant premises, including public buildings, European owned shops and warehouses and the larger residences had been stripped by looters. All the public services had broken down and, up to the time of my arrival, little had been restored.

The fall of Rangoon is a curious story. The XIVth Army, which had fought down through all Burma, was still some distance from Rangoon when a force, mounted at Akyab, set out to capture the town by an amphibious operation. This force overwhelmed the defences at the mouth of the Rangoon River, and continued upstream towards the town. They were met by two R.A.F. officers in a sampan. Rangoon had been evacuated by the Japanese some days before, and this fact had just been discovered by these two officers. Flying over the town, they had seen the words, "Japs gone" and "Extract digit", painted in large letters on the roof of the jail, where Allied P.O.W.s were kept. They

---

[7] Now Sir Hubert Rance.

landed to investigate, and found the place empty of the enemy.

The interval between the departure of the Japanese and the arrival of the British was disastrous. With no one in control of the town, the irresponsible elements of the population ran wild, and looting, burning and even killing were the order of the day. Rangoon afforded a marked example of the difficulties to be met in taking over a modern city. The Burma Civil Affairs Officers seemed to have been somewhat in the dark as to when or how Rangoon would be taken, and so, apart from one police officer, who was with the 26th Division (the main assaulting force), they did not get to Rangoon until some time after its reoccupation, and they might have been much later, if they had waited for someone to send them there and not displayed considerable individual initiative. Colonel Rennick was the first to arrive, getting there on May 7th by sea, having failed to obtain an air passage from Calcutta. Others came in ones and twos and small batches from May 10th onwards. The delay in arrival of these officers, detailed to carry on the administration and services of the town, was most unfortunate, as things became much worse daily, until the Civil Affairs Staff got them in hand. It seemed to indicate a lack of appreciation of the vital importance of Civil Affairs officers in this kind of operation.

Rangoon (which was known as No. 1 Area), was indeed in a bad way. There had been no water in the town since March 22nd, as bombing had destroyed the supply. Consequent upon the lack of water, the sewerage system had broken down and become completely clogged. All conservancy vehicles had been taken by the Japanese some time previously for war purposes, and, so, there was no conservancy. The generating station had been bombed, and there was no electricity nor electric transport. For all practical purposes, there was no road transport either, except what the Army brought. At the port, 60 per cent of the wharfage and 80 per cent of the covered accommodation was destroyed, all the plant and all the moorings were gone.

In cases like the water and electricity supplies, it was not only the sources of these supplies which were destroyed, but also the other ends of the systems. Taps and valves, switches and lamps and all detachable fittings had been looted from buildings. Vital parts had been taken from any plant or vehicle, which might have had a chance of functioning again, and, to make matters worse, all, or almost all, records of every description had been lost or destroyed. Even the cast iron manhole covers in the roads had been removed.

The repair of all this destruction depended very largely on local labour and the labour situation was very difficult. Rangoon had been a town of some 500,000 inhabitants, but, during the occupation or just before the re-capture, many thousands fled to the country, and only fifty per cent had returned. The supply of labour was accordingly very short, and there was no means of keeping what was available in the work where it was most wanted. Every service required labour badly, but the labourers moved at will from the more important work to the easier jobs, or to private employment, which recognised no standard wage and was prepared to pay almost any rate, because any price could be asked for the smallest job. Having come from England, where men and women were, during the war, directed to work as required or frozen in their jobs, it seemed to me that some such temporary measure was urgently necessary in Rangoon, in its undoubted emergency. Such a measure would, in my opinion, have speeded rehabilitation and resisted inflation to a marked degree.

I had known Rangoon in peace time, and walking through its streets again was a bewildering experience. In places, one had to clamber over heaps of debris and, in other places, the path was carpeted with Japanese occupation currency notes, thrown away because they had been declared valueless. It would have been impossible to honour Jap currency, as the country was flooded with it. Rumour said that certain Japanese officials ground it out of hand machines as required, much like issuing bus tickets. The roads were riddled with enormous pot holes and mud, filth and water lay over large areas. Some small shops had opened, in an half-hearted manner, and it was surprising to see, among their scanty wares, certain British made goods, such as soap, razor-blades and tooth paste, which had undoubtedly been hidden for three years through fear of confiscation. Fear must have been the predominating emotion through those years, and, indeed, British Officers told me that the people seemed completely dazed when the British Forces arrived, everything had to be repeated several times before it was taken in.

A complete collection of Japanese publications and propaganda sheets as issued to the occupied countries would, I imagine, be most interesting. Some of the pictorial magazines, such as *Front, Sakura* and the *Light of Asia*, were most attractive and carried some amazing war photographs and sketches, and, here and there, pictures and notes on ordinary peace-time activities, all directed to the glorification of Japan. The notes were in English and, sometimes, in half a dozen Asiatic languages as well. The great themes were the strength and the kindliness of the Japanese and the British-American-Dutch iniquities in Asia. Thus, from the *Light of Asia*, the following note comes, accompanied by many pictures of Allied prisoners at work.

> *"The number of war prisoners captured by the Nippon forces totals 400,000. Native troops who were misled by America and Britain into fighting against Nippon were released and allowed to return to their homes, while the American and British war prisoners are well and working happily under the considerate treatment of the Nippon forces."*

Some of the picture papers were cunningly designed, so that, in order to open them, it was necessary to tear across pictures of the Union Jack and Stars and Stripes—a symbolical action.

Other magazines, like the *Nippon Times Review* and the *Construction of the Greater East Asia Co-prosperity Sphere*, were well compiled booklets of mostly reading matter. The latter, published in 1943, carried essays from people in the occupied territories, and a Filipino, who won a prize, wrote:

> *"The East was once master of the earth. Mighty in arms and renowned in culture, the world was at its feet. But the relentless grinding of the wheels of destiny transported power to the West, and, abusing that power, the West in turn brought misery and poverty, oppression and tyranny to the East...*

> *"As an elder brother to unfortunate sister nations who have fallen under the ruthless yoke of Anglo-American greed, Nippon could not countenance their continued exploitation, and could not remain unmoved by the sorrowful plight of the peoples of Asia. Guided by the lofty ideal of Hakko Ichiu or*

Universal Brotherhood, she could not tolerate the ruthlessness of those powers in their efforts to perpetually enslave the East...

"Verily, the Greater East Asia war is a Sacred War, fought in the name of justice and righteousness, liberty and equality.

"It has brought about the happy reunion of the great Oriental family of nations, made whole once more in the creation of the Greater East Asia Co-prosperity Sphere."

There were other prize winners carefully distributed among the subject peoples. One was from Rangoon, one from Singapore and one from Djakarta (Java).

Another interesting propaganda sheet was *The Mainichi*—"A National Newspaper for International Readers"—in which extravagant claims were made of successes for Japanese forces. It was also printed in English.

The list could go on almost indefinitely, but I think the point to note is that, for three and a half years, Japan sowed seeds of many varieties and intensively cultivated vast areas of not unfertile ground. It would be too much to hope that all of those seeds have died or that all the young growths have been strangled. What kind of maturity those which have survived will attain is of considerable importance, but is unpredictable, in view of changes in gardeners and in forms of manuring.

On August 1st, 1943, Japan gave Burma a nominal independence, but there seems to have been little that was independent about it. The Burmese took it seriously, and a Declaration of Independence was issued, over the name of

Ba Maw, President of the Burma Constituent Assembly, which began:

> *"To-day, after more than fifty years of British occupation, Burma resumes her rightful place among the free and sovereign nations of the world."*

The Declaration goes on to talk of British intrigue, bribery and fraud, of British greed, tyranny and cruelty, and of Burma's gratitude to Nippon. It declares that Burma is a member of the Great East Asia Co-prosperity Sphere and that the war, against the Anglo-American enemies, is its war. A separate Declaration of war was issued the same day.

More than a year later, in September 1944, Vol. 1, No. 1 of a stately publication, entitled *Burma*, was issued by the Foreign Affairs Association, Rangoon. While it continually admits the leadership of Japan it, on the whole, displays a lessening of Japanese influence and a preoccupation with Burmese affairs. There is much to ponder over in this book of which this paragraph is typical:

> *"The East Asiatic War is a challenge of the New Order in the East. It marks the end of an epoch of thought. What is more, it opens a new page in the history of mankind. The East under the leadership of Nippon has made a lasting protest with all the ardours of a religious faith against the grinding repression of the West with all its pathetic faith in mechanical science."*

As time went on, the Burmese began to see the possibility of Japan's defeat. This must have been an awkward moment for the so-called independent government. Even if it were allowed that this government consisted of patriotic Burmans, concerned with the welfare of Burma, and if it were assumed they knew Britain would grant independence, they still had little choice but to oppose Britain's return. This they did with all vigour. A new War Government was formed, which issued the following statement of policy:

THE MAHABAMA POLICY

Statement issued by the new Mahabama War Government upon its formation on Thursday, the 1st February, 1945.

Having succeeded in expelling the British with the help of the Nipponese forces at the beginning of the present Asiatic war Burma won back the independence which she had enjoyed without a break since her history began and lost for a period owing to British conquest. As a result the new National State of Mahabamanainggan or Greater Burma, enjoying full independence and sovereignty, came into existence over a year ago. This State was established in alignment with the war aims professed by all the powers now at war. None gave more emphatic expression to these aims than the Anglo-Americans who in their Atlantic Charter have declared that "they respect the right of all peoples to choose the form of government under which they will live; and they wish to see sovereign rights and self-government restored to those who have been forcibly deprived of them." This was subsequently enlarged by the American President on February, the 23rd, 1942, to include the "whole world." It was upon foundations categorically accepted on all sides that the Mahabamas set up their new State.

To-day, this State is engaged in a life and death struggle with the old British enemy who has thrown words aside and invaded its territory with the avowed purpose of annexing it again to his empire. The British have brought the war with all its brutishness back into the very heart of Burma. The result is that our people, whose only wish is to pursue their own lives and fortunes in accordance with the universally accepted war aims, are now being forced to defend not only their independence, but even their homes against the most bare-faced act of aggression ever committed. The aggressor has recently announced in a blueprint and also in parliamentary statements that in place of our present independence he would assert the old-time imperialist prerogative to settle our affairs for us, including the form of government Burma would have within his empire as well as the time when she would have it. In other words, no war aim or charter or any such thing would be allowed to come between him and his prize of war.

A new struggle for their existence has therefore been forced at this moment upon the Mahabamas. Every Mahabama knows that either compromise or surrender is now out of the question. No cause could be juster, holier, more basic than the Mahabama cause in the present battle for Burma. It is the clearest case of a conflict between right and might, the struggle of a small people against an enemy that wishes to enslave them because he thinks he has the arms and the allies to do so.

In order to resist the aggressor to the utmost the whole Mahabama nation is being reorganised on a war footing, beginning with the government. We, the members of the newly formed Mahabama war government, have to-day accepted the grave responsibility of leading our people at the time of their greatest trial. We give, both individually and collectively, solemn pledge to them, firstly, that we will be a national government for the service of the nation as a whole; next, that we will dedicate ourselves unconditionally to the first national task of defending the nation's independence against the Anglo American enemies in the closest unity with Nippon and the other East Asiatic nations; and lastly, that we will take up the parallel national task, also with the co-operation of Nippon, of substantiating the nation's independence all round so that its benefits, political, social, as well as economic, shall reach every Mahabama home in the fullest measure and the quickest time.

As a national war government we swear allegiance and service to these national tasks by accomplishing which alone will the peril now hanging over our state and nation be conquered.

At the same time we call upon the nation itself to follow us along the way we have shown. This is a Mahabama government and leadership, so every Mahabama must follow it; this is a Mahabama war, so every Mahabama must fight it; and this is Mahabama independence, so every Mahabama must enjoy it fully and concretely. We show here to our people the way that will lead them to victory in all things. Victory shall be ours in Burma as well as in

*East Asia; and then a new era of peace, prosperity
and free growth will begin for all East Asiatic lands
and peoples, and Mahabamanainggan will be for the
Mahabamas, Burma for the Burmese, forever.*

* * * * *

Yes, war-devastated Burma was an interesting study on
which one could have spent a long time. My time was,
however, very limited and my object was to find out, from
a hasty study of Rangoon, what might be expected in
Singapore and what could be done about it. I was not the
first in the field, for the Dutch had also sent a
representative, who had arrived the day before I had. The
Netherlands East Indies, with a number of large towns,
would also, in all probability, present similar problems. I
feel now as I did then, that even though, as it turned out,
conditions were different, it would have helped in Malaya,
if a closer and fuller study had been made in the liberated
territories of Burma and the Philippines, by the British
Authorities, before Malaya was reoccupied.

Back in Calcutta, I spent several days at a typewriter,
stripped to the waist, making out my report. With the
speed at which events were moving after my return from
Burma, it is unlikely that the report even got beyond the
nearest pigeon hole, it is most unlikely that it was ever
read by anyone who could direct policy, and it is
impossible that it had any effect on action. Nevertheless, I
like to remember that I recommended, among other
things, that:

*"(a) The Allied Air Forces be requested to avoid
bombing the towns in British territory, which are to
be liberated, except for such targets as are very
intimately connected with the enemy's military
strength. The general impression in Rangoon being,*

that the bombing there was more wide spread than necessary and had caused immeasurable difficulties for those who were subsequently charged with the rehabilitation.

"(b) That every effort should be made to avoid a hiatus, such as occurred between the evacuation of the Japanese and the arrival of the British. This might involve some concentration of the Intelligence Services in places where it was likely to happen, and maintaining a small force ever ready to be flown in at a moment's notice. The difficulties, caused by looting and other illegal activities, during the period when there was no government in Rangoon, could scarcely be exaggerated.

"(c) That Civil Affairs Officers should be in a liberated town at the earliest possible moment. The delay at Rangoon, due possibly to lack of co-operation with, or by, the fighting services, caused confusion in some services and delayed rehabilitation generally.

"(d) Both the Operational Forces and the Civil Affairs Officers should be made fully acquainted with the existence and functions of the Custodian of Property. It would appear that the lack of this knowledge, in Rangoon, resulted in in adequate records of requisitioned property and conditions, which sometimes looked uncomfortably like looting by Allied Forces.

"(e) That no exchange rate be fixed for Japanese occupation currency. The Japanese so flood occupied territory with paper money that, if a rate is fixed, the *liability will be enormous and many will profit dishonestly.*

"(f) That the labour situation be faced boldly. Fixing wage rates is not sufficient to ensure a proper distribution of man power, and, in consequence, rehabilitation is likely to suffer, as labour drifts irresponsibly from the more unpleasant and difficult jobs, which are frequently the more important ones, to less unpleasant and easier work, when there is an unsatisfied demand everywhere. In Rangoon, movements of this nature have taken place in spite of the crying needs of the situation, which require that resources be concentrated on the more important tasks. I am strongly of the opinion that, in an emergency such as is likely to be met in a city immediately after changing hands, some temporary measure of direction is desirable in the public interest.

"(g) That sewerage and conservancy be given a very high priority in men and materials, because neglect of these services in the tropics is likely to have deplorable results. The co-operation of fighting units, with all the resources at their command should be obtained in a drive to clear up. The town area should be sprayed from aircraft with D.D.T. as early as possible. Spraying in this way has had excellent results in Rangoon."

Calcutta's burning sun and lashing rain were at their worst, and it was with no regrets that I packed my 65 lbs of baggage in preparation for the flight to Ceylon. Once again the Hostel's arrangements worked perfectly in getting me to the airfield in accordance with Air Transport

Command's plan. That plan being, so far as I could judge, that intending passengers should arrive at the terminal building at least two hours before the time of departure.

CEYLON TO SINGAPORE

THE journey of about eleven hours by Dakota from Calcutta to Colombo was rather tiring, but full of interest. It is beyond dispute that Dakota machines did a tremendous job in South East Asia, but many a man, who had spent seemingly endless hours on the hard aluminium benches they were then fitted with, or perhaps on the equally hard floor, must have hated the sight of them.

On those routine trips, they were usually well filled with passengers and baggage and, sometimes, so packed that it was necessary to clamber over the baggage to get to one's place. Starting in the early morning and climbing rapidly, the first sensation was cold. The air was cold, and the cold metal benches made sitting uncomfortable. The best seats were often on top of mail bags or haversacks, and, if there were sufficient of them and one were lucky enough to get there first, it might be possible to make up some of the sleep lost by rising at 3 a.m.

On the journey, we came down and consumed meals at Vizagapatam and Bangalore. At the former place, there was burning heat and enveloping dust, and members of the Air Force ground staff were covered with prickly heat. It was a barren, deserted and insufferable sort of place. Bangalore, in the hills, was, by contrast, comparatively chilly, a very stiff wind was blowing and sand was in everything. One of the ground staff, who came to tend the aircraft, was shivering violently, as he had just been transferred there from the plains, some thousands of feet lower down.

From 'upstairs', as flying men say, we could see a fantastic land pass beneath us. From the Hooghly valley to Ceylon, there was little that was green. There were browns and reds and blues, there were artificial-looking hills and stupid-looking rivers, rivers which twisted and turned on themselves in absurd fashion and approached the sea, but never seemed to enter it. In fact, the mouths were frequently blocked by sand bars and the connections were subterranean. There were no roads and few tracks. Here and there, a little hamlet appeared looking entirely self-contained and seemingly scores of miles from anywhere.

Bathed in sunshine most of the way we experienced, nevertheless, periods of cloud and one lashing rainstorm. There can be few more fascinating sights than the view from an aircraft pursuing its course among great banks of white suntipped cloud. The tremendous bulks, the fantastic shapes, the exquisite colouring of these mountains and valleys of cloud take one's breath away. One moment, completely enveloped in a white blanket, the next, emerging into a pocket of brilliant sunshine with unbelievable blue above, and, all around, great heaps of the whitest wadding shot with tiny rainbows and swaths of refracted light.

When those peculiar fingers of land, which endeavour, fortunately in vain, to join Ceylon to India, had been passed we were over green country again, and landing at Colombo had, for me, something of the feeling of a home-coming. It was familiar ground.

Walkingshaw was still with me, having also been delayed in Calcutta behind the main body, and, once again, we made our way to a transit hostel. This time it was the annex to the Galle Face Hotel. What a treat it was to be there where the climate was infinitely better than Calcutta at this time of year, where one could sit on the green lawns of the Hotel on the edge of the sea, imbibe fresh breezes and feel clean. We had a bit of luck and spent two nights there, because No. 2 Area's transport and stores were being unloaded from a ship as we arrived, and it fell to us to shepherd this transport from Colombo to the camp, some sixty miles inland.

Watching over that convoy of trucks and jeeps, as they staggered through Colombo and along the roads of Ceylon, was an amusing and also an anxious job. Driven by Indian drivers, just disembarked from a ship on to strange territory and obviously a bit bewildered, the vehicles were anything but co-operative. Individually and collectively, they got on the wrong routes, stopped at the wrong places and times, went too fast or too slow, travelled either on the right-hand side of the road or with one wheel in the near-side ditch. Added to this imperfect display of driving, there were difficulties caused by our inability to speak to the drivers on account of the language, and it was largely due to Walkingshaw's excellent gestures that, in the end, they got without loss or accident to Kurunegala, the new Headquarters of No. 2 Area.

Kurunegala was at the foot of the hills, some twenty-six miles north-east of Kandy where the Headquarters of the Supreme Allied Commander and A.L.F.S.E.A. were established. About twenty-five miles east of Kandy and twelve miles south of Kurunegala, at the village of Polgahawela, there was a camp exclusively for Civil Affairs Officers which appeared to be still born. Some officers were there, and undoubtedly some work was done, but there never seemed to be more than a handful of people, which changed very frequently. At this time, there were Malayan Civil Affairs Officers with A.L.F.S.E.A. in Kandy, with No. 2 Area in Kurunegala, at Polgahawela camp, in the main civil affairs transit camp at Pallavaram near Madras, en route to India from England and other parts of the earth, perhaps, also, in Calcutta and New Delhi and, certainly, still in England. Where the files, papers and baggage were was a matter for conjecture.

At Kurunegala, things became very business-like and I began to see more clearly the shape of things to come. Gathered at that spot were the Area Commander and his staff, contingents from the Navy and Air Force and a nucleus of the Civil Affairs branch. All were planning for the day when they would arrive in Singapore, and co-ordinating that planning with each other. They represented the Administration, which would later control the Island in the interests of the operational forces and of the local inhabitants, according to requirements. The fighting forces would pass on beyond Singapore, but the Island would be a base through which would pass men and materials, and, in which, there would be hospitals, rest camps, repair shops and stores. It was necessary that Singapore should contribute, as far as possible, to the operations elsewhere, while, at the same time, put its own house in order.

The plan of attack on Malaya had been worked out, and many code words for the various operations were being whispered. A beach-head was to be established in the Port Swettenham-Port Dickson area by a great amphibious operation, and, from there, it was intended that an armoured force should push with all speed, down the main road to Singapore. At the same time, paratroops were to be dropped on the Singapore airfields, and an assault made from the sea. Great land forces, a large fleet and overwhelming air strength were being prepared for the operation, and, from what was later discovered about the Japanese dispositions and lack of preparedness, the attack would have been entirely successful, though, almost certainly, many casualties would have resulted and the town of Singapore would have suffered severely.

Apparently someone had been at work, for, this time, the Civil Affairs Officers were to get the opportunity of being in the town at the earliest possible moment. I was asked if I would volunteer for the 'Zipper' Operation—the name given to the task of the armoured column, which, it was hoped, would open Malaya like a zip and secure the Singapore docks, so that a sea-borne convoy might disembark. I was glad of the opportunity to be in with the first. Other Civil Affairs Officers were to be with the convoy, in order that the government in 'Shackle' (the code name for Singapore) would suffer only a very short break, if any.

No. 2 Area had taken over, as offices, a sizeable schoolhouse in Kurunegala, and working conditions were relatively good. There were two camps for accommodation, one in the school grounds and the other at the edge of a lake on the far side of the rather dirty little village. This latter camp was pleasantly situated in a cocoanut plantation with a sandy subsoil, and was surrounded, at short distances, by great, picturesque outcrops of rock rising, in some places, to a thousand feet or more. At the camp, still in the process of being built when we arrived, there were few amenities and it took quite a bit of hard work and scrounging to make one's basha habitable. The only light was from hurricane lamps, which, in the dark-walled bashas, did little to relieve the gloom. Food was poor and not too plentiful and water was scarce, as it seemed to be in almost all Ceylon that summer. Kandy suffered an acute shortage, and the lake there, like the one at Kuranegala, went down and down.

Even when one knows how water is purified for the consumer, it is still disturbing to see people, clothes and cattle being washed in the source of supply. This was what happened, if the lake outside our camp supplied Kuranegala's water, which appeared to be the case. Fortunately, we had a well within the camp.

There was not much time or opportunity for recreation, but those who had to work off surplus energy improvised various games, to many of which no name could be given. Cocoanut trees, cocoanuts, jeeps, steel-helmets and other articles to hand were employed as sports gear and the last half-hour of daylight was usually filled with the cries and exhortations of sportsmen. The lack of adequate light prevented all but the most enthusiastic from reading or writing after dark, so these hours were filled with song, light and serious, racy and sentimental. I felt it was a healthy life, and when I climbed, as I sometimes was able to do in the evening, one of those enormous rocks to drink in the cool breezes and look on a large expanse of beautiful Ceylon, I came back for my cold shower, feeling preposterously fit.

Office hours were lengthy, from about eight in the morning till six or six-thirty at night, but, for me, as most of my planning was completed, the work was light. There was no easing at the week-end, which was unmarked, except for a service held by the Padre, in a 10 foot by 12 foot basha, on Sunday mornings. Anything from ten to twenty officers might be present and it struck me that they were drawn from the oldest and the youngest in the camp. Is there a span in early middle age when church going is less attractive than at other periods? The Padre was topical and forcible at those services and the hand-blown harmonium had a brave following. This particular Padre was certainly worthy of his hire, for, apart from his functional duties, he seemed to get every odd job in the camp and carry it out with cheerfulness and efficiency.

A great deal of my time in office was spent in assisting, with my personal knowledge of Singapore, officers who were planning without that asset. Accommodation in the town was one of their problems and I was asked endless questions about all the buildings in Singapore, which seemed to afford quarters, offices or storage. Obviously, there were to be great forces in Singapore with many needs, and, indeed, I got something of a shock when I saw the final plan of the town divided between S.A.C.S.E.A., A.L.F.S.E.A., A.C.S.E.A., and countless other 'seas', which were to inundate the already heavily populated elysium. It was also part of my duties to study air photographs, recently taken over Singapore, and pick out the additions and subtractions, which the Japanese had effected to the Singapore I knew in 1942. This was fascinating. Although the alterations did not appear to be very many, it was exciting to discover them and to endeavour to assess their meaning or contents.

A fair amount of time was taken in going to and from Kandy for meetings at S.A.C.S.E.A. or A.L.F.S.E.A. Headquarters. It was pleasant driving up the twisty mountain road to the somewhat cooler air at Kandy. The road, which hung on the mountain side, saw the last moments of many a military vehicle and casualties to many more. It was a narrow, dangerous road and military drivers in S.E.A.C. were not conspicuous, as a rule, for their carefulness or skill. S.A.C.S.E.A. Headquarters were comfortably located in the Botanical Gardens at Peradeniya, but A.L.F.S.E.A. was, to my way of thinking, situated in an absurd terrain some three miles beyond Kandy on the steep banks of a river. The road gradients within the area were dangerously steep in places, and finding one's way about was a nightmare, until the place became familiar. Building, on a large scale, was still going on and continued after Japan collapsed, how long after, I do not know, for, I am told, this sort of work is as difficult to stop as to start.

Kandy was a hive of military activity and teeming with soldiers, mostly wearing S.A.C.S.E.A. and A.L.F.S.E.A. flashes. The former looked from a distance like the hind legs of a goat, but was, on closer examination a Phoenix rising from flames. Very appropriately chosen, still, I wished the goat likeness had been eliminated. Here I got my first glimpse of the man responsible for it all, Lord Louis Mountbatten. He was driving his own jeep adorned with the five Allied flags, the flags of Britain, U.S.A., France, Holland and China. That the post of Supreme Allied Commander was well filled, there can be no doubt, Lord Mountbatten had, from what I heard and saw, all and more of the personality and ability required for such a post.

At Kandy, there were hotels, officers' clubs and an officers' shop. There were also ordinary shops of a good standard, and, although they were not nearly so well stocked as the shops in India, it was possible to buy odds and ends to help out camp existence. Altogether, a visit to Kandy was a pleasant break, especially if it could be combined with an evening in the town, good meals and possibly a cinema.

Simla, Delhi, Calcutta, Kandy, Colombo and other places, which later included Singapore, were centres where servicemen and women could and did have a comparatively good time. That means that they had some of the pleasures and comforts they would normally have had in civilian life; in some cases, it might even mean that they had more than that. Many sarcastic things were said

74

and written about winning the war from Delhi and elsewhere, and, understandably, they were mostly said and written by men who spent most of their time in the less comfortable places about men who spent most of theirs in the more comfortable places. I don't know if the pilots who flew over Germany said similar things about the ground staffs in England, or if the sailors at sea said them about the dockyard hands, but I rather think not. It seemed unique to the Army. The unequal distribution of unpleasant duties was something to ponder on, but it appeared unavoidable. An army must have its rear and most of the men there had been through the mill at one time or another. A few, of course, had not and they were just lucky, or unlucky, according to the point of view. At any rate, in my experience, the great majority of them worked very hard and, in spite of the amenities they enjoyed, they were anxious to get it over and get home. They may have considered it as the better of two evils but not as a first choice.

All that military world, in an operational theatre, was new to me and I took an interest in studying it. Not profoundly, but as work and circumstances permitted. The high-ranking officers, with very few exceptions, seemed extremely competent, pleasant and unassailably democratic. Other officers, relatively elderly, with established peace-time positions in civilian life, did things well, but frequently with no particular enthusiasm, though they seemed to be anxious to get it over and finished with. Men, who had grown from boys, in the six years of war, were still boys in many ways, although they were Lieutenant Colonels, Majors and Captains in the Army. They were keen to get into civvies, but rather dreaded the life they knew nothing of, and were apprehensive of the sort of position they might hold in it. That was one of the things which, in their own

The children of Singapore greet their liberators,
September 5th, 1945

phraseology, they just wouldn't know. The men from the ranks varied tremendously, some were very capable and some quite unreliable, but all good fellows in the generally accepted meaning of that term. The region they were being privileged to see, on the whole, meant nothing to them, it was just another place and one they didn't wish to be in much longer. They were descendants of John Bull and John Peel rather than of Raffles or Rhodes.

The military machine, as a whole, seemed well balanced and carefully organised, a world in which every man knew his place and generally knew his job. It should have been a model of efficiency, but it wasn't, at least not at all times. Perhaps, it had grown too quickly, and there had been too many changes in personnel and too many *ad hoc* arrangements, dictated by events outside its control, to allow it to achieve the efficiency of a compact, static peace-time department. If that was the trouble, then the fault lay in insufficient flexibility, or so it would seem. Anyhow the heads of the civil departments I had known always had more control over the output of their staffs than appeared to be held by Officers Commanding. It was surprising how frequently a proposal, which had been approved at a meeting where all the highest officers concerned were present, still did not get carried out, and how often instructions issued were not followed up by a check. On the other hand, in emergencies, when red tape was cut, the army certainly got things done quickly and well. It was at ordinary times, when there was no imminent danger or no emergency to be dealt with, that it seemed so hard to move or stop or guide.

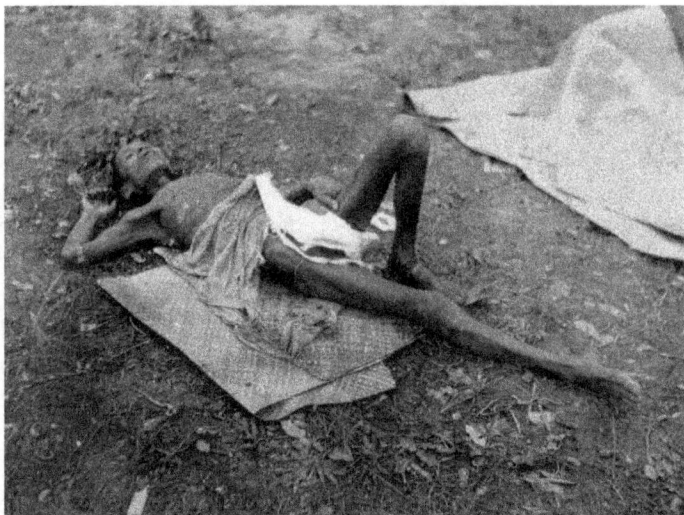

Reminiscent of the Belsen victims,
a Singapore coolie lies dying of starvation.

As an exasperating instance of this, my own endeavour to obtain some special vehicles is typical. Among the supplies I had listed a year earlier, as being particularly necessary immediately after reoccupation, were some thirty lorries with special bodies for conservancy work in connection with the sanitation of the large part of Singapore which was not served by sewers. These vehicles consisted of a standard army truck chassis fitted with a body of a special type, which, though unusual, was simple to construct. The army had accepted the responsibility for providing them and had been supplied with drawings some months before I arrived in India. With simple faith I believed that all was well until, some weeks after I got to Ceylon, when a signal arrived to say that one pilot model was about to be started and it was necessary that an expert be sent to Calcutta immediately to give guidance.

I had to go. Again that weary flight to Calcutta, again the Grand Hotel Hostel, again the heat, the humidity, the dirt of Calcutta. My instructions from high levels in Ceylon were to see that, in Calcutta, they knew beyond doubt exactly how those vehicles were to be constructed, and to ensure that a start would immediately be made, not on one, but on all that were required. That, as might be expected, involved a number of people including the manufacturers, the Tank Development Board, the Directorate of Mechanisation and others. I talked to all and ensured that the manufacturers were in a position to carry out the work at a satisfactory rate, that the Tank Development Board knew exactly what was wanted, that the necessary steel could be released and so on. Again, with simple faith, I returned to Kurunegala, where the arrangements I had made were confirmed by letters bearing important signatures. About two months after Singapore was reoccupied, the pilot model arrived alone in its glory. A lengthy correspondence ensued and, after another four months, I was assured categorically that the remaining vehicles would be sent. Another two months passed and I was informed, equally categorically, that there would only be the one I already had, no more would be made. I gave it up. These vehicles were urgently wanted all the time.

I arrived back in Kurunegala on the evening of August 8th, having travelled from Colombo in the SEAC Express, a comfortable train on which one could get a meal. It ran every evening, especially for South East Asia Command. The staff at Kurunegala, which had been increasing every day had, by then, reached a considerable figure. It was there that I first met, and began working with, Colonel Magnus Pearse, who was afterwards to be Chief Engineer, Singapore District. He and others, whom he had brought with him, had been on similar duties in Rangoon, and they had that useful experience to draw upon. Colonel Tydeman, an old friend from pre-war Singapore, was also there and was using his knowledge of the Singapore Harbour, on which he had previously been employed, for planning in connection with the port. Commander Martin and Commander Legg, other pre-war Singapore friends, were attached to the Naval Contingent and were enjoying the little extra amenities the Navy always seem to have, wherever they find themselves.

One day, without warning, James Beattie and Walter Dawson arrived from the Malayan Planning Unit in London, and, altogether, there was a fair sprinkling of men who knew the country. This surprised at least one officer who, in conversation with Tydeman and myself, said sarcastically, "the Army must be losing its grip to send you fellows, who know the place and may be useful, to Singapore." Still, I was wondering where my other officers were and when they would arrive, for the prospect at that time looked a bit grim for the technical services of Singapore. I had asked for a minimum staff of 57 officers, and the position, at that moment, was that only Beattie and myself were in Ceylon. Seven other former municipal employees were available, of those I had left six in London and heard nothing of since, and one was still in the U.S.A. Of the remaining 48, I could reasonably expect to get, on loan from the Peninsula Section, five former officers of the Malayan Public Works Department, who were probably in India, but the other 43 were nowhere on the horizon. From a list of service volunteers, which I had seen while at Hyde Park Gate, I had selected a number of officers, who appeared to have the necessary qualifications, and had requested that they be posted to me, but I had heard nothing further. My need for a full staff was more pressing than I imagined.

The camp mess had recently acquired a radio, which gave a very mixed performance. It had been taken down and put together several times by self-styled experts, but still refused to be consistent in its output, ninety per cent of which remained indecipherable. In spite of that, someone generally switched it on for the news, and occasionally something could be heard. The possibility of hearing much was, however, so remote that I had, long ago, given up groping my way, in the dark over rough ground, from my basha to the mess, to listen at 9 p.m. Two nights after my return from Calcutta, that was on August 10th, my hurricane lamp was burning so badly that I broke my nightly custom of reading for an hour before early bed, and went back to the mess at news time. The radio was clearer than I had ever heard it and the news it gave forth will live in history for all time. Japan had offered to surrender, provided the Emperor's sovereignty was not prejudiced. Well, if it wasn't the end, nobody in that camp doubted that it was just as good.

Bush telegraphy alone can account for the rapidity with which the news spread. In a few seconds the pitch black cocoanut plantation was alive with surprised, bewildered, exultant men racing and stumbling towards the mess. This was not like the end of the European war, which had faded out gradually with the cease-fire long imminent, this was unexpected and unbelievably good. Men, who had fought for five and a half years, had been wondering if their luck would hold for another half, all had been wondering what the next few months would do to them. The burden was suddenly lifted and they celebrated. Things went up or down according to their natures. Spirits and the roof rose, spirits of another kind and coconuts descended, and when the camp went to bed later, it had had a day.

The next day, Saturday, was also a full day. It went without saying, that we would be on the move soon, and, possibly, very suddenly. The military telephones got red hot as everyone tried to find out what was the next step. Speculation was rife. No one seemed to doubt that the ultimate surrender would come almost immediately, and, meanwhile, we waited impatiently for instructions. By evening, it was obvious that they would not come that day, and most of No. 2 Area found its way to Kandy to continue its celebration in better equipped and more spacious surroundings.

During the next three days, everyone acted as though the surrender were completed. The office was packed up and final arrangements made to move on a moment's notice. I received instructions to be ready to leave for Rangoon on the 16th, and, as it was necessary that I should have a few officers, at least, in Singapore as soon as I arrived, or very shortly afterwards, a signal was sent to the Base Camp at Pallavaram, asking that five officers be sent immediately to Kurunegala. The selected five, Morgan, Wilson, Inglis, Oborne and White must have been pretty slick, for they arrived on the morning of the 16th, an hour and a half before I left. They were all Public Works Department Officers of the Malayan Government.

On the afternoon of the 15th, I was summoned to Kandy to attend a meeting of the War Establishment Committee at A.L.F.S.E.A. The presiding officer was perhaps thinking of going home for he proved very unappreciative of the transport requirements for my work in Singapore and left me almost without a wheel. For that matter, he might as well have cut out the lot, for what I did get in the end was so little, and came so late, that it made no difference. Throughout the next year transport, or rather the lack of it, proved one of the biggest problems in rehabilitating Singapore.

After the meeting, I went to the Queen's Hotel for my evening meal and learnt that Japan had finally surrendered. That evening, Kandy was gay with bands of soldiers going about the streets singing and rejoicing. There was a carefree atmosphere such as I hadn't remembered seeing for six long years. It was good to see, but involuntarily my mind went back to the end of the previous war. On November 11th, 1918, I was, as a boy, rejoicing in the revels, which accompanied that relief. In the course of the day, I came on a young man sitting in his rooms studying and asked him, in surprise, if he was not celebrating the end of the war instead of "stewing at books". He looked up and said, "I don't feel like it, the period after war is always worse than during the war." I was so profoundly shocked, I could find no answer and left him.

On the morning of August 16th, Brigadier Pearse, James Beattie and I set out by road for Colombo. It had been arranged that we three should fly to Rangoon to embark with the convoy, which was to occupy Singapore, the others following shortly after by sea from Colombo. With us, to Colombo, came another officer of Pearse's staff to see us safely off and take the jeeps back. It was always useful to have someone to see one off on those air trips, as he took charge of that part of one's baggage, which failed to get on board. An allowance of 65 lbs. was given, and, of course, on a journey like that, when the next contact with possessions was very uncertain, one wanted to take every ounce of the 65 lbs. and a bit more, if possible. There was usually no means of having it accurately weighed before arrival at the airfield, and, then, there was that bit extra, which might or might not get through. In case one were told to off-load some weight, the man who did the seeing-off could avoid what would otherwise be a complete loss. It was seldom he went back without something, and frequently with a surprising amount.

On the road to Colombo, there were pleasing signs of the war's end. Here and there, little houses were bright with flags, and, sometimes, a small group of Ceylonese would cheer and wave as we passed. One officer set me thinking by saying, "These people don't know what it means to them. They will feel the draught, after all the money the Forces have spent here." Was that true? These people had lived relatively happily and relatively prosperously before the war and the servicemen came, could they not do so again? It seemed a truism, that neither their life, nor anyone else's, could ever be the same, but would it be better or worse in the changing East?

Colombo had declared a public holiday and was en fête. It was pleasant to mix with happy crowds at the swimming pool, the Galle Face Hotel and the Silver Fawn and talk to an occasional old friend. Most of them were, however, talking of relaxing and going home, which was a little disturbing to one going further away to what must prove, at best, to be a relentless grind for some time to come.

At least two Dakatos left for Calcutta the next morning. Pearse and I got on the first, Beattie on the second. Beattie got there first, and, by the time we arrived at the Grand Hotel Hostel, he had completed all the preliminaries and established our right to a good room. We had left Ceylon with a movement order giving us exceedingly high priority in travel, to ensure that we would not fail to catch the convoy, which was expected to leave Rangoon on the 20th. It seemed unlikely that, even with that, we could arrange to get on the Rangoon aircraft the next morning, as the booking for it would have been completed by the time we arrived in Calcutta, still, we meant to try. It was of no avail, but we were not unduly worried, as, by departing the day after, Sunday 19th, we should still be in time.

I have talked to all ranks, from generals down, about the seemingly strange methods of Transport Command's Air Booking Offices, and about the connections between the Indian Command and South East Asia Command. All have admitted ignorance. None knew exactly where the Indian Command left off or where South East Asia began, no one knew why certain people were taken on aircraft before others, who, almost beyond a shadow of doubt, were on a more important duty. The fact that our urgent transit authority from Ceylon carried little weight in Calcutta, or seemed to carry little, was attributed, by some, to the influence of Indian Command. Anyway we were kept waiting for days, until we had given up hope of catching the convoy at Rangoon.

Calcutta was just as hot and as humid as it had been on previous occasions, and prickly heat soap was just as necessary. An Army order compelled all ranks to wear slacks and long sleeves after 6.30 p.m., as an anti-mosquito precaution. It was much more uncomfortable than wearing shorts and half sleeves, but it was a sensible measure. What riled the Army was that sailors were apparently not subject to the order, and went about all evening in the lighter attire, while, of course, the women of the services exposed legs, arms and often shoulders to attack. In such a climate, nothing can be more annoying than to see others looking cooler and more comfortable than you are allowed to be.

The period of waiting for an air passage afforded an opportunity of seeing something more of the city. It had excellent stores and shops and a fascinating place called the New Market where anything could be bought at a price, which varied according to the rank of the purchaser. At a number of the stores such as the Army and Navy Store, Hall and Anderson's and Whiteaway Laidlaw's, there were good restaurants, and Firpo's Restaurants are world famous for atmosphere. Calcutta did not lack clubs, there was the very exclusive Bengal Club, the very attractive Tollygunge Club, which, with its surrounding green fields and gardens, formed a delightful well-kept oasis in a wilderness of dirt and neglect. There were golf clubs and swimming clubs and clubs to cater for other modern tastes, such as the Saturday Club and the 300 Club. There was an ENSA theatre, and any number of cinemas. There were churches and monuments to visit, and there was the Botanical Gardens, some distance along the river. The gardens had some extraordinary fine trees, but lacked colour when I saw it, and the grass was repulsively coarse.

By the evening of the 19th, we had given up hope of getting a passage through the normal channels in time to catch the convoy, indeed, we had heard rumours that the convoy had sailed that day, though other rumours denied it. Brigadier Pearse decided that he and I should try another way next day, so we got up at 3.30 a.m., and went on the airfield truck to Dum Dum in the hope of 'thumbing' a lift to Rangoon. We sat at the airfield till late afternoon, without success. We saw ENSA parties go off and many other people, who, in our conceit, we considered must be on much less important missions than ourselves. The position seemed absurd: we had been sent post-haste from Ceylon, so as to be in Singapore with the first forces to take over the vital services, we were part of the organisation for occupation, and yet, even with papers and all the authority the Brigadier could bring to bear, we could not get to the muster point. We might as well have been tourists trying to gate-crash. I think it was one of the many disadvantages of being officers, for I feel that if South East Asia Command had sent off two privates, with a high priority movement order, those men would have been shepherded to their destination in such a way as to exclude any hope of delay.

Back in Calcutta that evening, we paid another visit to the Air Booking Office at Victoria House and, by exerting all our powers, secured passages for the next day. Beattie, they would not take, and so he was left to spend, what he afterwards described, as his most miserable birthday. It did indeed seem hard luck. After being the first commissioned officer with me in London and the first in Ceylon, and having got so far towards being in Singapore at the beginning, it now looked as though his chances were gone and he was stranded—of all places—in Calcutta, left behind by the advance party, and far away from the main body. All we could tell him was to try his best to get to Rangoon by any means—and hope.

By one means or another, I had contracted a filthy cold in my head while in Calcutta, and the flight to Rangoon was agony. I had never previously experienced what it was like to climb to high altitudes and descend, while suffering from a bad cold in the head and it is an experience I don't wish to repeat. By the time we reached our destination, I was beyond caring about anything much, but it was, nevertheless, a relief to hear that the convoy was still lying in the river with the date of sailing, as yet, uncertain.

Over roads, which had deteriorated still further since my last visit, we made the usual round of offices to find out what was happening, and eventually arranged to go on board the next day. Lt.-Colonel Walker, who was in charge of the technical services in Rangoon, gave us hospitality that night. It had been a miserable day with rain and storm, and the town gave the impression of being exceedingly wretched. The terrible roads, the battered buildings, the lack of adequate electricity and water and the poor accommodation, which men were occupying, was all very depressing. I fervently hoped that Singapore would be in much better shape.

The next day brought ups and downs, fuss and bother about getting a launch to take us to the convoy some two miles down the river. In the end, and somehow, we found ourselves, with others, on board an R.A.F. launch, but I suspect that the R.A.F. transporting the Army on the Navy's element was just a chance occurrence and not an example of an organised combined operation. It was with a sense of triumph over organisation that I mounted the gangway of the *Derbyshire*.

Some months previously, when the success of the Burma campaign was assured, forces had been withdrawn from there to India to form a regrouped XIVth Army. Those left in Burma became the new XIIth Army. The regrouped XIVth Army, under the command of Lieutenant-General Sir Miles Dempsey, was training and preparing for the Zipper Operation, scheduled for September 9th, but was not, I gather, in a position at the time of Japan's collapse to occupy Malaya immediately. It seemed that the only force ready to embark, at that moment, was the 5th Indian Division at Rangoon, and so ships were sent there to form a convoy for the occupation of Singapore as a first step. The Division was embarked by the time we arrived, but, of course, for an operation of this nature, other smaller units had to be attached such as Port Parties, Medical Units, RAPWI (Rehabilitation of Allied Prisoners of War and Internees), Administrative Units and odds and ends like ourselves. These were gathering gradually, travelling most likely, as we did, on the every-man-for-himself basis. Then, and for several months after, there appeared to be an intense scramble by servicemen and former civilian residents to get to Malaya.

The *Derbyshire* was the headquarters ship of the convoy and the Commander of the 5th Indian Division, Major-General C. Mansergh was on board. At least one large apartment was fitted up as an office where last-minute planning and preparations went on and there were continual meetings and conferences. The 'Tannoy' broadcasting equipment was never silent. The ship's complement consisted of well over a hundred officers and a fair number of Indian troops. War-correspondents were also aboard in force, so, altogether, conditions were very cramped, and deck space at a premium. The food was good and plentiful, but water was severely rationed. Almost all had come on board with dirty clothes and very few of them at that, and, as there were no facilities for washing, we were not a very spick and span company. I had not, before, seen mepachrin-fed forces, where the effects showed up to anything like the extent they did among the battle-seasoned men on that ship. Mepachrin played no small part in winning the tropical fight against malaria, but it did have a ghastly effect on the skin, staining it all colours from brass-yellow to green-brown, and in a patchy way. Without pre-warning, one might have been excused for thinking this army belonged to another race of people, and a less aesthetic combination than jungle-green clothes and dirty brass complexions can scarcely be imagined.

After our rush to get there, we lay in the Rangoon River for another week, all the more impatiently because the reason was not disclosed. There were several good reasons, but, in my simplicity, I still doubt if they were adequate to weigh against the desirability of getting to Singapore at the earliest possible moment. General Itagaki, in charge of the 7th Japanese Army in Singapore, was reported to have issued a 'no surrender' call in spite of his country's capitulation, and so it seemed possible that early occupation would involve a fight. Then there was something about the surrender in Japan having to be signed before we entered Singapore, and also a period of waiting was incurred while the Japanese envoys came from Saigon to receive instructions as to our reception and to disclose information about such things as minefields. Even one British life is invaluable, but it seems questionable as to whether the immediate occupation of Malaya and the Netherlands East Indies would not have shown a credit in soldiers' lives, as it would certainly have done in the lives of Malays, Chinese and Indians in Malaya, and of sundry peoples in Indonesia. It would have, beyond doubt, eased a number of difficulties later met with.

While we were waiting for the event nearest to hand—the arrival of the envoys from Saigon—there was another arrival very welcome to me. Major James Beattie, triumphant over circumstances, stepped aboard the *Derbyshire*. He had come by sea from Calcutta and landed at Rangoon the previous evening. That was not an end to his trials, for, although we had left his name on shore with instructions for him to be sent out to join us should he arrive, he could, at first, find no one who had ever heard of him or would assist or even allow him to get to the convoy. His own description was most amusing, of how, in monsoon rain, he got evicted from one office after another, was finally sent to a transit camp sixteen miles out of the town, found there a tendency to postpone his release *sine die*, broke camp, borrowed a jeep, returned to Rangoon, invaded another office, refusing to leave till he heard something, thought better of it in the morning and went back to the first office he had called at. Speaking to the same officer as he had seen the previous day he said:

"If a message comes for me will you please let me know?"

"Yes, certainly old man."

"You have a note of my name. It is spelt B-E-A-T-T-I-E."

"Oh yes. That's all right."

Beattie turned and was at the door, when he was called back, "Here what did you say your name was?"

"Beattie. B-E-A-T-T-I-E."

"Why you're the man we have been looking for all over the place. Take this and get on board at once."

About 8.30 a.m. on Sunday, August 26th, we saw the two Topsy aircraft, painted silver with green crosses, which brought the Japanese envoys. They were escorted by Spitfires and were two hours behind the scheduled time. The twenty-two members of the surrender delegation were headed by Lt.-General Numata, Admiral Chudo (Deputy Chief of Staff to Field Marshal Terauchi, the Supreme Japanese Commander in South East Asia) and Lt.-Colonel Tomuria of the Japanese Southern Army Staff. They were met at Mingaladon airfield by Lt.-General Sir Montagu Stafford (Commander, Twelfth Army), Major-General W. S. Symes and Major-General F. S. Tucker. At the meeting, they were apparently confused, and saluted awkwardly after a hurried conversation between themselves—a typical example of Japanese behaviour when associating with Europeans. I remember, many years before the war, being entertained to lunch by some Japanese in a European-type hotel. They were all most anxious to behave as we behave, but never trusted their own judgment. All through the meal, there were whispered conversations going on, obviously about what to do, and then, after one of these, they would all do the same thing at the same time, such as grab their fish-forks or fold their napkins.

The Japanese delegation was driven from the airfield in closed station-wagons, and was billetted in two good residential houses. These houses, like others in Rangoon, were not too well furnished, and the members of the delegation had to sleep on charpoys. It is amusing to note that they brought their own rations and chop-sticks.

The talks between the Allied Staff, headed by Lt.-General F. A. M. Browning, Chief of Staff to the Supreme Allied Commander, and the Japanese envoys continued until 1 a.m. on Tuesday morning, August 28th, when the preliminary surrender agreements were signed. These documents provided for such matters as minesweeping, the relief of prisoners-of-war, air reconnaissance and entry into Japanese controlled waters. They also arranged for the evacuation of certain areas by the Japanese, and for the meeting, by British occupation forces, of Japanese officers and officials at specified times and places.

The remainder of Tuesday and Wednesday morning were used in last preparations, and on Wednesday afternoon anchors were weighed. We moved downstream to broader waters, where the whole convoy could get into shape. Included in the convoy were the ships *Highland Brigade, Devonshire, Corfu, Dilwara*, and many others, numbering possibly thirty, and including hospital ships and landing craft. The escort was provided by the East Indies Fleet Task Force, with Rear-Admiral Holland flying his flag in H.M.S. *Sussex*. On Thursday, August 20th, the convoy set sail for Singapore.

We were issued with life-belts, sea-sickness powders and mepachrin, as we kept our course south over a dead-still sea. Going at something under ten knots, the pace was exasperatingly slow for those, who, like myself, had had this journey in mind for three and a half years and were labouring under tremendous excitement to see Singapore again. After life-boat drill in the mornings, the days were largely idle, and, in my excitement, I found it difficult to relax, so that time passed very slowly. We were proceeding very cautiously, and every precaution was observed. The ships were blacked out at night, and paravanes were sweeping the sea at every bow.

I think there were many on board, who had the significance of the journey very much in mind. It was probably, for them, the last war-like operation, the culmination of a long hard road. If this went well, an epoch and the greatest adventure of their lives would end in triumph. They crowded to the service on Sunday morning, and heard the padre, Major Bennett, say in excellently chosen words, things appropriate to the occasion and calculated to make them think of the life and responsibilities which lay ahead. They sang, at his request, a tribute to and a blessing on those of their comrades, who could not be with them:

"O Valiant Hearts, who to your glory came
Through dust of conflict and through battle-flame;
Tranquil you lie, your knightly virtue proved,
Your memory hallowed in the land you loved.

"Proudly you gathered rank on rank to war
As who had heard God's message from afar,
All you had hoped for, all you had, you gave
To save mankind-yourself you scorned to save."

* * * * *

That Sunday, September 2nd, we sighted the north-west coast of Malaya.

On Monday, certain naval craft and other ships left the convoy and went into Penang, while we lay some distance off to await the result. Our luncheon menu offered us "Singapore Curry and Rice," and it occurred to me that it must have been a very long time since a British menu last mentioned Singapore. The dish itself bore no resemblance to a Malay curry, but the name was uplifting and when, after several hours, we proceeded on our way, I emerged from a haze of unbelief and concluded that I was really on my way to Singapore.

The 400 miles from Penang to Singapore, at our speed, took the best part of two days. I believed that I alone, due to my circumstances, sensed the eerie feeling of that journey, but long afterwards others mentioned it. The sea was absolutely calm, there was an unbelievable stillness in the atmosphere, and, in general, the sky was overcast and neutral. It is difficult or impossible to say what are the component parts of eeriness, but the still, featureless, black-green and threatening Malayan jungle on the port side, the smooth, featureless and blue-black sea all around, the hush which in contradiction to its name can be heard and the pent expectancy of those around must all have contributed. To me, it was a very real feeling, and one which I shall long remember.

One or two things marked this last lap of the journey. After leaving Penang, the ships were no longer blacked-out at night—a sign of growing confidence. When off Port Dickson, we saw great columns of smoke rising from among the trees, and we speculated on what they could mean. The bulk of opinion was that the Nips (the name by which the Japanese were always known in South East Asia Command) were breaking their agreement not to employ scorched-earth tactics, and some 'hard' things were said about them. Of a very different nature was the period just before darkness on the last evening, when, after the toneless, eerie day, the atmosphere became suffused with that exquisite amber light, which is not infrequently seen at Malaya's short-lived twilights. It is an arresting phenomenon of great beauty, which turns every material thing to gold and must even gild men's thoughts.

That day the *Sussex* had gone on ahead and entered Singapore waters. By arrangement, the Japanese commanders in Singapore went on board her to make final arrangements for the occupation. The story goes that, when the latter arrived at the Sussex, one of them said, "You are two hours late." The curt reply from a British officer was, "We don't keep Tokyo time here."

At the conference on the cruiser, the Japanese Command was represented by General Itagaki of the 7th Japanese Army and Vice-Admiral Fukutame, while the British representatives were Lt.-General Sir Philip Christison (G.O.C. Military Forces, Malaya), Rear-

Admiral Holland, Major-General Mausergh and Major-General Hone (Civil Affairs). It is said that at the end of the conference, Itagaki, the 'no-surrender' general, was in tears—a small contribution to the great flood of tears his country had engendered since 1941.

I was up at first light on September 5th, 1945, and, as the light strengthened, I could see, in the distance, Singapore. No raging fires, no palls of smoke, no bombing aircraft, no infernal din such as had been present when I saw it last. That was an easily discernible and pleasant difference, but, I soliloquised, there must be other differences and a lot depends on those.

THREE WEEKS

THE reader will remember that I deplored what happened in Rangoon in the period between the evacuation of the town by the Japanese and the arrival of the British to take over, a short spell of less than a week. In the case of Singapore, the Japanese had surrendered three weeks before British forces arrived. Most places on the Malayan mainland took longer to occupy, inaccessible areas took much longer.

Rangoon and Singapore were not quite parallel cases, as the Japs left the former town during war, with virtually no one in charge, a quite normal procedure. Our failure to get there earlier may have been a slip-up, but, in the circumstances, not inexcusable. Singapore was a different problem, and so, for the most part, was the Malay Peninsula. The Japanese remained in the more populated parts of those territories and were nominally responsible for good government, until such a time as we should arrive. That control—or, at least, such degree of control as had prevailed during the occupation—was not maintained is not, I think, altogether a fair charge against the Japanese. They were in a difficult position. Faced with hostility from the entire community, weakened by their defeat and fearing, as they had always feared, the bands of the now well-armed Guerillas, they were no longer masters of the situation. Contributing to this loss of power was the fact that they were largely deprived of their accustomed weapons of ruthlessness and brutality, which, if exercised then, would probably have rebounded on them swiftly. Also, their mental outlook must have been changed, for, with no future in the country for them, they would, understandably, care for little but their own personal welfare. That combination of circumstances and outlook, in the Japanese, allowed those of the inhabitants, who were so inclined, to become lawless, loot, steal, kill and rape.

It is not possible to get a picture of Malaya during those three weeks without going somewhat further back in its history. During the Japanese regime, all sorts of malpractices had grown up, some voluntarily, some involuntarily. Respectable people had to do things in order to live, which previously they would never have contemplated. Collaboration, or imagined collaboration, was behind a series of crimes, and the spirit of nationalism was behind another series.

When the Japanese introduced their currency into the country, they did it in no half-hearted way. There were floods of it. For this reason, and many others, it rapidly depreciated in value, while the pay of salaried employees, at best, remained at the same figure, until, as I frequently heard from victims later, one month's pay was able to purchase food for only two to three days. These employees, at first, maintained life by selling their goods, but, when that procedure was exhausted, many were forced to find other means. They accepted bribes where that was possible, they started dealing in the black market, and, eventually, in many cases, they stole. They often stole from the Japs, and, if there are degrees in stealing, that was probably the lesser evil, but, nevertheless, a wrong attitude of mind towards the property of others was created.

Those in search of money found many questionable things to do with promises of financial return, and, more demoralising still, often with hopes of gaining Japanese 'protection'. Gambling was officially sponsored and encouraged, spying paid well and procuring anything from a watch to a woman for the conquerors brought rich reward in money and favour.

In circumstances such as those in Malaya it was often impossible to draw a line between collaboration and non collaboration. There were attitudes at both ends which were beyond doubt, but about those whose behaviour was near the border line everyone had his opinion. That naturally made differences and suspicion among acquaintances and friends. Grievances, with a view to revenge, were stored up against collaborators and suspected collaborators for the day when the Japanese would no longer be there to protect them, and, thus, the foundation of trouble was laid.

The Japanese-sponsored Indian National Army was built partly on the spirit of collaboration, but mostly on the spirit of nationalism. A few joined that body solely to please the Japanese, but, almost certainly, the idea of Indian independence was uppermost in the minds of the majority of recruits. Irrespective of their motives, the members of this locally recruited body increased still further the enmities within the cosmopolitan population, and made certain races feel that Indians should have no place in a liberated Malaya.

Another body, from which the spirit of nationalism was not absent, was the Resistance Force. The three red stars displayed on its uniforms were supposed to represent a union of the Chinese, the Malays and the Indians, in other words, the Malayan peoples. Nevertheless, the Force was predominantly Chinese and was, on occasions, not without foundation, daubed Communist. Some sections of that guerilla force were said to have sworn that, when the Japanese were driven out, they would not hand over the country to any other power, but would declare Malaya independent. Without detracting in any way from the work the Force did, the attitude of some sections, after the surrender of Japan, helped not at all in restoring the confused country to normality.

A very broad and brief picture of Malaya during the summer of 1945 displays a country in the hands of a brutal and corrupt power, which was hated and loathed and feared by the overwhelming majority of the people of all the races which in habited it. Small percentages of each race collaborated with the Japanese to varying degrees. Others tried to make the Japanese believe they were collaborating, while in fact they were feathering their own nests. The majority, and especially those with many worldly goods, spent much of their time and energies in remaining as inconspicuous as possible. Of those who refused to collaborate, or to whom the opportunity was not given, a large number found living by honest means almost or entirely impossible, and so, in order to exist, resorted to dishonest or questionable practices, with an ever increasing moral deterioration.

Moral deterioration was a thing the Japanese were not interested in so long as they did not, themselves, directly and individually suffer. Indeed, they often encouraged it, even to the extent of allowing their own authorities to be robbed. The Police were equally complacent and, almost without exception, could be bribed. Bribery in the form of 'tea money' accompanied every transaction, whether it was renting a house, buying a railway ticket or avoiding molestation.

The Guerillas usurped a prominent position in the picture, as far as it applied to the Peninsula. They were a law unto themselves. They harassed the Jap in praiseworthy fashion, but, in addition, they played a part in the lives of the people. They took justice into their own hands and dealt with collaborators in their own fashion.

Their money and supplies must have come from many sources, not all of which, perhaps, were voluntary. Many peaceful people inevitably suffered in trying to steer a course between the two belligerent sides.

Rapid fluctuations in the value of the occupation currency, and equally rapid changes in commodity prices, added to the general difficulties. Prices had been fixed by the Japanese for many goods, but only Japanese, or Japanese employed persons, could buy at those rates. Some people, in desperation, committed suicide, others died through starvation.

That the Japanese expected an attack on Malaya in 1945 was certain, but they had no idea when, or from where, it would come. They also believed that the large towns would be bombed, in the same way as the towns in their homeland were bombed during that summer, and they made some quite inadequate attempts to lessen the effect. A thousand or so families were evacuated from Singapore, and many underground shelters of a poor type were dug. There were also signs that the Japanese contemplated retreating to the hills, especially to the Cameron Highlands area, and, if necessary, holding out in those natural forts to the last man.

The inhabitants were conscious of Japan's loosening grip, and this brought various reactions. The police were said to have handed arms over to the Guerillas, the Indian National Army began dissolving itself, and pre-war British currency was greatly sought after and hoarded. The increasing air-raids on Singapore encouraged the hope that the end was approaching, so that, with every raid and every report of a Japanese defeat from outside, the people grew bolder, and did what they could to embarrass the Jap and prepare themselves for 'the day'.

During 1945, events were such that hopes of liberation were founded on sound reasoning, but, during the years previously, hope of a quick release had always been present, even when there was no reason to support it. At first, it seemed to captive Malaya that the British would return within a year, but, as this hope receded, dates further ahead were voiced. The end of 1943 was suggested, then the middle of 1944, and so on. One Chinese family I knew gave the name 'Vincent' to a baby boy, which arrived early in 1944, in the belief that that year would be the victory year. When victory did at last come, the three weeks, during which Malaya waited for British forces to arrive, seemed almost as long as the previous three years.

It was probably fortunate that the Japanese did not immediately broadcast their defeat throughout Malaya, but kept the news back as long as they could till finally, on August 21st, they felt compelled to publish that hostilities had ceased. Although there were few short-wave receiving sets in Malaya not in Japanese hands, there had been rumours of the surrender since August 11th, rumours which emanated from the fortunate and brave people who had managed to retain one of those precious instruments. As might be expected, such rumours, even from remote sources, spread like wild-fire, but the people, as a whole, could not be certain that it was the end, while the Japanese kept silent and gave no indication.

When at last the news was revealed from official sources, it was like releasing bent springs all over the country. Amazing things happened, some of them much to be deplored. Private vengeance began to take its course, and there was no stopping it. Between race and race and between man and man, the accounts, which had been accumulating for three and a half years, were opened for settlement. The numbers of those who were murdered will never be known, and the greater part of the total vengeance, which was extracted in August and September 1945, will remain forever secret. The Guerillas were foremost in this work of 'cleaning-up' and, to their credit, they brought some semblance of justice to the operation. They conducted trials, which were said to have been fair and carried out with due regard for the dictates of justice. Nevertheless, all the people they wanted did not come quietly to be tried, and, no doubt, sentence was not always delayed on that account. As the Japanese withdrew to the large towns, the Guerillas took over the smaller towns and villages. They endeavoured to restore order, and even tried to fix commodity prices, but they judged and sentenced according to their own ideas, and not on the basis of established law.

A sentence of another kind, which was not to be carried out until September 5th, had been passed in India. It was a sentence of death on the Japanese currency. Although the people of Malaya didn't know about it, they suspected this money would suffer in some way under the British, and, among the many things which went wild, Japanese currency was conspicuous. Everybody wanted to get rid of it, and a spate of purchasing began. Buy anything and get rid of Japanese money was the thought in all minds, and this thought gained conviction when Allied aircraft dropped leaflets saying Japanese script was finished. Naturally, prices went up by leaps and bounds to fantastic heights, but business continued to be done. Doubtless, many who had consumer goods wished to hold on to them, but feared retaliation, and so made the best bargain they could, even for worthless money.

A third outstanding feature of the period was the wholesale thieving and looting which went on, both by organised bands and by individuals. Many bands masqueraded as Guerillas and got away with a lot, which, otherwise, they might have been denied, but many others made no attempt to pass themselves off for anything but what they were—gangs of robbers. Individuals found many properties unoccupied and unguarded and helped themselves. The police, if there were any left, were useless, and the Japs, when they had got what they wanted, cared nothing about the rest.

For many months afterwards, the looting of houses in Singapore came in for much comment. The pre-war European occupants had, when they returned, many hard things to say about the disappearance of their goods and furniture, and often, in my opinion, placed the blame in wrong quarters. Many accused the British Forces, which, though not entirely free from blame, were not culprits to anything like the extent of the accusations. When the Europeans were driven from their houses in 1942, most of them gave their servants a carte-blanche to help themselves, preferring that faithful servants should have the things rather than the Japanese. The servants and their friends, no doubt, accepted the opportunity. When the Japanese first came, they also took what they fancied and, when they left, they again helped themselves not ungenerously. On top of those three lootings came the period after the surrender, when the people round about any vacant property probably argued, "What the Jap has left is, in all fairness, ours." The Japanese had, in accordance with Allied instructions, I imagine, put a notice on vacated houses. The notice was in Japanese, English, Malay, Romanized Malay and Chinese, in that order. It read:

PROCLAMATION

This property, having been in use by the Nippon Armed Forces and/or Nippon jin, is to be put under the control of the Allies. Anyone looting or damaging this property shall be punished severely.

By order

THE NIPPON ARMED FORCES.

25th August, 2605.

The Japanese year 2605 corresponded with the Christian year 1945. The notice was not worth the paper it was written on, for, by August 25th, 1945, a threat by the Nippon forces had ceased to terrify people.

The Japanese and their satellites had, themselves, begun to be frightened. The former gathered together for comfort and strength, and removed from their everyday procedure aggressive symbols and actions. They even became generous and issued food and other commodities, which they had in store, to the people. The satellites changed their coats and faded away in the hope of losing their identity, and, in some cases, took active steps to associate themselves with anti-Japanese bodies or activities. Police, spies and National Armies threw away arms and uniforms, and all pro-Japanese organisations liquidated themselves and destroyed, as far as possible, all evidence of their existence. I think it would be incorrect to say that these bodies liquidated themselves reluctantly in all cases, for I believe that many, even though they had continued to work for the Japanese, were heartily sick of the regime and even disgusted with it.

In view of what I will have to say later, it might be well to insert here that a new idea had begun to take root in the minds of a number of the inhabitants. It was the idea of independence for Malaya. The idea was not confined to one race, but whether the implications had been worked out by any is doubtful. By August 1945, the Japanese had granted nominal independence to Burma and parts of the Netherlands East Indies, and what was more likely than that they would enact the same farce with Malaya? If Malaya could emerge from Japanese rule as an independent state, the problems of a number of its less reputable people might well be solved. The idea was, in consequence, no doubt, cherished in some quarters. In other quarters, where independence was not looked upon as an immediate issue, a new political consciousness had, at the same time, sprung up.

Not so universally as in February 1942, but still to a marked extent, the eyes of the world were on Singapore during the last weeks of August and the first weeks of September 1945. For the general observer, it was the culmination of the Far Eastern victory, for the peoples of the Commonwealth and Empire, it was the centre from which 400,000 prisoners-of-war and internees would be repatriated. How were those people faring during the period of waiting?

Some have written, and others will certainly write, of what went on in Japanese camps, and all their stories will be grim. For the purpose of this book, I can only say a very little about the Sime Road Camp in Singapore, where a large number of civil internees was held. Like others outside the camp, those people first fed on rumours of the surrender, then, significantly, their food issue began to improve. About August 19th, the Japs handed over the keys of the rice store, and, shortly after that broad hint, the official pronouncement came.

The Camp Committee wisely decided that the internees should remain within the camp, until British forces arrived, and one can easily imagine how they counted the hours. Some days before September 5th, a few parachutists and a shower of leaflets were dropped within the camp area, and, later, many parcels followed containing food, clothes and little luxuries. The camp also got food from outside, as the local people began trudging along the roads laden with all they could spare for the men and women they had previously known. The Japanese did not interfere with those friendly gestures, and the inmates of the camp benefited considerably.

Two days before the liberating forces arrived, the Union Jack was hoist within the camp. The ceremony was carried out by Lady Thomas, wife of the Governor of the Straits Settlements, as the Governor—Sir Shenton Thomas—had, early on, been taken, with other important captives, by the Japanese, to Formosa. Among the first to reach the camp, on September 5th, was a host of War-correspondents in search of stories. They got them. A military broadcasting Unit also quickly on the scene saw to it that, in a very short time, an internee was broadcasting to the world, and, thus, the dark veil, which had lowered over those people three and a half years previously, was lifted. Many hearts all over the earth rejoiced.

Within a few hours of the first landings, a message from the King was broadcast from a Singapore transmitting station. Included in the message were the following words:

"The thoughts of the Queen and myself have been constantly with you during the years of suffering so bravely borne, and, with the dawn of the Day of

107

Liberation, we rejoice with you that the lies which unite my people everywhere will now be restored... The traces of a cruel and ruthless oppression cannot be wiped out in a day and the work of restoration will be long and heavy."

Yes, the work will be long and heavy, and, not in all cases will it be restoration. From the ruins of the Far East, many new things will spring, and the best that can be hoped is that their growth can be directed. Growth is rapid in tropical climates, and, not infrequently, perfection is less in consequence. Had the liberating forces arrived sooner, fewer of the roots, cultivated by good government over a long time, would, I venture to think, have suffered.

SHONAN REVERTS TO SINGAPORE

THE *Derbyshire* cast anchor well out in the harbour, and, on board, there was a period of waiting. Troops from various ships were put ashore on the islands of Pulo Brani and Blakang Mati about 9 a.m., and, some time later, on Singapore itself. Their duties were to round up the Japanese on the islands and in the streets of the town, from the wharf area to beyond the Municipal Buildings. The sea had been taken care of by a previous order instructing all Japanese ships to be at least ten miles away from the convoy. While the first landings were going on, we listened for any sign of trouble, which we hadn't ceased to expect, but there was none.

On the *Derbyshire*, a party had been detailed to go ashore with the first launch. It included Brigadier Pearse, Colonel Regester, a number of War-correspondents and myself, and we waited impatiently for the launch to arrive. It came about 11 o'clock and we piled in, complete with arms and rations. Racing once again through the waters of Singapore Harbour gave me a strange exultant feeling, and I wanted to shout, but the lack of any signs of life and the uncanny stillness of the dull overcast morning were sobering. As we came alongside the Main Wharf, a War-correspondent and I, with childish enthusiasm did perilous jumps to be first ashore.

Two Indians and a Chinese boy, looking very dazed, appeared from a near-by shed. They were the only people in sight and I addressed them in Malay, getting no response but a stupefied stare. Walking to the Station Buildings, we passed two more Chinese and one exchanged a subdued "Tabek" (good-day), which, in the circumstances, seemed an inadequate greeting. The rain had come on and this, in addition to the deserted and partly destroyed dock area, gave a feeling of overwhelming desolation.

At the station, things were a little better. There were a few people about and small military units soon began to arrive to establish offices in the buildings, units such as the Port Commandant's and Transport Officer's. This station had been a comparatively new and handsome building with an exterior of light-grey artificial stone. It was now in a neglected and dirty condition and the exterior had been camouflaged with streaks of black oil or paint. I remember thinking how difficult they would be to remove.

The first job assigned to us was to proceed to the Municipal Building and take over the town from the Japanese Mayor and his principal officers, as soon as we got the 'all-clear' from the advance forces. As we had some time to wait for this, Pearse and I ate our emergency ration by way of lunch. During the meal, some lean and hungry children gathered round, but they couldn't be persuaded to come and take biscuits. However, when I threw away an empty meat tin, there was a rush for it and grubby fingers were wiped around the inside and sucked. Obviously fear had played a big part in the recent lives of those kiddies.

The Japanese had been ordered to send five hundred cars for use of the occupying forces, but very few arrived on the first day. Some came on subsequent days, but, I fear, the total figure was never approached, and, for a long time, the lack of adequate transport was a major factor in slowing up work and a real grievance in the lives of many,

110

who found it almost impossible to work efficiently or, later, to get to recreative centres without transport.

After our meal, we went to the Customs Building, a few hundred yards from the station along Keppel Road. This was an operational headquarters and things were happening. Some scores of Japanese had been rounded up and were sprawling in front of the building, while others, with white bands, were acting as interpreters. British officers and other ranks were bustling about, and a fair crowd of local people had gathered in the road. To add to the picture, some British prisoners-of-war had managed to slip out of a nearby camp and join the sightseers.

Here indeed was a study in types in a unique situation. The contrast in appearance between the victor and the vanquished did not, in all ways, favour the former. Sartorially, the Jap had the advantage, with the possible exception of head-gear. Their dark khaki tunics and knee breeches were of good material, clean and well-cut, their calf-length boots were magnificently polished and the whole was rendered very martial by bright buttons, shining leather and imposing swords. This uniform must have been very hot to wear, and it was somewhat spoiled by the white civilian-looking shirt collars, which protruded over the tunic necks with jarring effect and by the rather slovenly cloth caps. The British jungle-green, ill-fitting, cotton uniform showed up badly. Even when freshly washed and put on, it is not too pleasing or soldierly, and, on this occasion, there were few, if any, which had not been worn for days and had, long since, lost any claim to cleanliness or smartness. The Japanese were all about the same height, of good physique, short but sturdy, without being over fat. Obviously they were well fed and attended, whereas the British looked badly groomed, and of all sizes and shapes. It is difficult to compare faces, for, to us, all Jap faces are brutal, heavy and unintelligent, but, perhaps to other races, ours appear to have equally objectionable features.

The local people around did not, in general, appear badly dressed for an impromptu tropical crowd, though, here and there, there were exceptions, where marked difficulties with raiment were apparent. They did, on the other hand, look underfed and haggard and their shifty eyes were capable of many interpretations. The prisoners-of-war, who had made their way to this spot, displayed seriously under-nourished figures, but obviously they had donned their best clothes most prisoners-of-war and internees had managed to retain some garments for an occasion-and prepared themselves in every way for a party. They were still largely in a state of unbelief, finding it difficult to grasp the facts that they were no longer prisoners and that the period of horrors and deprivations had ended.

About 2 p.m., we got word that the way was clear for us to proceed to the Municipal Buildings. Pearse, Regester, Beattie and I set off accompanied by Brigadier Denham-Young from the operational forces. With guards, we made a small convoy of three cars. That drive will not be easily forgotten. We proceeded slowly past road barriers and other obstructions by way of Keppel Road, Cantonment Road, New Bridge Road, Hill Street, High Street and St. Andrew's Road. This route goes through the most densely populated part of Singapore, and, while not knowing what I expected, I was astonished at the rich display of flags from buildings and at the large, cheering crowds which lined the streets. They brought a lump to my throat. Those crowds were made up of both sexes, all local races and all ages. There were old men and women, who had lived all their lives, except the last three and a half years, under,

British rule and who, too old even to contemplate changing their allegiance in 1942, must have been rejoicing at the vindication of their faith. There were children, who, though too young ever to have seen a white man who was not a prisoner, were waving little Union Jacks to celebrate the coming to reality of fairy tales related by their parents. There were boys and girls and men and women of all the ages between, whose trust must often have been sorely tried, but, on this day, there was no mistaking the relief, pleasure and enthusiasm written on their faces. A better day, they hoped, had dawned.

As we turned into High Street, the crowd thinned and, in St. Andrew's Road, there was only a handful of people. The whole of the large open esplanade area was empty. Indeed all along the route, apart from those who had lined the roads and who must have come out of back doors secretively, the town had a vacated appearance. No shops were open and all doors and windows seemed to be shuttered, barred and bolted to the limit.

At the steps of the Municipal Building, we got out of the cars and despatched an officer to raise the flag on the roof of the building. As the Union Jack slowly rose to the top of the flag staff and unfolded in the breeze, we stood to attention and saluted. A dozen people at most saw that little ceremony, but I believe it deserves a modest place in the lost list of occasions on which the British flag has been raised throughout the world, over four centuries.

Within the building, we waited for the Japanese, who should really have been waiting for us. We chose to attribute their late arrival to arrogance or face-saving tactics, so that, when they did come, we kept them waiting under guard about the same length of time. There may, however, have been in their minds some confusion over time, as Malaya had been put on Tokyo time since 1942, and this was two hours or so ahead of Malayan time. The Japanese were reported to have been at the Municipal Building earlier and gone away on our non-arrival, and, if so, it was, perhaps, excusable. Why should there be these differences in time every few miles around the globe? It would seem that the only reason is so that we may all get up and go to bed when the clock hands are in the same position, and we won't give up this habit of mind. If Greenwich Mean Time were followed everywhere, clocks and watches would last long and much confusion would be avoided.

Naito, the Japanese Mayor, and six of his officers filed into the room and Colonel Regester proceeded with the formal ceremony of taking over the town. The Japanese were instructed in what they had to do and to whom each service was to be handed over. They displayed no arrogance or lack of co-operation, and took their instructions in an apparently willing spirit. They bowed themselves out, when dismissed, as they had bowed themselves in, and Shonan was again Singapore, without a deed-poll or other legal procedure, so far as I know.

I made a quick tour of the Municipal Offices, but found nobody. All, I was told later, had taken the day off, considering it safer to be at home in the circumstances. With my future job in mind, I turned taps and put on switches and was agreeably surprised to find water and electricity where they should be. It showed that men were working at the sources of the supplies and I should have liked to visit them, but darkness had come on and I was without transport to take me round. So it was a case of back to the ship with the others.

The *Derbyshire* was, by then, alongside the wharf and I was able to sleep on board the next two nights, which was very convenient. Each night at 10 p.m., General Mansergh held a conference, at which he informed us how things were going with the occupation and tried to help out with our individual problems. His lucid explanation of every situation was most interesting and instructive, and his personal charm made all contacts with him a great pleasure.

There were about seventy thousand Japanese on the Island when we landed. The process of taking over was to be done in stages, the Japanese being ordered to vacate the dock area and the centre of the town during the first day, to be outside the Municipal boundaries, that is beyond the outer ring roads, by the end of the second day, and to be all concentrated in the Jurong and Changi areas by the third day. Those guarding vulnerable points and stores, and those engaged on the essential services, were to remain at their posts until relieved, or replaced by British personnel. Apart from the fact that many Japanese crossed the Causeway to the mainland instead of going to the concentration areas, the occupation went according to plan.

Although the 5th Indian Division had a magnificent record in the war, it was a little unfortunate that the reoccupation of Singapore had to be carried out with Indian troops. In the town, there were large numbers of all races who spoke and understood a little English, and a British Division on this job would, if for language reasons only, have proved much more popular with the inhabitants. Even a greater spirit of good will might have been engendered, which would have paid dividends in the future. As it was, the Indians were welcomed as the forces of liberation, but easy relationships between the military and the local people did not result, as they otherwise might have done, in the first joy of freedom. Further, the language difficulty hindered other units of the army in carrying out their work, as every important building, depot and store was guarded by, and every vehicle driven by, Indians. In a normal military operation, an Indian Division came in contact, almost exclusively, with its own officers, who could speak its language, but the nature of this operation demanded cooperation with all sorts of units from all branches of the services, so that inability to converse with each other was a great handicap.

About noon on the day of landing, the first Proclamation signed by the Supreme Allied Commander was posted up. It stated, *inter alia*, that:

> "A Military Administration to be called the British Military Administration is hereby established throughout such areas of Malaya as are at any given time under the control of Forces under my command and shall continue only so long as I consider it to be required by military necessity."

> "Subject to the provisions of any Proclamation of the British Military Administration and in so far as military exigencies permit, all laws and customs existing immediately prior to the Japanese occupation will be respected."

> "All Courts and tribunals, other than military courts established under my authority, are hereby suspended and deprived of all authority and jurisdiction until authorised by me to reopen."

> "It is hereby declared that all Proclamations and legislative enactments of whatever kind issued by or under the authority of the Japanese Military Administration shall cease to have any effect."

The British Military Administration lasted 208 days.

At the same time, a nightly curfew was imposed upon all but military personnel. I do not think this curfew was ever rigidly applied, due largely to the lack of police and other organised units to enforce it, and it was removed on September 9th, because the General Officer Commanding was, at that time, satisfied as to the law-abiding qualities of the citizens.

I started the second day by going round the departmental offices of the essential services, and I found that large numbers of the staff had gathered and were, prior to my arrival, discussing the situation, which naturally, to them, was far from clear. It was a very heart-warming experience to meet all those good fellows again, and be so warmly greeted. That I should turn up in the midst of all that strange new world was, to them not only a surprise, but, I believe, also a relief. Before the war, Malaya's ordinary citizens never had much to do with Military Forces, but, during it, they had had more than enough, so that they were, perhaps, not overjoyed at the first appearance of the new uniformed regime. However, a soldier they knew was better than a soldier they didn't, and I had worked with them for sixteen years.

In the days that followed, it was an exceedingly pleasant, but a very trying, duty to meet former members of the staff, as those who had not been there the first day drifted back to the office, in ones and twos, and came to see me. Emaciated images of the men I had known before, some completely inarticulate, would grip my hand and hold on to it. Their lips moved, but no sound came, they burst into tears, fumbled for a handkerchief and disappeared in confusion. Others got as far as, "Thank God, thank God, God bless you," before tears drove them away. All, who overcome emotion sufficiently to speak, had long stories to tell of the dreadful times they had been

117

through, and some had, or imagined they had, dreamt of my return. It was a tremendous privilege to be able to console those men and help to get them on their feet again.

On the second day, although it started a hectic period which lasted for months, I felt compelled to snatch half an hour and make a brief visit to the house I had occupied up to 1942. It was still standing, but shut up, with an order by the "Nippon Armed Forces" on the door. There was nothing in the house, but from the back quarters, my old kebun, or gardener, and all his family emerged. I was as pleased to see those Malays as they were to see me, and our tongues wagged at incredible speed, without too much understanding of words by either side. The kebun asked all sorts of questions about my family and myself and displayed his children with the greatest of pride. He told me, with disgust written all over his face, of the doings of the Japanese and he illustrated some of them by waving a despising hand towards his beloved garden. Fortunately, he knew where my former cook and sais (driver) were, and undertook that they should come to see me with all speed. This, they did with beaming faces the next day. The boy I had employed had died, which was not surprising as he had been very sick and in hospital, when I last saw him.

My first visit to the camp for civil internees at Sime Road was, at the same time, both a relief and a shock. For years, I had heard of the filthy conditions, the semi-starvation diet and the brutality of the Japanese at this camp. The first two were not exaggerated, the brutality was, I understand, spasmodic. I had fully expected to see thin, starved, ragged men and appalling conditions of living, but seeing them, nevertheless, administered a shock. A number of my friends were quite unrecognisable, on account of the great beards which adorned their faces and the deteriorations in physique, while others were equally unrecognisable for the latter reason only. Some had grown old beyond what the years could account for, and, worst of all, a number had obviously changed completely; the change having started in frustration of the mind and worked outwards. All the same, there was something to be very thankful for, the deaths had been fewer than I had dared to hope, and, strangely enough, not an inconsiderable number looked fit and well and scarcely changed at all.

Five allied flags fly over the Cathay Building, S.E.A.C. headquarters in Singapore

"If you had seen us three weeks ago," one said to me, "you would really have got a shock."

There was a great deal in that, for, after the Japanese Tokyo surrender, the treatment had vastly improved and the guards had distributed more food to the camp. The local people had also, for some days, been bringing in food and other things, so that many had considerably improved in health and appearance, in the period between the first surrender offer and the actual liberation, due to the little extra nourishment.

The Japanese surrender party is brought in to the Municipal Building, September 12th, 1945.

How sections of the Asiatic population, at tremendous risk to themselves, helped the internees, during the whole of the occupation, is an heroic story, which it is not for me to attempt to tell, but which everyone who knows anything about it, however little, must applaud.

At the Sime Road internment camps, there were some 3,160 men, 1,020 women and 320 children. The women and young children were in a separate enclosure from the men. At first, incarceration was confined almost exclusively to Europeans of the Allied nationalities, but, later, and particularly during the early months of 1945, a number of other nationalities were sent to the camps. To some of the local people, especially those in prominent positions and those whose work brought them into daily contact with Japanese officials, internment was more desirable than liberty. I know of at least one man who pleaded on many occasions to be interned and eventually succeeded in obtaining his wish. This is not so ununderstandable as may at first appear. The Japs hated many of them for their known loyalties, and continually sought a chance to make them suffer. So long as they were at liberty, it was mental agony endeavouring not to make, or appear to make, a wrong step, but once interned they were comparatively unmolested, with much less opportunity of running foul of the Jap, with all its consequences.

The living quarters in the camp consisted of long dormitory huts, with about two feet between each so-called bed. There was considerable space around the huts where vegetables were grown, and, until the Japanese collapsed, the camp was efficiently organised for this and other work, each person being allotted his task. Naturally enough, when it became known that the war was over, the organisation wilted somewhat and some tasks were not so willingly carried out as previously. This would not have mattered much if the internees had been moved immediately after our arrival, but they were not, and so conditions in the camp deteriorated after September 5th, particularly in cleanliness, until the new authorities could get help arranged.

It is beyond all question that everyone in South East Asia Command and in the Colonial Office, who was concerned with the reoccupation of the Far East Territories, wished to do all that was possible and within reason for the captives in Japanese hands. There were, I know, great difficulties on account of the large numbers involved, but I still see no excuse for leaving the civil internees in Sime Road Camp after the liberation. Many of them waited weeks before shipping was available to take them home, and, during that time, they had to endure the filthy conditions of the camp with all its hated memories. Surely, the smallest dictates of humanity demanded that they should be removed at once and accommodated in civilised surroundings. It was a great let down, after all they had expected of the day when the British returned. The Service's found it possible to take over, at once, many hotels and other large buildings for various purposes, and it should not have been impossible to take over a few more and equip them for a short time, so that those people could get the moral uplift they so much required, and have a little comfort after years of soul destroying conditions. In my opinion a great mistake was made. A little more planning beforehand, and a little bed linen, would have made such a difference.

Before the reoccupation of Malaya, it had been decided that all the internees should be got away to a temperate climate for a period of leave as soon as possible, passages being supplied at the expense of the Government. The intention was excellent, and, in most cases, it worked out satisfactorily, as the public bodies and many firms were prepared to pay salaries during the period of leave, but there were some men who had their own small business in Malaya and no means of livelihood elsewhere. A few of those refused to go. Others went, but suffered poor financial circumstances during recuperation. It was not easy for them.

Very much to our surprise, a great number of the internees were not at all anxious to leave Singapore at once, and, indeed, persuasion had to be used in some cases. They had not, of course, known what was going on in the outside world. It had not occurred to them that the Army would arrive complete with organisations, which were prepared to carry on the functions of the Government, the Public Bodies and of some essential firms, while they were recovering. Interned officials had, indeed, prepared carefully worked-out plans (including leave rosters) for resuming their duties immediately at the point where they had left off in 1942. It was a praiseworthy idea, and their reluctance in abandoning it was easily understandable, but I think that many of them imagined that they were more fit than was, in fact, the case. The increased food of the previous few weeks and the stimulus of freedom had given them, by comparison, a feeling of fitness, which was dangerously deceptive. The chance of a subsequent breakdown was very real, and, if that had happened, the authorities would rightly have been blamed.

The period after liberation, prior to embarking for home, cannot have been very pleasant for the ex-internees, for, in addition to the rigours of their wretched accommodation, they had no transport to get about, few clothes and little money. They did not get much relief either on the homeward bound ships, as they were travelling under trooping conditions into winter weather, after, in many cases, seven or more years in the tropics. A fair amount of discontent was expressed on account of the accommodation allotted to them on ships. In general it was, of course, bad by peace-time standards, and who can blame those people if they were still living, to some extent, with the outlook they had had before the veil descended upon them. The position was sometimes aggravated by misunderstandings, if the following story, which I have on good authority, is true.

There were a number of passages available on a certain ship going home and the Camp Committee was asked by the Port Authorities (at that time a military unit) to submit names for those vacancies. A list was duly sent with the names in alphabetical order, and the Port Unit, not knowing anyone mentioned, filled the vacancies in the order given. The available berths ranged from relatively good accommodation on the top decks to very inferior accommodation below the water line. Those whose names began with 'A' were put on the top deck, and the 'W's' were consigned to the lower regions. That might have been all right if the 'W's' had not been senior civil servants, judges and directors in civil life, and the 'A's' had not been junior assistants and foremen but, as it happened, something like that occurred, and the balloon went up. An officer who was concerned with the matter said to me afterwards, "There's something to be said for the Army, you know at least where a man should be put."

Another story, on the same lines, was in the air. An ex-internee being asked how he knew the war was over said, "Well it was this way. I used to pass a certain senior civil servant in the camp each morning, and he always greeted me with, 'Hullo, Tom, old man, how are things going?' One morning he changed the greeting to 'Good-morning, Brown,[8] how are you?' so I knew the war was over."

The civilian internees had not always been at Sime Road camp. At first they were placed in Changi prison, and it was during their time there that the incident, known

---

[8] Not his real name.

as the 'Double tenth' occurred. Among those who were taken away by the Kempei-tai (Japanese Military Police) on that occasion, was Norman Coulson, who had been on my pre-war staff in Singapore. For some time after capturing Singapore, the Japanese had retained Coulson in his job, being unable to replace him, and, during that period of semi-liberty, his efforts to assist those in the prison were beyond praise. The Kempei-tai now tortured him to such an extent that he subsequently died. A few days after my arrival, a service, conducted by the Bishop of Singapore, was held at his grave and a wooden cross, made in the camp, erected to his memory. Hearing of the proposed service a few hours before it was due to take place, I made a point of attending. There were only about a dozen other people there, all civilians and most ex-internees. I was the only one in uniform. During the service, I noticed the Bishop looking very hard at me, and, immediately after it was over, he came to me and said, "I hope this is not in the nature of a censorship."

I tried to assure him that I had come to pay my respects to an old friend. He said, "You know we have come to distrust military men so much, that it is hard to think normally about them, even our own." In carrying out good works and rendering assistance where it was needed, the Bishop displayed, during the occupation, surpassing courage and suffered for it almost beyond human endurance. His words indicated an attitude of mind prevalent among many who had passed through similar ordeals.

Most of my former acquaintances were among the civilian internees, but there were also some who were prisoners-of-war. These had been in the Army or the Volunteer Forces when Singapore fell, and had nearly all been sent to work on the railway in Siam. They were still in Siam when the war ended, and, in general, went home by way of Rangoon. David Nelson was one exception, who had remained in Singapore throughout, being forced to work in a clerical capacity for the Nippon Forces or—as they called themselves—The Imperial Japanese Army. By secreting it among Japanese military papers, David had succeeded in keeping a very accurate record of the whereabouts and the fate of many Singapore people, much of his information coming from Japanese files. It was a very fine effort which proved exceedingly useful.

The boot was on the other foot now, and the Japanese were quickly put to work in Singapore. Care was taken that some of that work should be where it could be seen best by the local people, and one of the most conspicuous places chosen was the Padang or open area in front of the Municipal Building. This great playing field had been left in a mess. There were slit trenches, gun emplacements and scrap all over it, so that the former beautiful, green sward looked more like a rubbish heap than anything else. The formal surrender ceremony had been fixed for September 12th, and the accompanying parade was to take place on this ground. Some intense work was needed to put it into fit condition, and Japanese P.O.W. labour fitted the bill admirably. I, for one, rubbed my eyes in unbelief, when the Japs arrived to do the job wearing white gloves, which they did not remove while working. That habit persisted for some time, but was eventually stopped after it had brought a flood of protests from the populace. On the Padang, during those first days, the Japs worked hard and it was obvious that they were tremendous workers of fine physique. The people exulted in the turn of events, and missed no opportunity of letting the Japs know what they thought of them. One incident, the only one of its sort which I saw, pleased the crowd of onlookers immensely. A

British ex-prisoner-of-war was passing when he got an idea. He went up to a Jap worker and slapped him on the face. As face slapping of all and sundry had been the favourite and continually exercised pastime of the Japanese during the occupation, many who had suffered this form of humiliation were more than delighted at the retaliation, mild though it was.

A day or two after our arrival, I found it necessary to pay a visit to the water supply reservoirs on the mainland, some forty miles from Singapore. That was an interesting journey. The area had not been cleared of Japanese, and it was advisable to take reasonable precautions. Some technical officers accompanied me, and, with arms and food, we spread ourselves over a car and a jeep. The transport, we had at that stage, was so bad that it was not safe to rely on one vehicle for a journey of any distance. At Johore Bahm, we made a point of contacting an officer from Force 136[9] to question him about the somewhat lonely country we would pass through. He said that we should meet any number of armed Japanese, but thought everything would be all right. He added, "If they look unfriendly just raise your hand and yell 'aye, aye', that will do it."

He was right on both points. After leaving the main south north road, we came upon many thousands of Japanese soldiers who were heavily armed with every conceivable type of light weapon. The roadway was crammed with lorries, vans and cars, which bulged with officers and troops, and the jungle and rubber, on both sides, were alive with remnants of the once proud Imperial Army. They had come to this area with everything they

---

[9] A special Unit formed to carry out liaison with the Malayan Guerillas during the latter part of the war.

could lay hands on. Much of the motor transport, which should have been available to our Forces, had been used to bring them there, and many a dwelling in Singapore had contributed to the extraordinary assortment of goods they had brought along for comfort. Among the trees, they had pitched their tents and erected innumerable rough buildings with all kinds of material. Scattered around those living quarters were tables, easy chairs, wardrobes, beds and a hundred other types of household articles, including magnificent china and cutlery. There was even a gas stove to be seen, though the jungle was hardly a place where it could be put to its original use.

At one point on the road, where the Jap transport had got into a jam and angry shouts were filling the air, we tried the 'aye, aye' business and found, sure enough, that it subdued the turmoil and hastened our passage through. Apart from some threatening looks, there were no signs of enmity.

At the reservoirs, we found the local staff carrying on with extreme difficulty. It was a hilly area, safe neither from the Japanese nor from the Guerilla Forces and was, as likely as not, liable to be the scene of a clash between them. Those men were completely cut off from civilisation, having been without telephone or road communication in the recent weeks. They had no food, apart from what they grew locally, and they knew practically nothing of what was going on outside their little communities. In spite of that, they were carrying on the routine tasks of tending the reservoirs and pumping water, while their stocks lasted, without knowing what was happening at the other end of the pipeline. We had brought with us, from Sime Road camp, the civilian water engineer, D. J. Murnane, and he was hugged and blessed that day more than he had, I suspect, for some time, been accustomed to.

During the first week of our reoccupation, there were many exciting things to be seen in Singapore. It was fascinating to watch the town come to life again. On September 5th, it had, to all appearance, been dead and virtually deserted. Gradually, the little shops opened, you could almost see the boards coming off the windows, one at a time, day by day. Similarly, the street hawkers reappeared, each with his own peculiar noise-making instrument, a new noise each day indicating the revival of another hawking trade. The crowds in the streets got bigger and bigger and Singapore's only remaining transport, the rickshaws and tri-shaws, multiplied exceedingly.

It was not without difficulty, however, that internal trade revived. Japanese currency had been declared valueless and many thousands of people had, at first, nothing else. The new currency was put into circulation with remarkable speed, but it couldn't be done instantaneously, and so, for some time, bartering was largely substituted. Cigarettes could buy almost anything, but few people, except the Services, had any cigarettes and they, for the most part, were too preoccupied to barter during that week. I did, however, make one purchase with cigarettes, I exchanged two of them for a copy of the first issue of the *Straits Times*, which appeared, by a very excellent effort, on September 7th. I was told that, with the prices then ruling, I paid several hundred per cent above the published price, if not above its value. This particular exchange was made because I could find no one to change a dollar note. Officers on board the *Derbyshire* had been able to cash field cheques for new currency to the magnificent maximum of $13.43. How the figure was arrived at I don't know, but that was all we had for the first few weeks, so it was well that none was required. Those local people who had managed to retain or acquire British Malayan currency during the occupation must have been well off indeed during the first days after liberation. As for Japanese currency—it was known as 'banana money' on account of the picture of a bunch of bananas, which appeared on some notes—it could be picked up freely from the gutters.

Of the increasing numbers in the streets, only a few were bent on business or shopping. Most of them were people raising their heads for the first time in three and a half years to imbibe free air. The yellow slime, which had passed over South East Asia, had been stifling and this liberation was something to drink deeply of, and be curious about. In happy throngs, they moved about, no material purpose, none needed. Among them, were some servicemen, veterans of the Burma campaign, looking in astonishment at a town, which was not in ruins.

Conspicuous in those first crowds were men and women of the jungle forces wearing five-cornered caps and adorned with three stars. They were called indiscriminately "Resistance Forces", "Guerillas" or "Communists". They had harassed the Japs for years, and, now, they had come to Singapore in groups, for purposes best known to themselves. Some settled down to use their great energies in the work of rehabilitation, others found it hard to tame themselves for peace-time pursuits. No one cared much to get on the wrong side of them.

A few tiny cars and dilapidated lorries, filled to overflowing with humanity, dashed along the streets displaying flags, banners and grotesque figures, as only oriental celebrants can. Japanese, at work or still mounting guard on behalf of the Allies, were hissed, booed and spat at. No doubt, the people found it hard to understand why Japanese were still on guard at certain places, and carrying arms, and why Japanese officers still carried swords. Time altered those things, but taking over a city of a million people was a big job, and it was not done in a day.

What went on behind the inscrutable and subservient Japanese faces? Did they regret all the bloodshed, suffering and waste they had caused? Did they take to heart their humiliation? Did they repent in any way, or did they just think that, meantime, they had had their day, and it was good while it lasted? It was, of course, impossible to tell, but I got the impression that they didn't think about it at all, they lived from day to day and took things as they came. It was just as easy, and as meaningless, to bow to a Britisher as to cut off his head. After a week, came the big day, the biggest day in Singapore's history, September 12th, 1945. It was the day of the formal surrender of all the Japanese Forces in South East Asia to Admiral Lord Louis Mountbatten, Supreme Allied Commander, South East Asia. The day was overcast at first, but later there was brilliant sunshine. Singapore's polyglot population flocked to the Padang area in many thousands to see the ceremony, and were richly rewarded. It was carried out perfectly, and could not have been improved upon.

The Guards of Honour drawn up on the Padang, recently levelled and prepared by Japanese prisoners-of-war, represented all the services including, among many others, detachments from the British and French Navies and the 5th Indian Division. Marines flanked the steps of the Municipal Building, and, just inside, a party of Guerillas was drawn up. In addition to its other names, this force was known as the Malayan People's Anti-Japanese Army (M.P.A.J.A.), and, sometimes, as the Resistance Army.

While the Supremo (as he was familiarly called), was inspecting the Guards of Honour, the Japanese surrender delegation, consisting of General Itagaki, Lieutenant-Generals Numata, Nakimura and Kimura and Vice-Admirals Fukodomo and Shibata, arrived in cars bearing white flags. The cars were stopped some distance from the building and the delegation had to complete the journey on foot. The crowd was not slow to show its hostile feelings towards these men, and their humiliation must have been complete. They had even been deprived of their swords.

In those first days, it was considered necessary to impress on the Japs that they had been defeated. Their whole attitude showed little to indicate that that fact had been driven home. Before our arrival, when informing prisoners-of-war and others of the situation they had said merely "The war is over", or "The Japanese have ceased hostilities". There was a large volume of opinion, which considered that the Japanese felt they were not really defeated, but had voluntarily, as they said, "ceased hostilities". The Allied Command, in consequence, lost no opportunity of telling them the true position.

The signing of the surrender documents took place in the handsome Board Room of the Municipal Building. Never before had that room witnessed such an assembly, or been the scene of a function with a fraction of the importance of this. It was appropriately decorated with Allied flags, and two notable features were the fine plaque with the Royal Coat of Arms and a picture of the King. Strangely enough, those two articles had been taken from their original positions, and preserved by the Japanese in the museum. Other less pleasing features, but indicative of the importance of the occasion, were the many press cameras and arc lamps, which surrounded the room and peered down from the balcony.

The Supreme Commander was well supported by Allied representatives, in the persons of Admiral Sir Arthur Power, Commander-in-Chief, East Indies Fleet, General Sir William Slim, Commander-in-Chief, Allied Land Forces S.E.A.C., Air Chief Marshal Sir Keith Park, Allied Air Commander-in Chief S.E.A.C., Lieutenant-General R. A. Wheeler, Deputy Supreme Allied Commander, U.S. Army, Lieutenant-General Leclerc, Commander-in-Chief, French Forces, Far East and Air Vice Marshal Cole, Major-General Feng Yee, Brigadier Thimmaya, Colonel Burman representing Australia, China, India and Holland respectively. Among those representing the Malayan peoples and local interests were H.H. the Sultan of Johore, the Bishop of Singapore, Mr. Rayman, President of the Singapore Municipality, Dr. Lim Han Hoe, Dr. H. S. Moonshi and Mr. E. R. Koek.

When all had assembled, except Admiral Mountbatten, the Japanese delegation filed in through a sitting audience. The audience, including the Japanese, rose for the Supreme Allied Commander, who proceeded with the business in hand immediately. He said:

> *"I have come here to-day to receive the formal surrender of all the Japanese forces within the South East Asia Command. I have received the following telegram from the Supreme Commander of the Japanese forces concerned, Field Marshal Count Terauchi:—*
>
> > *"'The most important occasion of the formal surrender signing at Singapore draws near, the significance of which is no less great to me than to your Excellency. It is extremely regretful that my ill health prevents me from attending and signing it personally and that I am unable to pay*

homage to your Excellency. I hereby notify your Excellency that I have fully empowered General Itagaki, the highest senior general in Japanese armies, and send him on my behalf.'

"On hearing of Field Marshal Terauchi's illness, I sent my own doctor, Surgeon-Captain Birt, Royal Navy, to examine him, and he certifies that the Field Marshal is suffering from the effects of a stroke. In the circumstances I have decided to accept the surrender from General Itagaki to-day, but I have warned the Field Marshal that I shall expect him to make his personal surrender to me as soon as he is fit enough to do so.

"In addition to our Naval, Military and Air Forces which we have at present in Singapore to-day, a large fleet is anchored off Port Swettenham and Port Dixon, and a large force started disembarking from them at daylight on the 9th September. When I visited the beaches yesterday, men were landing in an endless stream. As I speak, there are 100,000 men ashore. This invasion would have taken place on 9th September whether the Japanese had resisted or not. I wish to make this plain: the surrender to-day is no negotiated surrender. The Japanese are submitting to superior force, now massed here.

"I now call upon General Itagaki to produce his credentials."

When the shaven-headed general had produced the required papers, the Supreme Commander read out the Instrument of Surrender.

THE INSTRUMENT OF SURRENDER

1. In pursuance of and in compliance with:

(a) The Instrument of Surrender signed by the Japanese plenipotentiaries by command and on behalf of the Emperor of Japan, the Japanese Government and the Japanese Imperial General Headquarters at Tokyo on 2nd September, 1945;

(b) General Order No. 1, promulgated at the same place and on the same date;

(c) The Local Agreement made by the Supreme Commander, Japanese Expeditionary Forces, Southern Regions, with the Supreme Allied Commander, South East Asia at Rangoon on 27th August, 1945; to all of which Instrument of Surrender, General Order and Local Agreement this present Instrument is complementary and which it in no way supersedes, the Supreme Commander, Japanese Expeditionary Forces, Southern Regions (Field Marshal Count Terauchi) does hereby surrender unconditionally to the Supreme Allied Commander, South East Asia (Admiral the Lord Louis Mountbatten) himself and all Japanese sea, ground, air and auxiliary forces under his command or control and within the operational theatre of the Supreme Allied Commander, South East Asia.

2. The Supreme Commander, Japanese Expeditionary Forces, Southern Regions, undertakes to ensure that all orders and instructions that may be issued from time to time by the Supreme Allied Commander, South East Asia or by any of his subordinate Naval, Military or Air Force Commanders of whatever rank acting in his name, are scrupulously and promptly obeyed by all Japanese sea, ground, air and auxiliary forces under the command or control of the Supreme Commander, Japanese Expeditionary Forces, Southern Regions, and within the operational theatre of the Supreme Allied Commander, South East Asia.

3. Any disobedience of, or delay or failure to comply with, orders or instructions issued by the Supreme Allied Commander, South East Asia, or issued on his behalf by any of his subordinate Naval, Military or Air Force Commanders of whatever rank, and any action which the Supreme Allied Commander, South East Asia, or his subordinate Commanders, acting on his behalf, may determine to be detrimental to the Allied Powers, will be dealt with as the Supreme Allied Commander, South East Asia may decide.

4. This Instrument takes effect from the time and date of signing.

5. This Instrument is drawn up in the English language, which is the only authentic version. In any case of doubt as to intention or meaning, the decision of the Supreme Allied Commander, South East Asia is final. It is the responsibility of the Supreme Commander, Japanese Expeditionary Forces, Southern Regions to make such translation into Japanese as he may require.

Signed at Singapore on 12th September, 1945.

Eleven copies of the Instrument were handed to General Itagaki, who, having produced two seals and a tablet of vermilion-coloured wax from his pockets, sealed them with his own personal seal and that of the Japanese

Army in the bottom left-hand corners. The Supreme Allied Commander signed them, using nine different pens, in the bottom right-hand corners.

Subsequently, in front of the building, Lord Louis, speaking through the microphone, said, "I have accepted this surrender on behalf of you all."

The ceremony ended with hoisting the flag to the top of a flag pole, specially erected on the Padang. It was a faded Union Jack, which has, since then, occupied a position in the room where the surrender was signed. Below the flag is a tablet, on which the following words are inscribed:

The Union Jack Presented to the People of Singapore
by
Admiral the Lord Louis Mountbatten,
C.G.V.O., K.C.B., D.S.O., A.D.C.,

Supreme Allied Commander South East Asia.

The Union Jack was carried at the capitulation of Singapore to the Japanese on February 15th, 1942. For three and a half years the prisoners-of-war in Changi Camp concealed it from the Japanese. On their release they presented it to the Supreme Allied Commander at whose order it was ceremonially rehoisted outside the Municipal Buildings when the Commanders of the Japanese Forces signed their unconditional surrender in this Chamber on 12th September, 1945.

Throughout the occupation, the Japanese had tried hard to impose their language on the Malayan peoples. They called this language 'Nippon-go', and everywhere one heard and read of 'Nippon-go'. When our forces returned, the people made what was, perhaps, a bad pun, but one which expressed a lot of feeling. On walls and hoardings around the town, the phrase, "British come-Nippon-go", was displayed in large letters. After September 12th, no one doubted that Nippon had really gone, although the aftermath had, and still has in part, to be reckoned with.

JAPANNED
SINGAPORE

WHEN entering Singapore Harbour on the morning of September 5th, I had wondered what differences would be found in this town and Island I had known so well. Beyond doubt, there would be physical changes, although, from my study of air photographs in Ceylon, I gathered there were few large-scale constructional developments of a permanent nature. In those photographs, I had not discovered any great new buildings, bridges or roads nor had I missed any outstanding features, which had previously been there. Still, the photographs were not capable of showing everything, and, untrained in the study, of such, there might be much that I had overlooked.

About possible changes in the people, I had been a little apprehensive. For over one hundred and twenty years, the guiding forces had been continuously British and the ideas and ideals before the people western. Almost overnight, the Island had changed hands and the new rulers were of a very different culture, giving lip service to all things oriental. During such a prolonged occupation, it must have been possible for them to effect some fundamental changes in local thought and habit. It took a little while to assess those, but the physical changes were immediately obvious.

Unlike Rangoon, the buildings in Singapore were structurally intact. Scars, left by Japanese bombing in 1941 and 1942, had largely disappeared and only the Naval Base and the civil docks had suffered from Allied attacks. Notable, among damage at the former, was the sinking of the enormous floating dock which had already been down once and up again. The civil dock area had suffered quite heavily, with damage or destruction to thirty out of forty-three transit sheds and seven teen out of thirty-three storage sheds. Landing there, one might have been misled into thinking that Singapore had had its share of hard knocks from the air, but, once outside the dock area, no further signs of bombing were visible.

Other signs of the occupation were everywhere. Few of them were individually of much importance, but, cumulatively, they made a great difference to the outward face of Singapore. The town before the war was clean and tidy and in good repair, but now it was dirty, neglected, overgrown and down at the heel. Since the first World War, most of the large buildings erected had been faced with a light grey artificial stone, and the Japanese thinking this conspicuous, appeared to delight in camouflaging it with black oil streaks. The station, various police quarters, barracks and other buildings suffered in this way, but, inconsistently, the Municipal Buildings and the Supreme Court were untouched, although the former was headquarters for, what the Japanese called, the Municipality Government or Tokubetu Si. Those black streaks changed a pleasant-looking building into a depressing sight. Other buildings, such as shop-houses and homes, had normally been colour-washed every year or two, but, in 1945, the face-lifting process was long overdue and the walls had adopted a variety of shades and patches, which were anything but aesthetic.

Buildings, which the Japanese had erected themselves, were numerous and shoddy. They were, no doubt, mostly for military purposes and intended to be temporary, but the siting of them bore no traces of the alleged Japanese love of beauty. They were everywhere. Ramshackle buildings of coarse brick, timber and corrugated iron were scattered haphazardly on all open spaces, golf courses, playing fields and parks. Inferior, chewed-up roads led into them and unsightly scrap lay all around, the whole being protected by crude barbed-wire fencing. The local people had not been slow to follow this jerry building lead, and, taking advantage of the slackened Municipal control, had erected its quota of similar structures on any ground not wanted by the Jap, other ownership being a minor consideration. Lean-tos and rickety stalls, overflowing open grounds, staked claims on public highways and back-lanes, securing immunity, for this contribution to the general disorder, by well-placed 'tea-money'. Hawkers by the thousand had openly pitched their emporia on any convenient roadway.

As the Japanese undoubtedly thought, during 1942 and 1943, that they had eliminated European influence from South East Asia, it is quite remarkable that they did not thoroughly clear from Singapore all outward signs of British rule. Apart from moving Raffles statue to the Museum and destroying the colonnade, they did not interfere with monuments or commemoration tablets. The Cenotaph, the Dalhousie Monument and others still stood. The Royal Coat of Arms, as carved on buildings, was allowed to remain and British signs and advertisements in conspicuous places survived the whole occupation. The Japanese added a few monuments of their own, notably the Victory Memorial on Bukit Timah Road at the ninth mile. This structure, placed in a very prominent position on top of a hill about 200 feet high, could be reached by ascending a wide and striking approach road of gentle slopes and imposing steps. This approach road remained a long time for all to see, but the memorial itself was blown up by our troops early in the occupation process. On September 6th, a similar fate befell the Indian National Army Memorial, situated on the Esplanade near the Cenotaph. The Fugi Regiment Memorial had a longer life being in a comparatively isolated spot some distance from any road. The site chosen for it was in front of the McRitchie Reservoir Bungalow, standing on a hill overlooking the impounded water about four miles from the town centre. There had been heavy fighting around this bungalow when the Japs took Singapore and the memorial column was probably inspired by their victory at that spot. A Japanese inscription on the column, according to an interpreter, read:

MEMORIAL TO THE FUGI REGIMENT WHO FOUGHT AND DIED

On the night of February 9th this Japanese Battalion crossed the Johore Causeway to the South West direction and attacked a strong British enemy front that was well defended from the Seletar Naval Base to Mandai Road. On the 13th February they had already advanced to the north of Singapore the key front of the British fortress. The British strongly resisted but due to the bravery of the Japanese soldier this place was captured. On the morning of the 14th February the British troops were retreating to the north-east of Katong Airport and Paya Lebar and were absolutely cut off.

On the 15th February the enemy were totally encircled and unconditionally surrendered. Mandai

*Hill is so called because of the bravery of the Japanese
soldier who fought so fiercely.*

Mandai Varna (Hill).

Unfortunately, the inscription is not enlightening and
indeed the wording, as translated, scarcely makes sense.
The name 'Mandai' preceded the Japanese. The column
was demolished early in 1946, by Japanese prisoner-of-war
labour.

In the same locality, and not far from this column, a
unique shrine had been built for religious purposes. It was
very beautifully conceived and carried out with superb
artistry, but that did not protect it from the same fate as
the others. I have heard it argued that these Japanese
structures might well have been preserved, not necessarily
in their original locations, but in some kind of War
Museum, however, the bulk of opinion favoured wiping
out all traces of the occupation. That was easy to do in the
case of structures, but not so simple with less material
things.

Contrary to what I had expected, there were few
notices in the Japanese language to be seen around the
town. They were not entirely absent, but certainly they
were not conspicuous. The street names had been left in
English and Chinese, and so had the traffic signs. Here and
there, Japanese notices were to be found outside shops,
warehouses and depots, and, I understand, they had been
much more numerous until a week or so earlier. During
the week before our arrival, the owners had judiciously
taken them down and substituted notices in English. The
Japanese had not interfered. The attempt to introduce
Nippon-go in Malaya was a conspicuous failure, in spite of
much effort and the offer of substantial rewards. It is true,
that many people who had to work with the Jap learned

143

some words and took care to refer to places, buildings and officials by their Japanese names and titles, but, beyond that, it seldom went. Imposing an alien language on a people by design appears to be impossible, and even reviving a national language, as we have learned in the British Isles, presents difficulties.

It was a pleasant surprise to find that the roads and streets with a few exceptions, were still in very good condition, which, after the dreadful state of those in Rangoon, was something to be very thankful for. Apart altogether from the discomfort and dirt of bad street surfaces, there are few things which give to a town a worse appearance. The relief was modified, however, by the filth and scrap which lay on, and around them. The main streets were bad, but the side streets and back lanes were appalling. Conservancy, under the Japanese, had almost entirely broken down and the people had, in consequence, deposited their rubbish in the most convenient spot, which usually turned out to be the street. Great heaps of scrap and putrefied organic matter lay everywhere, the monsoon drains were all badly obstructed and frequently entirely blocked. Resulting smells were none too good.

Modern armies, in retreat, always leave a trail of wrecked machines, and the Imperial Japanese Army was no exception. Broken down trucks and cars, bits of tanks and mobile artillery littered the roads and dumping grounds, and, in some areas, crashed aircraft added its quota. The Balestier and Aljuneid Road areas were prominent among the larger recipients of this kind of scrap, but the Island boasted many dumps. An old vehicle is a particularly stubborn thing to dispose of *in toto*. A certain amount of it will disappear very easily, as Singapore found, but the balance, which occupies the greater space, seems eternal. It was many months before the roads were cleared of wrecks, and when they were, more dumps had been created in Singapore's few remaining open areas. No mathematical calculation is likely to reveal when those dumps will cease to exist.

In keeping with Great Britain, Singapore had lost most of its cast-iron railings and nicknacks, but, as these had not been numerous, no corresponding improvement was effected. More serious was the loss of its cast-iron lamp standards, which had been removed in great numbers, and the diversion to other purposes of long lengths of pipe railing, which formerly protected the careless from falling into deep drains. The pipe railing was not very beautiful, and appearances gained by its removal but, in many places, it had certainly been justified by the indisputable danger to life and limb. One wonders whether it will be reinstated, or if some more pleasing substitute can be found. The deep monsoon drains, which line the streets of Singapore, are necessary to deal with the heavy rainfall, but they are very ugly and wasteful of space. Better planning of canals and underground conduits, in the very early days, might have saved a lot of the trouble they now cause.

When one left the centre of the town and reached the out skirts, deterioration from pre-war tidiness was particularly apparent. What had formerly been neatly cut grass verges were now, for the most part, planted with stringy papaya trees and unsightly tapioca plants, round the roots of which lalang (very coarse grass) grew unchecked. In several places, the footpath slabs had been taken up and coarse vegetables planted in the ground below—an indication of the struggle against hunger. That struggle had likewise caused the conversion of all tennis courts into vegetable gardens, a transformation which in England might pass unnoticed, but, as almost every better class residence in Singapore had its court, was, there, very conspicuous. The neat well-kept compounds, for which Singapore had been justly famous, were overgrown, unkempt and riddled with human burrows.

The Jap when frightened was a prolific burrower, and many a hole in Singapore Island bore witness to his fear. The digging disease had only come upon him, in Singapore, comparatively late. On first arrival, he had despised the meagre efforts of the inhabitants to protect themselves against his bombs, and had ordered all air-raid shelters to be filled in or dismantled. He told the people that the Allies had been driven so far away and Japan was so invincible that Singapore could not be raided. The white man had gone for good. With the passage of time and the reappearance of Allied aircraft in Malayan skies, the Jap radically changed his tune. Dig and dig again became his motto, and almost every available inch of ground was perforated to make a hide-out or thrown up as a blast wall. The quality of the workmanship was not good, and most air-raid shelters were inadequately constructed and inundated with water. In some cases, these diggings were enormous, great tunnels under hills and high ground without sufficient side or roof support. There were tunnels under houses standing on hills, to which entrance could be effected either from the floor of the house or from the foot of the hill, and into which the house itself would, sooner or later, have fallen.

The Jap had dug himself in on the Island in another sense of the phrase. He had covered great areas with camps and stores. The latter were particularly interesting in the nature of their contents, embodying as they did, in addition to normal equipment, great stocks of articles, for which there was no conceivable use. One depot will serve as an example, it consisted of some sixteen brick warehouses scattered over two hundred acres of rubber plantation. Each building was about 100 feet long by 24 feet wide by 20 feet high, and all were filled, from floor to truss level, with leather saddles and bridles, canvas and leather straps, canvas saddle-bags, holsters and similar harness. There seemed to be enough of those articles to equip all the cavalrymen and cowboys left in the world, and that in a country where a horse is a curiosity.

Diggings and dumps were not the only engineering enterprises they set their hand to. They made some traffic roundabouts and some roads. In pre-war Singapore, so many authorities seemed to have an interest and a finger in the design of a traffic round-about, that obtaining agreement to construct one was a major operation. Buying the land and encroaching buildings added a few more years to the time lag between its conception and its construction. The Jap had no such difficulties, he decided overnight that there must be large islands at three junctions, Orchard Road-Clemenceau Avenue, Tanglin Road-Napier Road and Paterson Road-Grange Road. People in the way were told to vacate their houses or property within two days, the buildings were demolished, the islands constructed and full-grown royal palms transplanted into the centre without, in all probability, a single file having been referred to the next fellow. The thousands, who now circumnavigate those islands daily, are mostly unaware that they are Japanese monuments. I do not think it a rash assumption that they will remain, testifying by proxy to Singapore's some-time traffic control awareness.

One spate of road building which overtook the Japanese is worthy of mention although it has now largely disappeared. The most beautiful inland part of the Island is undoubtedly the area occupied by the adjoining catchments of the three reservoirs, known as McRitchie, Peirce and Seletar respectively. These catchments were semi-sacred, no buildings or roads being allowed within their precincts, but golf clubs, club houses excepted, were not considered as violating that sanctity. The Royal Singapore Golf Club enjoyed the use of part of the McRitchie Reservoir catchment and the Island Golf Club had similar privileges on that of Peirce Reservoir, the remainder of the catchments were exclusively forest.

The Japanese decided to make part of this semi-sacred area really sacred, and constructed the unique shrine I have mentioned earlier, which stood on a hill overlooking the McRitchie Reservoir. That shrine faced the Golf Club from across a branch of the reservoir, opposite the second green of the course. The approach was by a series of roads, a bridge and a flight of steps.

Three of the approach roads ran across the golf course and one skirted its perimeter. This latter passed the Club House entrance continuing on a straight course for some distance, then, bearing right, emerged at the water's edge near the top of the reservoir branch over which the bridge was built. From there, it ran back alongside the reservoir to the bridge approach, joining with the more direct routes at a well laid-out and tree lined junction, which was beautified by formal beds of shrubs and flowers.

The bridge, spanning the water gap, was arched in faultless lines. Its parapets of rounded red and yellow timbers, with modest ornamentation, added blending colours to the green background, and reflected a picture in the still water which was a joy to look at.

From the other end of the bridge, a short path led to the great wide flight of dressed granite steps, which gave access to the shrine, magnificently situated on the levelled top of a hill, and, in itself, a charming example of Japanese architecture in wood. Equally charming was the little tea house, which stood half way up the long flight of steps and moulded its curved timbers, latticed windows and slatted roof unobtrusively into the trees. The paths around these buildings and at the foot of the steps were carpeted with carefully selected white and black pebbles and flanked, on both sides, by tall Japanese lanterns carved from wood in exquisite taste.

Where the forest was cleared, it had been done without vandalism, so that the best trees, where possible, had been left standing to enhance the beauty and give a satisfactory feeling of maturity and composure. The whole was Japanese construction and landscaping at its very best.

Dual considerations, for the catchment area and for the jealous followers of the Royal and Ancient game, succeeded in obliterating those signs of Japanese devotion, and, now, there is no trace of the roads which impudently crossed the fairways, concrete bridges, which supported them over golfing hazards, have yielded to dynamite, and their remains have served to fill a hole some other way. Of the other works, little remains, looters found uses for the timbers of the buildings, and, I fear, many a Chinese gravestone was once a Japanese granite step. The long arched bridge has disappeared as completely as its reflection in the water.

This offering to the Gods was made by the Japanese before their deities began to desert them. When that defection commenced, they hurriedly returned to their road-making and constructed a network of many miles through the catchment forests, as far as Peirce Reservoir and Thompson Road. Hidden from the air by overhanging trees, those roads afforded concealed approaches to many hide-outs for men and material, and, no doubt, if more time had been allowed to them, a very elaborately protected area would have been completed. As it happened the work was left unfinished and the traces are rapidly reverting to jungle.

When the roads were usable, they enabled the Japanese and others to cut down and remove timber from the forest catchments, but the loss of trees there was scarcely noticeable to the casual observer. It was a different story on other parts of the Island, many areas being thoroughly denudated of all timber of any height. Indeed, as an old resident, I found that one of the most startling things was to look over the Island from any vantage point. The changed landscape was arresting, before the reason for it became apparent. Where thick forest and jungle had been, so far as eye could see, there was left only low scrub, interspersed with red wounds, where the Jap had burrowed, or with blackened sites of camps and dumps. This lust for wood sprang from two sources, one official and one unofficial. The Japanese wanted wood for their camps and stores, they wanted it for the wooden ships they built in great numbers, and they used it as a substitute for steel and other materials in various activities. The local people used it for firewood, and, also, as cheap raw material for a number of small industries. With the break-down in control, they took it, in all probability, from any place they pleased. The local wood was mostly poor, and a very inferior substitute for imported timber and firewood, but the Japanese were not in a position to import, due to shipping losses and lack of organisation within their sphere of control.

It was sad to see the green tree-clad Island laid bare and vandalised over large areas.

The work which the Japanese did on airfields is worthy of mention. The Civil Airport at Kallang had been extended across Grove Road, almost as far as Tanjong

Katong Road, and this extension, together with dispersal points and emergency air strips, made the Katong area unrecognisable. The closing of Grove Road forced a long detour on those who wished to get from the town to Tanjong Rhu or Katong and was, consequently, very unpopular. It must be recognised, however, that the Kallang Airfield, as originally built, was useless for modern long-distance land machines, although, when opened about 1937, it was considered as extremely up to date and capable of catering for all aircraft for a long time to come.

Changi Road had also been crossed near the 11th mile by a completely new airfield, which the Royal Air Force has now adopted and proposes to retain and improve. This, I understand, will ultimately be the best military airfield on the Island, but at what a cost! The alienation of the whole Changi area is an irreplaceable loss to the civilian population. The pleasantest part of the Island, and often the coolest, it was, before the 1930s, a complete change to get there from Singapore, and enjoy a secluded holiday by its white sands and blue sea. A narrow red laterite road led to it, with little but vegetation on either side until one reached the little village at its end near the sea. The few holiday bungalows on the shore were well tucked away, and the whole approached, as nearly as possible, to what one imagined a tropical paradise to be. This retreat was particularly useful, as it has always been so difficult to get away from the turmoil and heat-haze of Singapore which, with the never changing climate, rapidly breeds monotony and staleness, against which the individual must constantly fight. Singapore's growing importance and consequent militarisation before the war, first broke the spell with a great barracks, and, now that an airfield has been added and the road brought up to modern standard, the whole route and the fairyland at its extremity has become, or is quickly becoming, urbanised.

Although the process of desecration of the Island had begun before 1941, the Japanese occupation hastened it out of all proportion to the time they spent there. With airfields, camps, dumps, electricity pylons and temporary buildings they destroyed the landscape, by tree-cutting they ruined many a pleasant spot, and, in general, an artificial mess was left where natural beauty had prevailed. The fine Botanical Gardens, with many rare specimens, were badly neglected, and, for some reason, had become so unattractive that even the monkeys, which had drawn many visitors, particularly children, had vanished. Farrer Park, Katong Park, Keppel Golf Course and the little Golf Course at Tanglin Road (formerly used by the Japanese themselves) were built over, or used as dumps. The same fate befell almost every 'lung' of the Town, and, against this despoliation, there was nothing which they did that could be said to have improved the Island. A few of their works may be useful, such as the airfields, but many a project, into which much effort was put, could only be abandoned. The roads in the catchment area and a new dock, which they had commenced to build at Pulo Damar Laut, were among the more ambitious works of their hands to be discarded as useless.

A great fleet of transport fell to the Japanese as booty, when they captured Singapore. There must have been tens of thousands of vehicles, many new and the majority of the rest in good condition. On those, they appeared to rely throughout the occupation, and did not import many of their own, but, through lack of spare parts, or technical skill, or both, the fleet diminished rapidly in numbers, and had almost faded away by the time they surrendered. The few, that were left, were in a deplorable condition.

One innovation which the Japanese introduced, or permitted to be introduced, was the tri-shaw, which consisted of a bicycle with a side-car attached for a fare-paying passenger, This had largely replaced the former rickshaw and, subsequently, the British Civil authorities gave it their blessing, discrediting the rickshaw in its favour.

It is a surprising reflection on Japanese ability and organisation that, although in control of most of the world's rubber and many oil fields, they managed to produce only thin solid rubber tyres for bicycles, and forced many motor vehicles to run on coal gases or inferior petrol from vegetable sources. Transport was a big problem for the local people throughout the occupation. Public vehicles dwindled, and cars ceased to be available for almost all, other than Japanese and their quislings. A few clever people transformed cars into vans and obtained permission to use them as business vehicles, but, for most, it was a case of a Japanese bicycle with solid tyres or nothing.

The insides of buildings and houses did not escape the general deterioration, though the degree of damage varied greatly, some suffering very little, if at all, while others were completely stripped or converted into dumps. A few cases will serve to illustrate what happened. St. Andrew's Cathedral and the Roman Catholic Cathedral escaped almost intact, the former being very proud that a service had been held there every day, with one exception, from the fall of Singapore to its reoccupation. On the other hand, the Presbyterian Church in Orchard Road had been stripped of everything, the organ smashed, the pulpit, pews and furnishings thrown out in a dump, and the building then used as a store for soap, matches, paint and the like. The Municipal Buildings and the Supreme Court escaped lightly, but the Victoria Memorial Hall, the Government Secretariat, the P.W.D. offices and the Old Supreme Court were stripped and used as stores. In general, typewriters, duplicators, office mechanical equipment and lifts had suffered severely, or disappeared altogether, but records and files were preserved in many cases, though not, by any means, in all. The Government records of land transactions were intact and most of the Municipal files survived. So far as I can ascertain, many banks and business houses were equally fortunate due to a variety of causes. In some cases, files survived simply because no one bothered about them, in other cases, they were hidden by the local employees at risk to themselves, and, occasionally, preservation was due to the good offices of some less destructively-minded Japanese. An outstanding example of preservation by this inconsistent race was the care taken of the Museum with its precious relics. Raffles Museum and the attached library were well looked after, and, indeed, the Japanese added to both from local loot, so that a number of private possessions and books were afterwards found there. In contrast to those examples, the records and books of many establishments, including the clubs, early became scrap paper.

In the vaults, cellars and basements of some public buildings a number of dumps of semi-precious articles were found such as silverware and paintings, and stores of consumer goods were distributed widely over warehouses, public buildings and private residences. The lack of system in most dumps was very apparent, all sorts of goods being heaped together in disorder, boots and electric bulbs might share a container with soap and aircraft parts. Tinned meat would, as likely as not, be side by side with hair oil and postage stamps, while over and around the lot, scrap of every description lay unsorted.

Private residences of former Europeans suffered, as a whole, more than any other type of building. When left vacant in 1942, much was taken from them by the local people before the invader arrived, and, later, before they were claimed by Japanese officials, their soldiers had a free hand. When the Japanese settled down to occupy Singapore, the officers and officials were allotted vacant European residences, together with everything they contained. So far as I can gather, the contents of a house, from then on, were considered the property of the Jap to whom it had first been allotted and, if he moved—which he frequently did—he took those contents with him to his next residence, leaving only the things he didn't want. The man who had occupied the house to which he went did the same thing and, in consequence, the belongings of the former European owners rapidly got spread about. Those belongings were further dispersed by Japanese 'generosity' to lady friends (in SEAC language—'comfort girls'), informers and others philanthropically inclined towards the conquerors, each being rewarded according to his or her merits by a piano, a gramophone or a fish fork. This 'generosity' reached its 'highest' levels when Japan surrendered, the men in possession then, having little chance of retaining the articles for their future enjoyment, made a virtue of the necessary separation. If there was anything left in the European houses after this flood of giving, it was, during the interregnum, at the mercy of gangs of robbers and the neighbouring people, who, perhaps comparatively innocently, took helpings of what they considered belonged to no one. Naturally, small articles disappeared more completely than large pieces of furniture, but the latter were not immune to Japanese methods, so that, between house moving and the oft-practised art of converting furniture to firewood, few pieces remained *in situ*. For some time to come, it is probable that when Mrs. Smith calls on Mrs. Jones she will, quite innocently, be offered her own armchair to sit upon.

The looting of houses and buildings did not, unfortunately, stop with the removal of furnishings and equipment which were normally movable. It extended to permanent fittings, particularly those connected with electricity, water and gas. Electric switches, wiring and lamp holders, water boilers, taps and geysers, gas and electric stoves, all came in for the attention of looters, and they spared neither walls nor floors in removing them. Those things had a marketable value and by devious means, they later got to the market, intact or in pieces.

I do not wish to convey the impression that every European house was completely despoiled, that would not be correct by any means. A great many were entirely empty of movable goods and stripped of most permanent fixtures, but houses were found with every degree of damage, from the emptied and battered to the few which were completely intact. There were not many of the latter, but they did exist, and their preservation was due to a series of lucky circumstances. In a relatively obscure position perhaps, they were securely locked by the owners and left in charge of conscientious servants, who managed to keep them unviolated, until the authorised Japanese officials came to claim them. Those officials then, by some good fortune, remained in the same houses throughout the occupation, and left them intact for the servants to take charge of once more. A house, which was recovered as it was left, must have had good servants, relatively good and stationary Japanese, and a lot of luck.

The kebuns (gardeners) were about the most stable appurtenances to a house, and many of them were to be found where they were left. Living in back quarters and concerned with the garden only, they allowed the world and its vicissitudes to pass over their heads largely unheeded. They grew most of their own food and came into contact with the occupiers of the house as little as possible. On the other hand, the inside servants ceased to have jobs when the house was vacated, and so moved on, finding it safer to be away from premises, which tempted robbers and looters and from any responsibility which anyone, British or Japanese, might subsequently consider them to have acquired by virtue of remaining. Many servants did their best to protect property, but circumstances were too strong and the property disappeared. If they took a few odds and ends themselves, who will blame them? I, for one, much preferred that my servants should benefit from what I lost than that the Japanese should have it. That, I think, was the view usually taken, for the affection and esteem between master and man, in the pre-war Malaya, was very marked, and, throughout the occupation, the fate of servants and employees was a constant worry to most Europeans. The joy of the reunions, after that break, was a great tribute to the happy relationships which had existed.

The local people, who greeted us so enthusiastically on our return had been through a lot, and much of it had not failed to leave marks. There had been mass murders and individual murders, mass torturing and any number of individual victims. Rape, beating, theft and looting had gone on continuously, and there had been hunger and want. More than anything else, there had been almost universal mental agony and suspicion, no one knew when the next horror would come, or from where, and no one knew whom he could trust. After three and a half years in an atmosphere such as those things engendered, one would expect to find a people changed, but what form the change would take was not so easy to guess beforehand.

Up to a point, the conditions which prevailed in Malaya were known to the outside world before the liberation and there may have been some, in that outside world, who endeavoured to gauge the effect those conditions would have on the people. Numerous questions would immediately present themselves. Would our defeat in 1942 have destroyed all faith in the white man? Would our delay in returning be held against us as a measure of our lack of concern for their welfare? Would the Japanese, who had an unsurpassed chance of winning the people, have alienated all sympathy by their cruelty or would the fact that they, too, were a coloured race have excused them? Would the hunger and want of the people be blamed on the Japanese or on us? Would the habits of dishonesty and racketeering, which had been forced on the inhabitants become permanent? Would the population emerge subdued and ineffective, or would it be more politically conscious and rebellious?

The answer to all those questions can scarcely, even yet, be given satisfactorily, but there was much about the physical and mental condition of the people which showed up early. First, and very comforting, was the warmth and spontaneity of the welcome they gave us. There was no doubt whatever that it was genuine, and those of us, who had been privileged to live in the country before, very quickly became aware that personal relationships had in no way suffered by all that had happened. Indeed, they seemed to have improved, and, I venture to believe that, never before had the various peoples of Malaya, white and coloured, been so close together as during the first months after liberation. The internees spoke in glowing terms of what had been done for them, during the dark days, by those outside the wire and the latter seemed to wish for nothing better than that the British should again be among them. The flood of emotion and goodwill persisted through the period of golden haze, which followed the liberation. There was ample cause for it on both sides, tyranny and fear were gone, friends were reunited, the war was over and surely the period of want was ending.

That we were received warmly on our own account is beyond question, but I do not propose to suggest that we were not welcomed for other reasons as well. Naturally, the people wanted many things, especially food and clothing in abundance, and they hoped we would immediately provide those. That we did not do so was not our fault, but, as the months went by, the failure, while not impairing personal relationships, took some of the radiance from the liberation. Signs of malnutrition were everywhere, great numbers suffered from beri-beri and almost all were deplorably thin and hungry. They had lived, for the most part, on meagre quantities of unpleasant tapioca with some greens of poor food value. Other diseases were also prevalent such as malaria, tuberculosis and venereal disease, and medicines for treatment had not been made available to the people. Clothes had been very scarce and wardrobes were empty, either through wear and tear or through the necessity of selling what could be spared in order to buy such food and medicine as could be had. The clothes a man appeared in were usually his best and only clothes, except, perhaps, some abbreviated garment which he donned when he was not appearing. The exigencies of circumstances were most notable in the absence of Malay songkohs. These caps are worn as a religious rite, and are not lightly abandoned by a conservative people. In addition to being starved for food, the inhabitants were starved for news. Very little from the outside world had reached them for three years, and one of the first requests I got was for papers, periodicals or any reading matter. There was a great blank in their knowledge of what had happened in recent years, and, in consequence, a cramped outlook. There was also a great lassitude, which, combined with the other things, reduced their working efficiency by a large percentage. They all needed a holiday, good food and more clothes, but immediately after liberation, the moon would have been more easily obtained. Fortunately, the liberation itself gave them a mental stimulus, without which I doubt if most of them could have carried on.

In working with them from day to day, one noticed a number of little things, an inclination to bow in Japanese fashion when they met you—the Japanese had rigorously enforced this, their method of salute—a disinclination to take responsibility, a pathetic gratitude for any little gift such as cigarettes or an old coat, and, unfortunately, due to Japanese inflation, a lack of appreciation of the value of the new currency.

The outlook of many towards money and work had certainly changed under Japanese tuition. Under their regime, honest work was about the last thing to bring due reward. It was the resort of those, who were not sufficiently clever or sufficiently immoral to adopt the new code. Blackmarket dealing, thieving, gambling, informing and procuring were the richly rewarded occupations, and far too many people served apprenticeships to them. When the Japanese ceased to rule, the last three failed to attract as before, but black-marketeering and theft retained many followers and have, even still, numerous devotees. That was one of the more serious legacies of the occupation, involving moral deterioration and mental degeneration very difficult to eradicate, especially in a world of continuing shortages. People involved in those occupations got money in an underhand way, without a corresponding amount of work, and developed a contempt for normal methods of living, which may persist and find new outlets, when the black-market and theft have ceased to pay. If a large section of the populace is involved, as was the case in Malaya, the results may be grave and of long standing consequence. To connect some of the possible results with politics, would not be stretching imagination too far.

In the earlier part of this book, I have stated that Malaya, before the war, was singularly free of political and racial issues. The Japanese occupation altered that. The country emerged with a new political conscience, which, however desirable a political consciousness may be, was sure to be attended, in the future, by disunity and enmities, if not by bloodshed. It could scarcely be otherwise in a country where the native peoples are outnumbered by an alien and very progressive race of a different colour. I am convinced that there is no more affinity between two racially-different coloured peoples than there is between white and coloured. The fact that the Japanese were coloured did not, in any way, help them with the brown, yellow and black communities, whose countries they had invaded. I would go even further than that and say, that a coloured people would, if compelled to be subject to a foreign power, select a white one in preference to one of any other colour.

Malaya's new political consciousness was, at the liberation, strongest among the Guerillas. The first incentive for those men was hatred of the Jap, but the second, I guess, was a desire for political power. With the genuine and responsible members, this desire was, I have no doubt, to be pursued along legitimate and constitutional lines, but, unfortunately, all such movements attract to their ranks many questionable characters, and the Malayan Peoples Anti-Japanese Army was no exception. How far the less responsible element would have tipped the balance towards gaining power by force of arms, if circumstances had afforded the opportunity, I do not pretend to know, but I deduce from many incidents that the issue was a close thing.

Wielding pick and shovel, Japanese soldiers appear in a new role to the people of Singapore.

I have nothing but admiration for the superb bravery and endurance of resistance armies, but their careers are generally attended by so much misery to non-combatants and so much unrest later, that one may legitimately question their ultimate value. A Jap or a German was shot

*A victory column, erected by the Japanese after their
occupation of Malaya, is broken up by Japanese P.O.W.s.*

by a guerilla, and a whole village wiped out in reprisal. A
train or a lorry was blown up and dozens of innocent
people were slaughtered as an example to others. Was the
case of the Allies aided to a commensurable degree? I do
not know, but I take leave to doubt. When peace came,
were the mental attitudes, which had developed, an asset?
Did the war and the post-war period, considered together,
benefit? Those are questions, which must have been asked
many times in Malaya, and variously answered in the
minds of both people and rulers.

How far the more extreme views of some of the
Guerillas had, by the autumn of 1945, permeated the rest
of the people is difficult to say. It had been acknowledged,
for some time, that the Chinese were anxious for a larger
say in the governing of the country. The Indians, as a
whole, were concerned much more about India than they

were about Malaya, for few of them looked on Malaya as their home. The Malays were in a very difficult position, being outnumbered in their own country and doubtful if, without British protection, they could maintain a leading position. Nevertheless, they were not insensible to nationalist urgings. Either because of, or in spite of, the Japanese occupation all the various peoples of Malaya had, when we arrived, developed a consciousness of government beyond anything they previously had.

The reason for that may not be unconnected with economics. For a long time before the war, Malaya had been a very rich country with good pay for regular employees and abundant opportunity for business. Under an efficient and benevolent government, and with no pressing wants, the average citizen had been content to use his or her energies in acquiring money and enjoying life. It was seldom that anyone had difficulty in finding work, and, with the lenient climate, the absolute necessities of life were few. Most of Malaya's wealth came from rubber, tin and shipping, the first two were exported mainly to Europe and America and shipping flourished by virtue of the country's unique position, free trade and the freedom of the seas.

When the Japanese came, these three industries ceased to be sources of wealth, the Japanese-controlled territories could not use anything like the quantities of rubber and tin, which could be produced within them, and the big outside markets were no longer available. Many millions of rubber trees ceased to be tapped, and only a few of the tin mines were kept going in an economical manner. Shipping fell off to almost nothing, as exports and imports dwindled, and the Japanese lost more and more ships. Hundreds of thousands of people employed, directly or indirectly, in those trades must have been thrown out of work, and the flow of real wealth reduced to a trickle.

The opportunities of reward for honest work having dried up, and the many sources of man's pleasure, from spending on luxuries to simple gatherings of friends, being rendered impossible or suspect, the minds of many turned to the whys and wherefores of things, and, without the opportunity of studying a wider world, sought ideas for altering the one at hand, which might give promise of better things. Thus in a confined space and under abnormal circumstances, seeds, which in the larger view were those of contraction rather than expansion, were sown.

Japan commenced its war with the avowed intention of clearing the white man from Asia and establishing an economic unity in the Far East. When Tenno-Heika laid down the sword, there were more white men in Asia than had ever been there, at any one time before, and instead of economic unity, there was economic chaos. In every land where the Jap had been, there was disorder, starvation, raggedness and poverty, and, in achieving this, he had caused an immeasurable amount of agony and bloodshed. The ultimate outcome of his holy war is not yet fully apparent, but whatever evolves, it will not be a Nipponese-governed Greater East Asia Co-Prosperity Sphere.

MILITARY
ADMINISTRATION

ON September 5th, immediately after the British Forces landed, Proclamation No. 1—the Military Administration Proclamation—was posted up in the area under control. In this Proclamation, the Supreme Allied Commander assumed for himself and his successors full judicial, legislative, executive and administrative powers and responsibilities and conclusive jurisdiction over all persons and property. He established a British Military Administration throughout the areas of Malaya under the control of his Forces, and, subject to his orders and directions, delegated to the General Officer Commanding Military Forces, Malaya, all the powers, responsibilities and jurisdiction assumed by him. He gave to the General Officer Commanding authority to delegate further to any officer under his command such powers, responsibilities and jurisdiction as he deemed necessary and empower him to delegate in turn to his officers.

The General Officer Commanding delegated to the Chief Civil Affairs Officer, Malaya (Major-General Hone), full authority, power and jurisdiction to conduct on his behalf the military administration of the civil population of Malaya. The Chief Civil Affairs Officer then empowered, subject to any orders and directions from him, Brigadier McKerron and Brigadier Willan, as Deputy Chief Civil Affairs Officers, to exercise all functions of government over the civil population in the Settlement of

Singapore and on the Malay Peninsula respectively. Thus were the two Divisions, the Singapore Division and the Peninsula Division, of the British Military Administration, Malaya, set up. It was not long before they were universally referred to as the 'B.M.A.'

The British Military Administration (Singapore Division) established its headquarters in the Municipal Building. Its task was to heal the wounds of Singapore and attend to the body corporate, through convalescence, until normal health had been almost restored. Like other doctors, the B.M.A. put its name and consulting hours on a board at the door and was liable to be called out day or night.

The Municipal Buildings had been the headquarters of the Japanese Municipality Government which had, in its own way and with modifications, carried out much the same duties as the B.M.A. now took over. Before the Japanese era, the building had been confined exclusively to municipal affairs. The additional services, which the Japanese decided to control from this headquarters, forced them to make considerable alterations in the accommodated personnel, so that a number of Municipal Departments were pushed out, and some purely Government ones, such as Police, Education and Food Rationing brought in. With the impromptu manner in which the Japanese flitted—they appeared to have been exceedingly unstable both individually and departmentally —many records, and much furniture and equipment, formerly in the offices, had gone astray and that which replaced it, or had otherwise appeared, by September 1945, included the property of many services and individuals previously located elsewhere on the Island. Some of the Jap officials must have had ideas about their own comfort, for a number of the former austere and utilitarian offices had been converted to very comfortable compartments, which resembled boudoirs, with settees, easy chairs, mirrors, occasional tables and thick carpets. The B.M.A. accepted what the gods gave, and, with a minimum of alteration, settled down to serious work.

It is not easy to describe in a few words the extent to which a city varies from normal in a process of changing hands after the fashion of Singapore's reoccupation. The chaos which ensues is a result of the modern way of life. Centuries ago, man was much more independent, not relying to anything like the same degree on national and local government. Nowadays, most of the essentials and amenities of his existence are provided directly or indirectly by government. Imported or transported food and clothes, piped water, centrally generated light and power, roads, public transport, civic protection for himself and his possessions, and so on, are provided for by some form of government, or supplied under its auspices. The money he uses is government currency, and its value depends on government activities. When government fails, therefore, the whole state of man is thrown into confusion, and so it was with Singapore.

When we arrived, almost everything had stopped. There was no money, no public transport, no Post Office services, no newspapers, no trade, no courts of justice and to all intents and purposes no police protection. It was not just as if those things had stopped for a holiday, it was much more serious than that. The organisations, which had, at one time, existed had largely disintegrated, and there was no directing personnel to guide the operations of what was left. That was one of the larger differences between Singapore and, say, a town in Europe. The chief executives of all government and municipal departments and of most large public enterprises had been British, until the Japanese took over. When the latter surrendered, those organisations were decapitated and the B.M.A. had to supply new heads and rebuild the debile bodies.

What was, perhaps, the strangest situation of all was caused by the Currency Proclamation, issued immediately after reoccupation. That Proclamation made all Japanese currency useless and thus, at one stroke, deprived one million people in Singapore of all purchasing power. It was the only possible course, but its implications made one gasp. Strangely enough there was very little protest from the public against the decree, which must have seemed to many harsh and fantastical. For days, and in some cases weeks, there were hundreds of thousands of people without any money whatever, a strange position, in which barter and loan were largely resorted to. Those who had retained some of the former Straits Settlements currency, or had, with good business instinct, acquired some during the occupation, were well off in that period. For a short time, British money was much sought after and its purchasing value was high, but one psychological factor kept it within bounds. A man, with some trivial thing to sell, who had been accustomed to demand for it, say $100 in Japanese money, found difficulty in accepting its real value of $2, even though he got dollars with the King's head on them.

Among the first duties, undertaken by the B.M.A. on arrival, was the closing of all banks which had been operating under the Japanese. That, together with assessing their resources, must have taken some time, as the problem of locks, keys and combinations all over the town was a major one. So many keys were lost and so many combinations unknown, that finding out the contents of vaults and safes could not have been easy. It is probable that, as happened in other places, many bank

170

safes remained unopened throughout the whole occupation and possibly contained pre-war currency. Some Chinese and Indian banks re-opened on September 17th, and the British followed suit on October 1st.

Immediately after the Japanese currency had been pronounced useless, it was obviously the duty of the B.M.A. to get the new currency into circulation with all possible speed. That was done with amazing rapidity in the town, but it was a little slower in isolated rural areas. It was done by a variety of methods, which included advances to local firms, grants to charitable institutions and poor relief. In addition, all employees of the B.M.A. were given advances in pay, amounting to as much as three months, for some employees of the former Government and Municipality. So successful was the introduction of the new money, that before a month was out, one could wonder if too much had not been issued, in view of the shortage of goods on which to spend it. To add to that which was newly issued, a large amount of the pre-war currency came out of its hiding places, when it was declared legal tender. Japanese prisoners-of-war alone were relieved of some three million dollars, which they apparently had faith in.

The drastic action of fixing no exchange value for Japanese notes proved the right one, and there are now very few responsible people who question it. Incidentally, it probably saved the tax-payer in Great Britain many millions of pounds, if one can draw conclusions from what took place in Germany, where the mark with a value enriched many servicemen at the expense of the British exchequer.

The restoration of law and order was not so simple as getting people to accept money. Up to a point, it progressed satisfactorily, but it will be a long time before all the lawlessness resulting, directly or indirectly, from the occupation can be eliminated. All the conditions necessary to ensure that there would be a long battle against crime were present when we arrived. Great numbers of the people had lost law-abiding habits, indeed, to break the law under the Japanese was, in many cases, to acquire merit in the eyes of the local inhabitants. It needed bravery, and it usually inflicted a thorn in the side of the hated rulers, so that it came to be looked on very largely as a virtue. In other cases, it was a necessity, but whether virtue or necessity, it increased by leaps and bounds until the country was inundated by a wave of crime. There were individual criminals and gangs of criminals, and many were armed. Arms had been relatively easy to come by, as many Japanese, and possibly some of the two thousand Germans found in Malaya, had, after the surrender, sold arms to local gangs or bartered them for food. Armed men all over the country imposed their will on others, they stole goods, extracted money and vengeance, kidnapped and dealt in blackmail and arson. Felonous acts were not confined to the land, for gangs of pirates also flourished to despoil local shipping.

To fight the wave of crime, the B.M.A. had at first only a negligible force. The police and detectives, under the Japanese, had become almost entirely demoralised. Many of them were Japanese recruited, and had never been trained to British police methods. Those of the old force, who remained, had been forced to absorb Japanese methods. Altogether, the position was a peculiarly difficult one for all concerned, old members of the force must have sworn allegiance to the British when they originally joined, sworn allegiance to the Japanese in 1942, and again to the British in 1945. During the occupation, they had been largely employed in searching out pro-British activities, and, after our return, their attention was reverted to anti-British activities. Colonel Foulger, who was at the head of the Police Section, had not an easy task.

As a precautionary measure, a curfew was imposed during the hours of darkness immediately on our arrival, but it was removed a few days later on September 9th. The removal was probably a gesture of good-will towards the people, encouraged by the difficulty of enforcing it in a town, where it was a major problem even to inform the inhabitants of its existence.

The forms of crime, which were most noticeable to others than the police, were armed robbery and theft. Nothing was safe, if left for a moment unguarded. People were held up, houses and stores broken into, and the total volume of goods, which thus changed hands illegally in the first few months, must have been staggering. This, of course, was encouraged by vacant premises, the lack of adequate locks and the temporary dumping, in vulnerable places, of materials recently imported. The docks were particularly subject to loss and particularly tempting, as much of what arrived there had been scarce or non existent in Singapore for years, and, in consequence, was almost priceless. Cigarettes, for example, disappeared in enormous quantities, as cigarettes could buy the earth.

Vehicles and vehicle parts came in for a great deal of attention from thieves. If it had not been so disastrous, it would have been amusing. Cars, jeeps and lorries disappeared from in front of offices, from residences and from garages. Leave a vehicle and in the twinkling of an eye it was gone. Taking out the ignition key, the rotor-arm or some such part made no difference, the thieves came equipped with spares, and went off with the vehicle. The cars, which the Japs had left, were all in bad condition and broke down frequently, and so, in the early days, before an order was issued to the Services making it compulsory for at least two people always to accompany a vehicle, a man would frequently leave his broken-down car or jeep unattended, in order to obtain assistance. When he returned, as likely as not, the tyres and several of the more easily movable parts were gone. Tyres were in great demand, and sometimes, when, for one reason or another, the whole car could not be removed the four or five wheels went alone. Numbers of local drivers had to be employed by the military and cases occurred in which both vehicle and driver disappeared, the disposal of the former being good enough to set the latter up for life. As it took some time for the B.M.A. to get a record of all vehicles, it was, at first, as easy to sell a stolen car as a bunch of bananas, but even after all vehicles had been registered, the thefts continued, for the various parts could be sold for fabulous prices, when disassembled.

One side of police work was rounding up collaborators. Although a very lenient policy was adopted, there were many who were suspect, or said to be suspect, and a strong feeling was abroad among the community that collaborators should be dealt with. With British ideas of justice, this was not so easy, as it was extremely difficult to get witnesses. Those, who could testify, were afraid to do so because they had not, as yet, sufficient protection against possible retaliation. A difficult situation was thus created, the loyal people clamouring for action against the disloyal—they argued that they might just as well have enjoyed the advantages of being disloyal, if disloyalty brought no punishment and loyalty no reward—the authorities anxious to do so, but unable to comply on account of the lack of witnesses. The whole situation caused not a little discontent, and possibly encouraged some to take the law into their own hands.

That many private feuds were going on was obvious. They could be seen in mild form among the office employees, and they could be heard in more violent form at night. In the residential area where I lived, there was, for months on end, scarcely a night when shots were not exchanged somewhere in the neighbourhood. Although generally confined to a few rounds, on occasions, they appeared to be pitched battles, lasting half an hour or more. Sometimes, the shots came from sentries, sometimes, from houses, where the occupants were protecting their possessions, but most frequently, I judged, they were the results of a feud dating back to the Japanese occupation.

The police had an uphill task, but they recruited and trained, they enlisted the help of men from the 5th Paratroop Brigade for a period, they worked in with the Military Police, who were brought to Singapore in large numbers, they got radio-equipped cars going, and gradually gained strength, yet eighteen months after the reoccupation, the battle had still to be won.

Not least among the battles which the B.M.A. fought was the battle of supplies, particularly food and textile goods. Fortunately the Jap left some stocks of food behind, food which he had stored, as though expecting a siege. This helped in the initial stages, and partially filled the hiatus caused by the unexpected early surrender. Food, which had been scheduled to arrive at a time dictated by the anticipated campaign against Malaya, was now late, but of course the overriding difficulty was the world shortage. It was naturally hard to get the people to grasp the fact of a world shortage. Shut off from outside news, they had thought, during the occupation, that outside Japanese-controlled areas, food was in abundance, and they expected liberation to bring unlimited supplies. The let down was a deep disappointment. Rice was what was particularly wanted, and rice, of all commodities, was relatively the scarcest.

The B.M.A. fought hard to better the people's food and ensure an equal distribution of what was available. In the days before the new money had got into the hands of the public, free issues of rice and other food stuffs were made, and, thereafter, rice, salt and sugar were rationed. Luckily, it was possible to take over the Japanese system of rationing, and a certain amount of delay was avoided on that account. The initial rations issued were considerably higher than the nominal amounts allowed during the Japanese regime, but they were subsequently to drop, due to the universal shortage. On the whole, supplies of foodstuffs, other than rice, steadily increased, but it was a long time before the rice position showed much improvement, and, at periods, it was very bad. As rice was the basic food of 95 per cent of the people, the lack of it coloured the outlook on many subjects.

Coupled with a general shortage of supplies was an acute shortage of transport. This impeded distribution and curtailed the importation of such things as vegetables from the mainland. The battle was long and hard and the position sometimes serious, but in spite of the real hunger, which some suffered, good will towards the Administration was slow to alter.

The Administration for its part did what it could, with what it could get. Special rations were given to heavy labourers, special milk issues made to children and control imposed on basic foods, as far as available staff permitted. Inevitably, however, a colossal black market sprang up or revived and those who could afford to buy in it did not want. Price control on non-rationed foods was a failure, it could not have been otherwise with insufficient food inspectors, police and courts. This black market, which operated largely through hawkers in the streets, could provide almost anything—at a price. Hawkers multiplied much more rapidly than rabbits, and it was impossible with limited resources to block or control them. They became one of Singapore's biggest problems.

The general shortage of food would have been worse but for the numerous gardens and allotments which had been cultivated during the occupation and the livestock farms, which the Japanese had developed, to help the diet. The latter were taken over and looked after, but there was a general tendency by the people to abandon their small bits of cultivated ground, in the hope that they were no longer necessary. Very soon, the Administration had to start a "Grow more food" campaign, which was not particularly well responded to by the disappointed population.

Little can be said about textiles, except that no appreciable quantity arrived for a very long time. The price of cloth in any shape or form was fabulous, if it could be got at all. Enormous prices were asked for everything, including local produce, the cost being from ten times the 1941 prices upwards. Bananas fetched 10 cents each, eggs 45 cents, a tin of cigarettes $10, a mosquito net $160 and a small car $10,000.[10] In the course of the general fight against shortages, the B.M.A. plastered the town with posters illustrating a family. "Waiting till cheaper goods arrive." Hope deferred for many months brought a trail of difficulties, and, in the end, lowered the B.M.A.'s stock. Filling the shops could not be easily or quickly done, which was unfortunate, but more unfortunate still was the fact that, when consignments of goods did arrive, it proved almost impossible to get them to the public at the prices

---

[10] The Singapore dollar is worth 2/4.

which should have prevailed. All sorts of devices were ultimately resorted to, such as opening official canteens and eating-houses and distributing goods direct to departments and firms, which, in turn, distributed them to employees. The black market in Singapore was very stubborn.

Malaya had, like most other occupied countries, a problem of refugees and displaced persons. Singapore, as the largest town, had the biggest share of Malaya's quota, and even that was, before long, increased by happenings in the Netherlands East Indies. Although the work connected with the distressing problem did not all fall on B.M.A. shoulders, sufficient of it did to make it a major task. The number of people, who had to be moved, one way or another, was tremendous and a large proportion of that number needed feeding, care and hospitalisation for a lengthy period. The many thousands of prisoners of-war and internees were in the care of RAPWI, an ALFSEA organisation, but some of the latter naturally looked for assistance from the B.M.A. Next in numbers were the Javanese, whom the Japs had imported as labour gangs, but all countries of South East Asia and the Malay mainland had helped to swell the ranks. Of the total number, many were destitute, but perhaps the condition of the Javanese was worst of all. They were picked up from the streets in a wretched or dying condition, having been treated like slaves and abandoned like dirt.

While preparations were afoot to return the Javanese to their country, events in that country forced upon Singapore a large contingent of the white Dutch from the Indies. They were men, women and children who had been forced to flee for safety. Liberated from the yoke of Japan, they were threatened by Indonesians, who, striving for independence, wished to evict the white population.

They came in thousands to Singapore and many British felt, as I did, that, apart from any other considerations, we owed them hospitality and refuge in return for their willingness to receive many of us in 1942. Before the end of 1945, Singapore had become a huge transit camp with thousands of troops going both East and West, thousands of displaced persons seeking passages to all points of the compass and thousands of refugees seeking safety.

In such circumstances, all the services, including those operated by the B.M.A., were strained to the limit. Partly due to the early surrender of Japan, and, partly, to the general shortage of suitable men, the B.M.A. was always inadequately staffed. The strain on the available officers was terrific and did not fail to show up, here and there, in the form of sickness or partial breakdown, but, in the main, they bore their burdens gallantly, burdens made heavier by insufficient transport, poor living conditions and the lowered efficiency of the local subordinate staff. The subordinate staff was desperately tired and undernourished and should have had a period of rest and recuperation, which it was impossible to give. To most members of that staff, the greatest possible praise was due for their conduct throughout and after the Japanese occupation. The B.M.A. appreciated that loyalty, but was unable to do much to reward it, as every staff question was tied up with the position of its members as permanent employees of Civil Government and Municipality, although, for the time, they were employees of the War Office.

It was a curious position and not a very satisfactory one. As all costs during the Military Administration were chargeable to War Office funds, the subordinate staff and the operatives had to be fitted into Army classifications and designations, many of which did not correspond at all well with those of the Civil Authorities. ALFSEA had prepared a "Malaya Territorial Supplement" to its "Instructions Regarding the Employment of Civilian Labour" and had cast it in a mould more suitable to temporary employment under military units without any civil functions. When it came to be applied to the permanent employees of the Civil Government it was like a very badly-cut suit, that only fitted at the points where it happened to touch. My own opinion is, that it was prepared without sufficient advice from those, who were familiar with the conditions of employment in Malaya, and also, while it was impossible to tell beforehand what the cost of living would be, it was insufficiently flexible to remove hardships, caused by the abnormal rise in prices which occurred.

Labour suffered most, because, after purchasing its inadequate rations, there was nothing left with which to buy occasionally in the black market. It had, however, one advantage over the more highly paid clerks and technicians, in that it was not tied so closely by the promise of long term benefits, such as pensions and provident funds. Of that advantage, it made full use, and the story of Rangoon was repeated. Men left essential work and took employment privately, where double or treble the wages could be earned. They left key jobs in the public service and earned ten times as much in the black market, or, which was often the same thing, by illegal hawking. By refusing, temporarily, to direct labour, no matter what democratic principles prompted the refusal, I felt the Administration was not doing its best for the public or the future Civil Authorities. The intentions regarding labour were excellent. The minimum wage was virtually doubled, the formation of Trade Unions was encouraged, Trade Union experts were brought from England to advise, and a start was made with the machinery for regular negotiation in disputes. Nevertheless, during the unquestionable emergency, when Singapore was in a state of flux, inflation and political upheaval, when labour, largely illiterate, was subjected to all sorts of irresponsible propaganda and was unready for full scale Trade Unionism, a stabilising measure was necessary, and, if it had been imposed, I believe that the black market would have been much reduced, inflation curtailed and rehabilitation speeded. More important still, labour could have emerged from that temporary restriction with properly organised Trade Unions and Trade Union machinery, which would have obviated the chaotic conditions that Singapore later experienced, due to endless strikes, some times by unrecognised labour formations. The good citizen worker would not have suffered by such a measure, on the contrary, he would almost certainly have gained through lower prices, and his voice would have been more readily and sympathetically heard.

Troubles which the B.M.A. experienced with labour were not entirely due to the economic situation. If supplies had been plentiful and men had been paid a good living wage, it was unlikely that politics would have caused any trouble. As it was, the economic stress provided a fertile field for political agitators to work on, and strikes occurred which varied from mostly economic to wholly political. The politically unsatisfied were not at first numerous, but they made the most of their opportunities and those opportunities, in Singapore, sprang largely from economic causes. When we arrived, almost the whole of the Chinese community co-operated with the Administration enthusiastically, and, while they were eager for more political power, they trusted that it would come constitutionally. An enormous Victory Procession was held, by all sections of the Chinese, on September 15th, and, in countless ways, this community displayed its loyalty and readiness to work with the Authorities. The Indian community was, as might be expected, less united. The Indian and Malay Muslims held a Victory Procession on September 22nd, but the Hindoos were less demonstrative and, in fact, a section of them, later, made a ceremony of placing a wreath on the site of the destroyed Indian National Army Memorial. The Malays, so far as one could judge, were loyal and co-operative, but the Malay community in Singapore was small. The loyalty of the Eurasian community had always been beyond question.

To all communities, it must have been obvious that a new order had come. The newspapers of all races, and all languages, resumed publication and were not submitted to any censorship. Societies and associations of all descriptions were allowed to flourish, advice and criticism were invited and welcomed at every turn, and, as early as mid-November, an Advisory Council, representing all communities, and all legitimate interests, met at the invitation of the Chief Civil Affairs Officer.

The negative state in which the Military Administration inherited Singapore was changed at bewildering speed. The town came to life, and things were started much more quickly than anyone had a right to expect. In the vanguard of the services, which commenced to tick over again, was the Press. The *Straits Times* appeared in a one-page edition on September 7th, having changed from an afternoon to a morning paper. Soon, newspapers had resumed their ubiquitous existence, some being helped initially by the *Straits Times*. Even with the stress of events, someone was concerned about culture, for the Museum opened to the public on the 12th. Trolley-buses began to run a skeleton service on the 16th, and the

Post Office commenced some functions on the 17th. For about a month, letter post was free, as stamps were not available for sale until October 19th. The cable office, hard on the heels of the Post Office, reopened on September 18th. The local banks started business on September 12th, and the British banks on October 1st. It was by a particularly good effort that twenty-one schools recommenced on September 25th, and, four days later, the Railways ran the first trains from Singapore. Broadcasting, which had commenced on the first day, rapidly got into full stride, and, in a few weeks, gave programmes in English, Malay, Tamil, Hindustani and three Chinese dialects.

The early resumption of those services, and many others, was a tribute to the ability and enthusiasm of the B.M.A. officers and of undertakings sponsored by the Administration. It had to be paid for in sweat and toil, as it went far beyond what had been contemplated in the planning days. The task, as then seen, was to plan and organise for the maintenance of a minimum emergency standard, sufficient to prevent disease and unrest in a town that had been fought over and largely destroyed. Instead of that, the B.M.A. gradually found itself being required to carry out almost all the functions of a civil government in peace time, plus a number of others, consequent upon the abnormal circumstances. It was, in fact, a civil government in uniform, bound by the peace-time laws of the country in almost everything it did, and, at the same time, conforming with military codes. It had only a fraction of the peace-time government staff, and many of its officers were new to their duties. Much of its organisation had, necessarily, been moulded hastily to its dual functions and was greatly hindered by extreme shortages of equipment and supplies. Added to those disadvantages, was the legacy of chaos left by the occupation, which increased the task of ordinary administration by imposing one of rebuilding.

It is not easy for an Army to gain the confidence and respect of a large and mixed population of various races, colours and languages which has just emerged from its first experience of military rule as from a nightmare, yet, that confidence and respect were gained, and the leading article in the *Straits Times* of October 24th, 1945, which is quoted below, confirms it.

ARMY RULE

Perhaps the highest tribute that could be paid to the British Military Administration is the simple statement that the man in-the-street still does not realise just how military it is; he still is not yet conscious of the fact that the G.O.C., Malaya, is virtually the military governor of Malaya, with all the powers of a military governor—and that again is no small compliment to Lieut.-General Sir Miles Dempsey. So far from there having been any attempt to rule the population of Malaya in the spirit of army discipline, the man-in-the-street still does not know that the ground-plan of the present temporary government shows General Dempsey at the head, with two staffs under him: the staff of the Fourteenth Army and the British Military Administration. To bring out further the main outline of the picture, it should also be stated that this dual machine of power and organisation under the G.O.C's hand has been directed during the last six weeks to four main objectives: firstly, the disarming and concentration of the Japanese Forces; secondly, the repatriation of Allied prisoners-of-war and internees; thirdly, the relief and rehabilitation of the civil population; and, finally preparation for the restoration of civil administration at the earliest possible moment.

We have seen for ourselves the progress that has been made along those four parallel lines. Malaya will soon be cleansed of the alien taint more completely and quickly than we had believed possible, and we trust that the hundred thousand Japanese troops and civilians who are to make a temporary home of their own on an island in the Rhio Archipelago will be given the object-lesson they so badly need in civilised standards of treatment of prisoners. As to the second objective, the flow from the prison camps homewards has been proceeding from Singapore steadily at the rate of one to two thousand a day, and all who have been working with RAPWI—not forgetting the airmen, nurses and ground staff who made speedy rescue from Siam, Sumatra, Java and Borneo possible —are to be congratulated not only on the efficiency but on the spirit with which they have performed their mission of mercy. Coming now to the civil side, we see for ourselves the manifold activities of the British Military Administration in Singapore, and latterly-thanks to a series of very informative dispatches from the special correspondent of the Straits Times *who has been touring the ex-F.M.S.— we have been learning something about the admirable tone of the administration which is being set up by Military and civil affairs officers in the Malay States. Finally, there need be no doubt that the military authorities mean what they say when they promise return to civil government at the earliest possible moment: the promptness with which the change-over has been made in Burma is proof of that, if proof were wanted.*

In the meantime, we could not ask for a more genuinely sympathetic, considerate and liberal attitude towards the civil population by the military government. Five years ago we would not have believed that the establishment of a theoretically autocratic military government could have been compatible with the restoration of true freedom in Malaya. But in practice it has been so. No civil governor in Malaya has ever had so much power as General Sir Miles Dempsey, and none has ever used it less. We have all found a good deal to criticise and complain about in relation to the British Military Administration viewed as the practical day-to-day equivalent of the Straits Government and the Singapore Municipality, but we have every reason to be thankful that they came in with their cut-and-dried scheme of civil reorganisation, and, considering that half their personnel are still waiting to be transported from India, they have got the essential services going and tackled a multifarious array of social and economic problems with very considerable success in the short space of six weeks. But..., when all is said and done the war is over, the world is at peace and, irrationally or otherwise, we confess that we pine for the day when this militaristic costuming on the civic stage will disappear and the old Malayans in the B.M.A. will get into comfortable white suits again.

* * * * *

The reader will note the desire expressed in this article for a return to civil government. It was, of course, a very natural desire, if only for the sake of again having something which was familiar. I do not think that, at the time of the article, the desire was very strong, but, as time went on, it certainly grew. Later, it became fashionable to blame all the ills the town was heir to on the B.M.A. and to suggest that they would be removed when civil government returned. It was not unlikely that many of the increasing demands for the end of the B.M.A. originated with those who were impatient for political or other power, which under a military government they could not exercise. The Army was no less anxious to be rid of its commitments, but somewhere wise councils prevailed and the matter was not unduly hurried. In the first place, the civil officials, who had been interned, were all on leave, and, in the second, the town was far from ready. If rumour was true, Burma was not a very happy example, for many held that the change there had come too soon for the best interests of the country.

Irrespective of when the millennium would come, the B.M.A. (Singapore Division) under the sure guidance of Brigadier McKerron spared no effort to put the town in a position to receive it. The same could be said of the rest of the Army which, without the same incentive as the B.M.A., helped generously where it could, consistent with the requirements of the Forces.

WORKS (SINGAPORE)

SEVERED from the B.M.A. by the decision arrived at in India, the Works Division was responsible to the other side of the G.O.C.'s Command. As I was intimately connected with it and believe that it played a part in the rehabilitation of Singapore which was not unimportant, this chapter will be devoted to its activities.

The Army was faced with an enormous amount of engineering work on the Island. The work fell naturally into two categories, firstly, that which was exclusively for the Forces, such as the construction or repair of camps, depots and air fields, and, secondly, the operation and maintenance of the essential engineering formerly under the control of the Civil Authorities. The Chief Engineer's Command was split into two distinct branches for the two classes of work, and the organisation, which took charge of the utility services and other essential engineering formerly under the control of the Civil Government and Municipality, was known as Works (Singapore). It was the final development of the Malayan Planning Unit Subsection of the same name. The two engineering branches, although distinct, assisted each other where necessary, which was particularly useful during the early weeks, when neither had many officers and the pooling of resources, to tackle first jobs first, was the only way to accomplish anything.

Only a mere handful of engineers arrived on the first day. In addition to the Chief Engineer (Brigadier Pearse), Major Beattie and myself, there was Lt.-Colonel Lendrum and, possibly, one or two others. James Beattie and I were the only representatives of the Civil Affairs side, and others gathered very slowly on account of endless difficulties they found in getting from India and elsewhere to Singapore. Eventually Works (Singapore) comprised a Deputy Director Civil Affairs (Works), two Commanders Royal Engineers (C.R.E. 129 and C.R.E. 130), seven Works Sections (Works Sections 956 to 962 inclusive) and a few extra pieces. The Cs. R. E. acted as deputies to the D.D.C.A. (Works), and each Works Section took over one or more of the former civil departments. It was a case of fitting civil organisations, as far as possible, into a military form.

On the Peninsula, the moulding of Civil Affairs engineering officers into C.R.E. Units may have been quite satisfactory, as one Works Section could cover all the work in a limited locality, much as had previously been done by the District Public Works Officers. The services on the Peninsula, being generally of a less specialised nature, P.W.D. officers in any area had been expected to know enough of all branches of engineering to get along, but, in Singapore, the essential services were highly departmentalised and only experts in one particular branch of engineering had staffed each department. It was, not easy to fit that kind of organisation into the standard Army formation, but it had to be done and eventually things settled down. The subordinate staff and the general public, no doubt, found it very confusing, when, for example, instead of addressing the familiar Water Engineer, they had to refer to Garrison Engineer 961, or, if they wished to go over his head, to C.R.E. 130, D.D.C.A. (Works) or C.E. 148 instead of the Municipal Commissioners.

The Works Division suffered at the beginning, and all the time through lack of senior staff and transport. It was, of course, not unique in that, but it was among the worst sufferers, especially as it was faced frequently with matters, which had to be attended to immediately, such as a breakdown in water supplies, electricity, gas or sewerage. At the outset, the staff position looked impossible, with only two Civil Affairs Officers to take over the work done by over a hundred in peace time. I knew that about a dozen officers were on the way, but of the balance of the establishment which had been authorised, I knew nothing. Fortunately, the small contingent of five P.W.D. officers, who had come to Kurunegala the last day I was in Ceylon, arrived on September 6th, only one more arrived during the next four weeks, and, by the middle of November, there were still only twenty-seven. About ten more were subsequently added, but at no time throughout the existence of Works (Singapore) was it much above half strength. Works Section 962 (Electricity) was perhaps the worst example of under-staffing, for its strength ranged between two and five officers, during the whole of the Military Administration, against a peace-time establishment of some twenty-six.

The position in the first months was worse than it ought to have been, owing to the difficulty that officers experienced in getting transport from India to Malaya. There were a number of officers at the Pallavaram Camp near Madras kicking their heels anxious to get across, but held up by causes outside their control. Even when they did arrive in due course, the staffing problem was not nearly solved, because there was not enough of them nor, in all cases, had they the qualifications required. Efforts to obtain additional staff from other units in Malaya met with little success, though the one or two officers, who were lent, were very acceptable.

On account of the nature of the engineering services, a great deal of transport was required to ensure efficient working, or, for that matter, any working at all. In all liberated countries, transport proved a major problem, but as Singapore was liberated without the town being fought for or heavily bombed, it was reasonable to expect that the shortage would not be so great. Expectation was disappointed on account of deplorably bad Japanese maintenance, and the local efficiency in looting. In the Works' garages great dumps of vehicles were found, but almost all were non-runners and only one, here and there, could be put on the road after extensive repairs. It was exasperating to see so much useful work, which could have been done, if only the vehicles had been available, and it was excessively annoying to have officers tied to their chairs through lack of transport, when they should have been getting on with some important job miles away. On account of the supreme shortage of public transport it even became necessary to collect the clerks from their homes and bring them to the office in load-carrying vehicles. Two and a half months after the liberation, Cs.R.E. got their unit transport, which was the first break in a desperate situation, though it provided only a fraction of what was required.

At one of the conferences held before Singapore was reoccupied, the Japanese had been instructed to keep all their engineers on the essential services, until such a time as British engineers could take over. That order was, on the whole, obeyed, and on September 6th—the first day we got down to the job—Pearse and I interviewed the Japanese heads of departments. Earlier that day, one small, but very essential thing, had been done, the public clocks had been changed from Tokyo time to Malayan time. At the interviewing, we tried to get from the Japanese a picture of the condition of all the services, but the results were not very satisfactory, partly on account of the language difficulty. Some of the Japanese produced reports in English which had been carefully prepared, but it was early obvious that most of what we wanted to know, we should have to find out for ourselves. In the end, we kept those Japanese hanging round for a few days, in the hope that they might be useful, but they turned out to be figure-heads only and of little value. Others, mostly technicians, who were employed away from the office at the Power Station, Gas Works and various Pumping Stations were helpful and were retained as long as it was found desirable. Some half dozen at the Electricity Power Station were the last to go, they had proved so co-operative and helpful that, on leaving, a special recommendation was made for their early repatriation to Japan.

Japanese labour was very much sought after by all who had outside work to do, but, in spite of the large number of prisoners taken, there was never enough to supply the demand as only a fraction of the total was available. I do not know the reason for that, but I suspect it was connected with the difficulties of housing and guarding prisoners on the Island. Accommodation was extremely short and the Army found great difficulty in providing guards. Most of the P.O.W.'s were sent to an island in the archipelago to establish a colony and fend for themselves, which, I believe, they did with outstanding thoroughness.

The desire for Japanese labour was prompted by two things, first, the general shortage of labour and, second, the physical fitness and good working qualities of the prisoners. They were a very sturdy lot, and, initially, they strained every muscle in their efforts. There was, however, before long, a notable falling off in their output, for they were quick to find that the British were not a driving race and they took advantage of the forgiving hearts of the guards and employers until it was possible to discover, on many occasions, an almost undisguised go-slow policy among them. On the other hand, Singapore, during those months, would have had a bad time without them. There was so much to be done that the supply of local labour was quite inadequate, and, in addition, a large percentage of it was inefficient, due to under-nourishment and other occupation troubles. It was also suffering from political propaganda which played a big part in a number of strikes. Strikes properly carried out are legitimate, but when they are forced on men against their will and are accompanied by intimidation, they can scarcely be said to be properly conducted. When they affect essential services, like water supplies and electricity, for a million people, they become very serious, and it was in such circumstances, among others, that Singapore benefited by having a supply of prisoner-of-war labour.

The labour position in Singapore had always been complicated by the various races which inhabited it. Any labour force on the Island might be composed of either Malays, Tamils, Lascars or Chinese, but the working qualities of the four races varied very considerably, and the same rates of pay for all would have been an injustice to both employed and employer. On the other hand, racial discrimination was undesirable, so public bodies were beset by a problem, rendered still more involved by the objection some races had to time work, and others to piece-work. The hours of work, for the Japanese P.O.W.'s in Singapore, seemed to me, and possibly to them, very short. During a visit I made to some factories in Japan a number of years ago, I gathered that the Japanese worked extremely hard and very long hours in their own country, and, judging by their smiling countenances in Singapore—

although a Jap smile may mean many things—they felt quite happy to adopt British working hours, remuneration and discipline. Works (Singapore) employed many, and there was ample opportunity to watch them at work.

The excellence which the Japanese could display at hard physical work did not extend to the way in which they operated the engineering services on the Island during the occupation. They made some extensions, especially with the electricity system, but no fundamental improvement. They moved machinery and other installations at any whim, neglected maintenance almost entirely, and bequeathed a jumble such as needed to be seen to be believed. They left, in every conceivable place, great heaps of derelict plant and other scrap, stuff brought from the four corners of South East Asia for no purpose, so far as one could see, other than to clutter up the depots, machine shops, power houses and stores in Singapore. Machines, of every description, had been run to a standstill, or very nearly, and all installations were falling to pieces, through lack of attention. Great heaps of filth lay in the streets, back lanes and open spaces, and no respect at all had been shown for cleanliness or order. Only one conclusion could be drawn from the deterioration and confusion of the undertakings, it was that, for the previous six months at any rate, the job had been too big for them. They had been overwhelmed, and had, to a large extent, lost control. That any services continued to function, even partially, was due to the ability and conscientiousness of the local subordinates, each in his own sphere.

Why the Japanese had allowed this state of affairs to develop is difficult to understand. Granted they were fighting a war and could scarcely be expected to lay down new machinery or effect improvements or replacements, except where absolutely necessary, but Singapore was vital to them for many reasons. Three thousand miles from Japan, it was their base for operations over a vast area, and the biggest and best equipped workshop south of China, to which all their forces must have looked for assistance. They could not afford to let it run down, yet they did. Perhaps they felt defeat coming before it was imminent, or, perhaps, in some subtle way, the internal pressure of the inhabitants had borne upon them.

When on September 5th, I had turned taps and worked switches in the Municipal Buildings, I got a feeling of relief on discovering that water and light resulted. Often, in the days that followed, I almost wished they hadn't, for their presence in that spot did not, as I soon found out, mean that they were everywhere in abundance. On the contrary, there was a very limited supply of both, and some other amenities were even more below requirements. It might be said that it was better to have a little than none at all, and with that I quite agree, but the fact that some people were adequately supplied and comfortable made those, who were not feel ill-treated and shout all the louder. If it had been possible to say, 'no one has any water for baths, no one has this or that' and blame it on the Japs, then human nature is such that the position would have been more readily accepted. As it was, Singapore, with a bigger population than ever before made demands on certain services much beyond what, in their best condition, they would have been able to meet.

They were not in good condition, far from it. The water supply, which was of first importance, was approaching the stage where there would have been almost a complete breakdown. About four-fifths of the water supply had to be pumped, the other fifth coming to the town by gravity from Pulai Reservoir on the mainland which normally had in storage about 1,000 million gallons. The Japanese allowed the pumping machinery to get into such a bad state—a number of pumps had broken down completely—that the amount being pumped was about half of what it should have been. Instead of repairing or overhauling the pumps, they had drawn from the gravity source additional water to make up for what they could not pump. The result was that, when we arrived, the Pulai Reservoir which normally takes a year's rainfall to fill was entirely empty. The two service reservoirs in the town, on Fort Canning and Pearls Hill, were also empty, and as they maintained the pressure to buildings on high ground, buildings so situated got little water till things improved.

The filtration plants had virtually ceased to work, largely through lack of cleaning and attention; and no chemical treatment at all was being carried out. It said a lot for the original purity of the Singapore water that no epidemics of water-borne diseases had resulted. The Japanese had told the inhabitants to boil their water for cooking and drinking purposes, and, until things could be put right, it was necessary to continue that instruction, though I doubt if it was followed by more than a fraction of the population. A grave risk was run, but the town got away with it, possibly due in part to the extensive inoculation, which had been done and to an immunity built up over the previous three years of slackening standards.

While many buildings were without water, a great deal was running to waste all over the town. There were leaks every where, and, in houses which had been looted of taps, many pipe-ends were running full bore. Every water consumer in Singapore had been metered, in the same way as gas and electricity are in England, and water had been charged for by the thousand gallons used. That was, normally, a check on waste, but, by September 1945, most of Singapore's meters were unserviceable or had been tampered with, and so many people who would otherwise have turned them off, carelessly left taps running. In particular, taps were left turned on in buildings to which water only came at intervals—generally at night—by people who wished to take advantage of any such period. When the water did come on, the occupants were probably out or asleep, so that baths and basins overflowed and much was wasted. The Forces were not free from blame in the matter of wasting water, although Unit commanders did their best to help with the problem. Officers and troops, billetted in houses and barracks, where, for the first time in a long period, they had piped water, were apt to use it lavishly, and, as they did not pay for it individually, even after others were being charged, the waste was difficult to bring home.

With the increased civilian population, the influx of troops, the great volume of shipping, the reviving industry and the waste, the need for water was higher than ever before, and the system was such that rationing in any simple manner was impossible. Against all the adverse circumstances, Major A. C. Wilson, who was in command of the Water Works Section, together with his few officers, fought a gallant and unceasing battle to keep Singapore water-happy. By the time Civil Government returned, the ubiquitous filth had been cleared away, reservoirs replenished, filtration plants rectified, dosing restarted, pumps overhauled and waste largely eliminated. Thirty-one million gallons a day, or about thirty gallons for every man, woman and child, were being supplied, and every drop could be drunk safely straight from the tap.

To Major Charlie White, who was in command of the Electricity Works Section, the laurels must go for an overwhelming job well done. With only 15 per cent of the staff, which was considered necessary in peace-time, he kept Singapore supplied with light and power against great odds. His two or three officers, of course, shared in the honour, but the lion's part of the work fell on him. He was up against the problem of violently increasing demands and shortage of generating plant, such as the Central Electricity Board met later in England, but, in addition to that, he had to cope with an undertaking which had been running down for a long time, through lack of proper maintenance, and with a distribution system, which had been mauled about indiscriminately.

Pages would be needed to describe the chaotic condition of the electricity supply undertaking, and, then, much would be left unsaid. An idea can possibly be obtained from a few brief facts. The same filth and dirt over everything, the same lack of essential maintenance, turbines running on oil which had been put in before the occupation, carbon brushes which, when worn below the holders, had been backed with pieces of wood, and boilers choked and disintegrating. The distribution system had been extended far beyond the capacity of the plant, over a hundred new substations had been incorporated, and an overhead 22,000 volt supply run to the Naval Base. The hap hazard wiring, which was everywhere obvious, was enough to drive any electrical engineer crazy. Inside many houses, long lengths of flex made spiders' webs connecting every type of electrical gadgets, wires in hundreds emerged from windows and doors to hawker's stalls and outside lights of every description. Many hundreds or thousands of clever people had connected their supplies to the mains outside the meters, and, over all consumption, there was a light-hearted irresponsibility. Wires, lights and gadgets entwined buildings in the town with a gay abandon, and one judged that many a suburban house had been combed to make a down-town display.

As with other services, the demand went up and up, the black-out had gone, the people were light-hearted and wanted light, industry revived, and the Burmese-campaign veterans had itching fingers for a switch, after many weary nights with hurricane lamps. In spite of lack of staff, ever-recurring underground faults, looting of substations and a hundred and one headaches, which would have sent most men to hospital, Charlie White continued to give Singapore electricity with very few interruptions, while at the same time cleaning, bandaging and healing the wounds of the system. By the time he laid down the burden, the daily output had more than doubled.

Gas had failed in Singapore months before we arrived, and, although the installation was small, it was a big job to get it going. The same story of neglect applied to this undertaking. As gas leaks are dangerous, no little care was required in resuming distribution. Until Vin Kelly arrived on October 8th, no one, who had any knowledge of gas, was available. Vin, however, had many other duties, and, at first, he had no gas coal. Gas was important, because the street lighting was by gas and hospitals, catering establishments, and many better class buildings used it for cooking purposes. After some delay, coal was obtained from the Navy and a Gas Engineer was located in Kuala Lumpur, where there was no gas. By some paperwork, the Gas Engineer—Major P.R.J. Orchard—was transferred to Kallang Road and the lights went up in Singapore's streets at points, where the Japs had neglected to remove the posts. Orchard, eventually, got assistance in the person of an R.A.F. officer, who was also a gas engineer, and, in consequence, it was possible to extend gas supplies to many consumers. As a great favour, this man had been lent by the Air Force, which continually asked for his return, because, if my information is correct, he was required as Entertainments Officer. The Air Force could be put off for a while, but, ultimately, the officer's return was demanded and there was nothing for Orchard to do, but reduce his commitments. Instructions were issued that non-essential consumers should be cut off and gangs of men were sent out to 'de-gas' most residential premises. Entirely by accident, the first place to be so cut off was the residence of a very high ranking R.A.F. officer. The telephone lines got red hot, and in no time Orchard's assistant was back on the works.

We were fortunate with the sewerage system which was comparatively intact. Its installations and machinery had suffered less than most from bad maintenance, but still a great volume of overhauling, cleaning and rehabilitation was necessary. Major E. M. Oborne did this efficiently, without making anyone conscious of a complicated service which is usually forgotten by the public. That is great praise. Unfortunately the complementary service—town cleansing—was among those which had been most neglected, and Major J. Stables, working single-handed, had a thankless task. Under him came the organisations for rubbish collecting, street cleaning, nightsoil collection and the licensing and control of hawkers.

I have already said something about the filthy state in which the town was found, and I need not enlarge upon it. The multitudinous hawkers have also been mentioned. A limited number had always been authorised and licensed, and, at first, their increasing numbers seemed to be almost a good thing in that they brought food to the people, which, at that time, was an over-riding consideration. The trouble was they continued to multiply at an alarming rate and there were not the resources to control them. The black market encouraged them and they encouraged the black market, while at the same time increasing the labour shortage. Entirely undaunted by fines and confiscation of goods, hawkers who had been cleared from a street by the Police, again filled it fifteen minutes later. Profits were so big that periodic fines and losses made little difference.

Nightsoil collection is not a drawing-room subject, but the absence of it would have made the drawing-rooms, in a large part of Singapore, uninhabitable. Many dwellings in the town were not served by the sewers, and the dry middens were cleared by an efficient system of air-tight buckets and special wagons. The Japanese ran out of buckets and wagons, but, unconcerned about that, they cashed in on the situation by selling the right to collect to contractors. It sounds strange, until one hears how the contractors made large profits by disposing of the contents of the buckets at high prices to market gardeners and allotment holders. The commodity was used as a fertiliser, in a manner which the British Medical Association would scarcely approve.

Stables was badly handicapped by lack of transport and labour. The special wagons from India did not arrive, and wagons of any sort were lamentably scarce. Men could not be recruited, as this was at the head of the list of nasty jobs, with many pleasant ones waiting to be filled. The service suffered more than any other from the instability of labour, and yet, from a health point of view, it was vitally important. Much as one would have liked to use Japanese prisoners on nightsoil collection, it was not possible to do so to any extent, as the work involved the men wandering off alone round the backs of houses. Prisoners were used on other dirty jobs, such as clearing heaps of filth in the streets, a task which helped to demonstrate to the people over a wide area that Japan had really, at last, lost precious face. The Rochore Canal, a particularly dirty stretch of water, also received a spring cleaning from the P.O.W.s, and, during the operation, the inhabitants of the district fought good-humouredly for ring-side seats. I do not know the ethics of giving dirty jobs to prisoners, but the work had to be done and it did not seem wrong that those, who had enslaved, tortured and fouled, should be required to clean.

Irrelevant as it may be, I feel compelled to mention that Singapore, on one occasion, had its rubbish collected and its streets swept by men at the other end of the local social scale—commercial magnates, professional men and government officers. During a strike of dustmen about 1937, the white-collared, chair-borne, limousine-transported 'tuan besar' (literally, 'big masters') took off their coats and manned the municipal rubbish lorries for the benefit of humble shopkeepers in the streets broad and narrow. That took considerable enthusiasm and courage.

The roads, streets and bridges on the Island had come through the occupation in relatively good condition, but, nevertheless, they required much immediate attention to prevent them deteriorating to a point where enormous expense would be involved in putting them right. The threat of deterioration was enhanced by the great volume of very heavy military traffic, which began to invade them. This was something which had not been reckoned on when they were built, and Major Alan Inglis with his Roads Works Section had to think and act quickly, in order to preserve Singapore's excellent road surfaces from the fate of those of Rangoon. The Works Section was handicapped in all directions by the condition in which the Japanese had left the quarries, crushing plants, asphalt plants and road-making machinery. Many of the road-rollers and much miscellaneous plant had disappeared, and most of what was eventually found had to be dug out of airfields or hauled from the jungle, where it had lain in a broken-down and useless condition.

The heavy task of re-conditioning all the dilapidated machinery and transport fell on Major S. G. Duncan and his Mechanical Works Section. The reader will have gathered that his mechanical hospitals were full to overflowing, and that many a complicated surgical operation was necessary. Unfortunately the operating theatres had also been ravaged and denuded, so that many a piece of plant and many a vehicle had to be set to work again, after being patched up with—what was picturesquely described as—pieces of string and chewing gum. The mechanical mind of the Jap was in a class entirely by itself.

Major E. G. Gardner, with Singapore's looted and defaced buildings on his hands, had a colossal and widespread task. There were many hundreds of public and publicly-owned buildings to be made habitable by his Works Section, using odds and ends of materials, which had first to be found. A looted and stripped house requires a surprising number of different things before it can reasonably be called a dwelling place, and, when those things have to be searched for or bought in a blackish market, the process of conversion is apt to be long, difficult and expensive. When offices and similar buildings had been made useable, there still remained the problem of accommodation for the civilian officers, who were expected to return in hundreds with their families, when the Military Administration ended. In most cases, the best that could be done was to prepare accommodation of about the Army's standard, before the days of Lord Montgomery's humanising influence.

While Gardner was making great efforts to render existing houses habitable, Mr. W. B. Pidge, who had arrived from home for the purpose, was working on plans for the large-scale erection of prefabricated houses which were intended to relieve the deplorable shortage of accommodation for the less well-off members of the community. There was a crying need for houses, which ranked with food and clothing in the minds of many, and new houses seemed to merit a very high degree of priority. House building was, however, a matter of a long term nature and concerned the future Civil Government more than the B.M.A., but it was the endeavour of the latter to hand over Singapore, when the time came, as nearly normal as possible and in a position to go ahead with development.

It was with that object in view, that the long lists of supplies made out in London, had been ordered and, fortunately, they began arriving in January 1946. At first, there was a trickle and then a flood, which necessitated a special sub-department being set up under Mr. Wallace to deal with collection, checking, distribution and so on. The work grew to enormous proportions, as ship after ship discharged an endless variety of engineering stores and plant at the docks—as yet not completely organised, and still subject to looting. In our great need for such stores, it was very satisfactory to find that the many wearisome hours spent in London, guessing problematic requirements, were bearing excellent fruit. Without that foresight in 1944, we would indeed have been badly off in 1946.

The stores were all the more necessary, because it seemed exceedingly difficult to get anything from India, on which so much dependence had been put. It had been expected that the military organisations there would have been in a position to procure and send to Singapore many things, which were urgently needed. They complied in a few cases, but on the whole the results were disappointing. Perhaps, the things we wanted could not be obtained, but most of the engineers thought, rightly or wrongly, that when Japan collapsed, the Army in India had folded its tents and slipped away or gone to sleep beneath them. That did not lessen the debt Singapore owed to the Army in Malaya for supplying, from engineering depots on the Island, large quantities of standard stores, without which it would have been impossible to carry on during the first few months.

With the arrival of stores from Great Britain, things began to get on a proper footing. The prices of those materials were known, and that, in itself, was a great advance, for, previous to that, work had been carried out with materials, in all conditions, taken from Jap accumulated stores, on which no market value could be placed, because there was no 'white' market and no government-fixed price. For the accountancy minded, there were many such problems. Things, which were normally priced on long experience of production and supply costs, lacked that experience, so that figures had to be guessed. It was only gradually that the machinery of costing could be got going, and, in the interval, strange things happened which included free water, light and cleansing during the first month or so.

The B.M.A. was the military substitute for the Civil Government and Municipality, and, if taken out of uniform, only the close observer would have recognised the difference. A large number of its officers and almost all its subordinate staff were pre-war employees of the two bodies. The others, with few exceptions, hoped to be employed by one or other of them later. Works

(Singapore), although replacing seven Civil Government and Municipal departments, was not part of the B.M.A., yet, its officers and subordinate staff were in the same constitutional position as those of the B.M.A., and many staff matters were controlled by and dependent upon the B.M.A. It was a confusing position, in which the B.M.A. naturally found it hard to appreciate the separation, and with which Works (Singapore) found difficulty in conforming. To avoid trouble, a great deal of duplication was necessary and much referring of one side's wishes to the other. In attempting to get the best of both worlds, the organisation was perhaps typically British, and, certainly, it needed much British compromise to make it work. It was made to work, and indeed did a good job—or so is my belief.

The success which accompanied the rehabilitation and operation of the essential services in Singapore was due to the men who manned them, and to those others who helped from outside the Works organisation. First, among the latter, were Brigadier Pearse, his successor Brigadier Anderson, and their officers from the Royal Engineers and Royal Electrical and Mechanical Engineers, in the other branch of their Command. The ex-internees, who had previously operated the services, gave help which was invaluable, during the days they were awaiting passages home. With their intimate knowledge of the undertakings, they were able to start Works officers on the right lines and point out snags, in a way which saved many laborious hours for the newcomers.

With one or two exceptions, the subordinate staff had not been interned or imprisoned, but it had, as a whole, suffered severely both physically and mentally. That it carried on immediately and willingly in a convalescent condition, amid a host of difficulties and uncertainties under new masters, is something which should not be forgotten. During the first months after liberation, the commissioned officers got very few hours off duty, work started shortly after 7 a.m., and the last conferences were frequently called for 8 p.m. During Saturday afternoons and Sundays, they were also on duty, and it was not uncommon for members of the subordinate staff to be present, entirely without compulsion, and even without being asked. They came, giving up their leisure, because they felt they could be useful.

At Christmas time in Singapore, it had always been the custom to exchange greetings widely, and so, at the approach of Christmas 1945, I circulated the following message, which was perhaps, rather hastily and inadequately worded:

CHRISTMAS MESSAGE 1945

The Christmas Season is an appropriate time for me to tell all members of the Staff and Labour Forces how much I appreciate their hard work and loyalty since September 5th, 1945. In such a huge organisation as Works (Singapore), it has not been possible for me to keep in close personal touch with all my Staff, but I believe that I know enough to appreciate fully the efforts made by almost everyone.

The conditions under which we have worked have been abnormal and very exacting, and the general conditions of life after 6 years of war, including 3½ years of enemy occupation, have been far from easy. This was bound to be the case and it is my earnest hope that those who carry on in a spirit of service shall not regret their decision in the future.

No one knows better than I do that there have been many private grievances, and perhaps some cases of temporary unavoidable injustice. We are, however, still fighting a war. Not against a hostile alien army, but against the numerous internal forces which would reduce this town to disruption and chaos. In such a war, just as in battle, the job should come first. When that war is won, other matters can take their rightful place.

I thank you one and all for what you have done. I wish you a very happy Christmas, and trust that 1946 will bring back to you, in no small measure, the life you desire.

* * * * *

The replies which came back expressed, in various ways, loyalty and service. The following is typical:

"All members of the Headquarters Subordinate Staff greatly appreciate your sympathetic and encouraging remarks and have pleasure in reciprocating your best wishes for the forthcoming festive season. It is our greatest joy and will always be our endeavour to put forth our best to serve you."

However, another reply, which I got, seemed to go closer to the bone. It was:

"I, a staff of the Municipality, appreciate your sentiments contained in your Christmas Message. I realise only too well your arduous and exacting task, and Loyalty to Duty has been ingrained in me since childhood, hence I can assure you of that Loyalty always.

"A very Happy Christmas and New Year to you and those dear to you."

(Signed) "UNAVOIDABLE INJUSTICE".

While on the subject of messages, another, which came to the Senior Officers on the eve of Chinese New Year, might be quoted:

"1st Feb., 1946.

"On the eve of the first Chinese New Year of freedom and liberation from the mental tortures of the dark years, we, on behalf of the Chinese Members of your Works Sections, take this opportunity of extending our sincere thanks to you and your Works Officers for their sympathy and consideration shown to all members of the staff in the very difficult months since September 1945. As a token of respect and regard to the Senior Officers of your Works Sections, please accept this little humble reciprocation from us.

"As Civil Administration will return very soon, we wish to add the following:—

"(a) To those Officers who are remaining in service here whether it be in the Government Service or Municipal Departments we once again assure you of our utmost cooperation in the discharge of our duties.

"(b) To those Officers who are leaving these shores, we wish to extend them our best wishes in all their future undertakings."

The message was handed in at a conference of Senior Officers, and the "humble reciprocation" was a cup of tea and a biscuit each. It seems to me that, by quoting these, I can show more adequately a reflection of local feeling than I otherwise could in many words.

I fully believe that the same spirit pervaded the vast majority of the Works labour force, but for reasons, which are discussed elsewhere in this book, it was not so constantly on the job. Strikes and threats of strikes were ever present, and they threw a big additional burden on the shoulders of both senior and subordinate staff. Other heavy duties in connection with labour and with subordinate staff, which were not part of peace-time work, were imposed on the organisation by the exigencies of the times. Foremost among those were accounting and wage paying operations, which had formerly been done by Treasury officials, and the necessity for distributing food consequent upon the labourers' special rations.

The work and responsibilities of seven large peace-time departments, together with all the extra duties dictated by the times, were, in their militarised form, incorporated in two C.R.E. Units, under Lieutenant-Colonels Vincent Kelly and George Morgan, who had as A.Cs.R.E., Majors Rolf Jensen and Harold Begbie respectively. Upon those men, were concentrated tremendous tasks, in a run down and confounded metropolis. On the successful execution of the tasks, all other rehabilitation activities of the Administration and many military enterprises largely depended. None was let down.

LIBERATION'S
AFTERMATH

IN the occupied countries of Asia and Europe, the inhabitants looked forward to the day of liberation with intense longing, and, in imagination, must have pictured a wonderful life starting at the point where they left off and progressing rapidly to a more just and happier world. Each individual would have expectations unique to his or her circumstances, but two hopes, at least, would be held in common. The hope of freedom from tyrannical authority, and the hope of freedom from want. The liberation of Singapore brought the former to its people, but it did not bring the latter immediately to all, nor did it ensure anyone restarting where he had left off. Singapore was in fact a changed town and it was necessary, in many things, to go a long way back on the road of progress to find a suitable point for a fresh start.

If the people of Singapore had been asked, in the middle of 1945, to record what they expected the Island to be like when it was again free, it is probable that not one in ten thousand would have been near the mark. Cut off from the outside world, unaware of the staggering world shortages and of the condition of other occupied countries, they had little on which to base a prophecy. Even if they had known about those things, they would, presumably, have been ignorant of the plans of South East Asia Command, which played the biggest part in altering the outward face of Singapore, during the months which followed the end of the war.

The 5th Indian Division, with its attached Units, was but the small vanguard of the great forces which later came to Singapore or passed through it. What the total numbers were I cannot say, but, certainly, they amounted to hundreds of thousands, and, whether permanent, semi-permanent or transitory, they gave Singapore the appearance of being a huge service camp, which indeed it was. The state of complete militarisation was emphasised by the fact that all functions of government were carried out by men in uniform, and by the absence of the normal European civilian population. To complete the picture, every third building seemed to be in Service use, all the streets were crammed with military traffic, and military notices confronted one at every turn. For all that, the degree of militarisation which Singapore 'enjoyed' was less than it would have been if Japan had carried on the fight longer, and, certainly, it was not so exacting.

One might reasonably ask in what ways it was exacting. It did not impose on the people any rigorous discipline, nor deprive them of any food or essential commodity. Indeed, one could say that, during the Military period, very few of the local people lacked anything they would otherwise have had, and, on the credit side, they derived inestimable benefits. When the European population returned the picture was somewhat different, but that came later.

The greatest demand, of the Forces on Singapore, was for accommodation. They required houses and buildings to live in, offices to work in, places of entertainment and recreation, and great areas for vehicle parks and stores. To those things, they helped themselves generously enough, but even so, they did not have anything like the standards usually required in civil life. Had they not occupied many buildings, most of them would have lain vacant and been subject to further looting and damage, because far the greater part of what was requisitioned belonged to the absent Europeans. Very little of the accommodation, which would normally have been occupied by the local people, was appropriated, nor were the inhabitants subjected to much requisitioning of transport or goods. It was fortunate for the Services that the peculiar circumstances in Singapore left so many of the larger buildings and houses vacant, otherwise it is difficult to guess how the accommodation problem would have been met. Besides those premises, which were actually vacant, there were others, such as clubs, which for various reasons could not immediately resume former activities. They also came in handy when the population was at its highest.

Some idea of the extent to which Singapore property was occupied by the three services and their followers may be obtained by the mention of a few of the more conspicuous places used by them. The Supreme Allied Commander lived in Government House, and his S.A.C.S.E.A. staff worked in the Cathay Building. Over that building, which was the tallest and most prominent on the Island, flew the five Allied flags, with lively display, amid Singapore's upper air. Possibly, also in search of good air, the main body of A.L.F.S.E.A. went to Changi's seaside Barracks, a location which was later exchanged with A.C.S.E.A. for Tanglin Barracks, when the R.A.F. decided to retain and extend the new airfield, commenced at Changi by the Japanese with British P.O.W. labour. Many houses in the neighbourhood of both Barracks were taken over for officers, who could not be fitted into the cantonments.

I have mentioned that the B.M.A. (Singapore Division) occupied the Municipal Building, but many branches of it were to be found in other premises. Its officers at first lived in flats at the junction of Grange Road with Orchard Road, but later moved to the houses at Goodwood Hill. R.A.P.W.I. occupied the Goodwood Park Hotel close by. When the B.M.A. officers left the Grange Road flats, the staff of No. 2 Area moved in from Fullerton Building, where they had been living above their offices. The Headquarters of No. 2 Area, after a period over the Post Office, established itself at Fort Canning and became 'Singapore District', the necessity for a code name having vanished.

The Navy, for the most part, returned to the Naval Base, but it also set up a Naval Headquarters in Union Building, and took over the Adelphi Hotel for the accommodation of officers. The R.A.F., desiring a town address, put its Base Commander and his staff in Meyer Chambers.

Quickly on the heels of the combatant forces came the many components of the rear, which assisted and amused the military machine. Rejoicing under clusters of initials, they dug themselves in and proceeded to discharge their praiseworthy functions. N.A.A.F.I., the most widespread and the most jealous of its place in the sun, took over, among others, premises in Raffles Place, including those formerly occupied by Little's and Robinson's Stores. It also established canteens in many places, and catered in most of the entertainment centres for Service personnel.

The Army Y.M.C.A. made its home in the despoiled Singapore Cricket Club pavilion and looked across the disordered Padang at Toc H in the Recreation Club's building. The Y.W.C.A. established a hostel in the Rex Hotel in Bras Basah Road. E.N.S.A. Headquarters was the

Victoria Theatre, and, in addition to this theatre, the Pavilion and Alhambra Cinemas were operated under its banner. There was a special theatre in Waterloo Street for the Indian Forces, who also had their own canteen in a large residence off Orchard Road.

Service canteens and clubs sprang up everywhere. Many of the Christian churches had one or other, or a combination of both, and, sponsored by the War Office, had access to service supplies. The Shackle Club in Raffles Place, the Union Jack Club and the Sailors' Institute were among the larger places set aside for non-commissioned ranks, who, in addition, used the Phoenix Restaurant and Ballroom in the Cathay Building on several nights a week. The main club for officers was the former Tanglin Club, but there were also good Officers' Clubs at Changi and Johore Bahru. The Singapore Swimming Club's property was taken over for the use of all ranks, and opened, after extensive repairs, on Christmas Eve. It was renamed the 'Lido'.

Almost every European-owned house on the island was requisitioned for service use. Most were utilised as dwellings or messes, but quite a number functioned as offices. In the latter cases, the compounds were almost sure to be turned into depots or car parks, and many a neat garden became a dump or quagmire.

Looking at one of those, a very, senior regular army officer said to me: "It's a shame the way the Army always makes a mess." It wasn't true, however, for the army, in Singapore, cleared up a dozen messes for every one it made. The buildings, the clubs and the playing fields taken over by the army were, in most cases, handed back in a better condition than they were found.

I do not hesitate to include the Women's Services among those which assisted and amused. They all came,

Q.A.I.N.S., W.R.N.S., A.T.S., W.A.A.F.S., F.A.N.Y.S. and Welfare. They were to be found in various places, including the General Hospital which had become 47 B.G.H., a military hospital, but the biggest assemblage was at the W.R.N.S. Headquarters at Ardmore Park, where the large block of flats and all the houses around were chock-a-block with Lord Munster's brigade.

Ask any serviceman or civilian, who was in Singapore during the year after liberation, and he will unhesitatingly tell you that there was an acute shortage of transport, yet the roads and streets were jammed with vehicles, as they had never been before. This apparent contradiction was accountable for in several ways. There were, it's true, very few cars among the civilians, as their vehicles had mostly been commandeered by the Japanese and gradually destroyed or caused to disappear. The same fate befell the buses, formerly used for public transport, so that very few remained intact, and the local population found transport a serious problem. Service transport consisted of vehicles taken from the Japanese, together with those which had been brought in by the Forces. Of the former, there was not a great number which could be used, and, while a great amount of transport was brought in, it was far short of being adequate for the tremendous tasks which were in hand, or for providing personal transport for the large number of Service men and women. In the narrow streets of the town, and on the few country roads, it gave the appearance of being unlimited, but there were few men with a job on hand, who could not advantageously have used more.

The military load-carrying vehicles were not suited to Singapore, many of them being much bulkier than had previously been permitted in the streets. It can easily be imagined that little room was left, when a duck, a transporter or a 20-ton wagon invaded a street already monopolised for two-thirds of its widths by hawkers and rickshaws. On the other hand, jeeps were very suitable for navigating the congested highways, and their drivers made full use of the fact.

Driving of military vehicles was, for a long time, deplorably bad, and there were innumerable accidents. Indian drivers again seemed out of their depth and quite ignorant of traffic regulations, or of the ordinary methods of traffic control. Their apprenticeship had probably been served on the deserts of Africa or the tracks of Burma, where there were no annoying restraints, like red, amber and green lights. Indian truck drivers were not the only people at fault, and may indeed have caused less accidents than officers with jeeps and cars. Here the main fault was excessive speed combined, not infrequently, with lack of experience and dulled judgment. Men, emerging alive from a six year war, finding themselves in a pleasant place after much that was not too comfortable, and nearing demobilisation, are apt to have high spirits, which a turn of speed suits. Anyway, between one thing and another, the traffic chaos got so bad that endless regulations about the use of vehicles were issued. To drive a car or jeep an officer had to carry around a great bundle of permits and papers. Smoking, while driving, was forbidden, only one drive a week for recreational purposes was allowed, a curfew was imposed on military vehicles after 1 a.m., and no vehicle could be taken out without an attendant, or left unattended. The list of 'don'ts' and 'musts' increased week by week, until—if taken seriously—one could not go in a car without great apprehension. The traffic position was an illness, which needed drastic remedies, but, in spite of applying them, it took a long time to cure.

Road travel also had its amusing side. Japanese P.O.W.s (they afterwards became officially known as 'Japanese Surrendered Personnel') were always on the roads, being taken in lorries from one job to another. They were most punctilious about saluting, and in long streams of traffic they stood almost continuously at the salute, as one British officer after another passed in cars. Sometimes, it was fun to watch a 'brass hat' studiously trying to avoid Jap subservience, as his car endeavoured in vain, for a mile or two, to pass the Jap-carrying lorry in front, whose occupants sprang to attention and saluted every time his eyes rested upon them. One also, very selfishly, took delight in coming upon numbers of high-rankers stranded beside magnificent, but immobile cars, which had formerly been in Jap hands and were now paying the price. Dirty, scruffy little jeeps would take them in tow and the loss of dignity would be great.

Before leaving the subject of transport, it might be well to record that, in the end, the civilian population got back some of the vehicles, which the Japanese had originally acquired. Among the transport, handed by the Japanese to the British Army, was a number of cars belonging to Singapore people. They were, at first, used by various units, but, later all were transferred to the B.M.A., and, later still, handed back to the claimants, where ownership could be established. The number, which got back home by this devious method, cannot have been large, as thieves had, by that time, got most of those, which, otherwise, might eventually have been returned.

The soldier in Singapore lived on his rations and was not permitted to eat in civilian restaurants, nor to buy any food, except fruit, in the shops and markets. Rations, though adequate, were often dull, and it was pleasant to have mess meals relieved, albeit at great expense, by pineapples, bananas, chickos, mangosteens, pomelos and rambutans. The Army gave up its rice to the hard pressed inhabitants, and, in consequence, that item passed from its diet, after the first few delicious Malay curries. The purchase of drink locally was also forbidden, but the order failed to save a few from the fatal consequences of drinking locally manufactured 'hooch' containing wood alcohol. The service clubs and canteens were, however, reasonably well supplied with both food and drink, without permitting much indulgence in either.

There was little opportunity of playing games, even for those who had the leisure. Most of the tennis courts and playing fields had been dug up, or diverted to other use. The Padang furnished one football pitch and nothing else. Jalan Besar Stadium ground was playable, but Anson Road was piled high with Jap litter. All other football and cricket grounds had been rendered unserviceable by one means or another. The large area of Farrer Park was mostly in vegetable allotments. The golf courses were built on, or overgrown, and tennis courts, like those at the Ladies Lawn and Farrer Park, had ceased to exist. In spite of Singapore being an island, it was very difficult to go swimming, until the Lido opened up, and, even then, it was not easy on account of the transport shortage. Altogether, the Serviceman had to look largely to evening amusements for his entertainment, and to his own newspaper, *Seac*, for his reading. That small daily paper, in the extraordinary capable hands of Lt.-Col. Frank Owen, fulfilled a great need for non-party, non-commercialised news among the large garrison.

Malaya has never been a good country for the British soldier, as the heat and other conditions tend to breed discontent, unless many things are provided, which are usually unobtainable by non-commissioned ranks. Lots of clothes, plenty of baths, personal transport, and a fair amount of money are necessary, if a man is to keep clean, go anywhere or do anything. He finds also that it is difficult to get congenial civilian company, male or female, as most of the local people, he would care to be friends with, have much more money than he has, and enjoy all-important transport facilities largely denied to him. Added to any dissatisfaction due to peculiar local conditions, there was, in 1946, a feeling that the war was over and demobilisation imminent. Those circumstances made for unrest, and it was a great tribute to the men in S.E.A.C. that discipline of a good standard was generally maintained, even if clothes and appearance sometimes lacked smartness. Gone were the days when all ranks were permitted to rejoice in bare bodies, and many found bush-jackets irksome, in a climate more consistently sticky than Burma.

Not all had to put up with it for long. Group after group came up for demobilisation, ship after ship left, packed with men from the victorious army, going home, who carried, among their most prized possessions, a sword, which had once swung from the waist of a little yellow Nip, bent on Asiatic domination by any means, foul preferred.

Not all the Europeans in Singapore, during the Military Administration, were Servicemen. There was a small number of civilians, though, so far as the militarised appearance of the place went, they made no difference. They all came in under the aegis of the War Office, and were subject to military law. They wore uniforms without military insignia, drew army rations on repayment, and, to the local people, can have seemed little different from the soldier.

The imposition of that militarised world on a people, hitherto unfamiliar with it under the British, did not, so far as I could see, greatly perturb Ahmad the Malay, John the Chinaman or Ramasamy the Indian. In no time, they had conformed to its peculiarities, and even adopted some of its language and methods. With perfect familiarity, they would talk in initials mentioning H.Q., O.C., O.R., M.T., U.K., S.E.A.C., and all the rest, quite unconsciously, and, as likely as not, greet an officer with a salute. Army or no army, the business of living was after all the first concern, and anything, which helped to smooth that, was all in the day's work, provided it did not conflict with racial ideas or pride.

Behind the vacant appearance given by the bolted doors and shuttered windows of the first day, there must have been a large multitude of people. No census was available, but the many ways, in which population was to be roughly assessed, indicated that Singapore's had increased. On the whole, that was contrary to expectation, for evacuation and other means of reducing numbers had been tried by the Japanese. Forces working in the other direction had been greater. Men and women, from smaller towns and villages all over the country, had fled to Singapore to hide, when they had become suspect to the Jap, or incurred the wrath of the Guerillas. In that way, many of the best and worst had come to lose themselves in the crowded city. On top of that, there was the normal growth of an oriental community, which at all times is rapid, when protected by any degree of modern medical care. There was no reason to believe that enemy occupation had reduced the number of births, rather the other way. The best protection a woman had against the Jap was to be pregnant, and, where not already present, the invader showed no objection to initiating that condition himself.

The cowered multitudes, who had been through the dark days, sprang to activity very quickly, once they had taken a measure of the new Authorities. Those with law-abiding intentions worked hard in office or business, and the otherwise inclined showed an enthusiasm for breaking the law, which was, at least, remarkable. Forgetting the latter for a moment, one had a deep sense of pleasure and gratitude at the way the great majority rejoiced, got down to work, tightened their belts and carried on. Loyalty to the British Government, and to former British employers, was very touching, and the spirit of co-operation, combined with a readiness to tackle their own problems, most commendable.

The spirit of rejoicing and the new enthusiasm in the people was demonstrated in many ways, during the first weeks after reoccupation. Every community and every organised body celebrated with processions or receptions, and individuals gave their parties. The Chinese, always first in these matters, had two enormous processions, one being a Victory procession on September 15th, and the other to commemorate the occasion of the "Double-Tenth". The latter had always been held before the Japanese came, but, on October 10th, 1945, it broke all records for numbers. That same day, the Chinese Chamber of Commerce gave a large reception to celebrate the Allied Victory, and, around that time, innumerable Chinese residents gave parties to their friends. The parties were notable for the excellence of the food and drink, most of which had been bought at terrific price in the black market. Roast suckling pig was a favourite dish, and champagne and expensive whiskies were served to wash it, and many other luxuries, down.

The Muslim community, which included Malays and Mohammedan Indians, held their procession on September 22nd, and, later, the Indian community, as a whole, found an excuse for a reception in the Victoria Memorial Hall. One Indian sent a cheque for $10,000 to the Supreme Allied Commander, for whatever cause he deemed suitable, and said it was in "very sincere appreciation and thanksgiving for deliverance". The Medical Auxiliary Service paraded on September 13th, Guerillas paraded at various times, and in fact, before long, to find anyone who had not paraded would have been difficult. The fever was not confined to local people, for the Services had it also, and parades, large or small, seemed to be taking place all the time, so much so that the Municipal Building, in front of which they all passed, rang continuously with the sound of bands. It was a peculiar atmosphere of prolonged exhilaration.

Another sign of general enthusiasm was the rush to get places opened up and things started. Shops took down their shutters, and made a brave display of the few goods they had. One-man industries, especially those where scrap was the raw material, quickly commenced to resound with the noise of hammers. Hawkers flocked to the attack, and they, together with thousands of little coffee shops, many in business for the first time, prospered exceedingly, though the latter had little to sell but coffee. Places of entertainment were among the first off the mark. The Great World and the New World Entertainment Parks and the Cathay Cinema were all going by the third week in September, the New World without its Cabaret, which had been bombed out of existence in 1942, and the Cathay without its air-conditioning. The first night-club to draw the well-to-do crowds was in the building, formerly used by the Dutch Club in Cairn Hill Road, and, a little later, the Atomic Club burst into Singapore's night life with a great blaze of light. Pre-war residents saw with interest that Mr. Bailey had opened up still another Cocoanut Grove, but it was a sole effort as his partner, Cowan, had for some time been enlivening the U.S. Forces. The Capitol Theatre, which had been diverted far from its original use by the Japanese, did not again entertain until early in 1946.

Other more serious activities also got under way quickly. The Cathedral, which had never been closed, held a Thanksgiving Service on September 23rd, attended by more brass hats than that building had ever previously blessed. It must have been a unique service in that a Bishop, who had been imprisoned and tortured, preached to the heads of great forces, which had come to free him. The Presbyterian Church and the Wesley Church had been stripped and used by the Japanese as storehouses. Both started services very quickly in other places, the Presbyterians joining with the Chinese Church in Princeps Street, and the Wesleyans using their Church Hall. Due to the amazing energy of Padre Jack, the former were back in their own building by September 23rd though, for some time after that, they also had to use their Church Hall. It almost goes without saying that the Salvation Army was very quickly on the scene. The Roman Catholic Cathedral, like the Anglican Cathedral, had been permitted to carry on throughout the occupation, and liberation found it ready to resume normal activities.

One other building of a religious nature, the Y.M.C.A. in Orchard Road, had been put to a very sinister purpose by the Japanese. It was made into headquarters for the Kempei-tai, their secret or military police. Though brutality and sadism were not confined to any particular section of the Japanese, the Kempai-tai, as a body, acquired the worst record. In that building, they constructed the inhuman cells, where so many of Singapore's residents were incarcerated and treated, in most cases, with appalling cruelty, resulting in many deaths. Those cells were a gruesome sight with their walls completely covered with the marks of bugs, which the unfortunate occupants had squashed in self defence.

Raffles Hotel became a hive of activity, but in a very different way from pre-war times. Instead of being the rendezvous of a cosmopolitan and wealthy crowd with finicky tastes, it gave temporary shelter to hundreds, perhaps thousands, of ragged unwell people, rescued from internment camps in Java, Sumatra and the other islands of the Netherlands East Indies. The N.E.I. were, at that time, in turmoil, and life there for Europeans and some others was, perhaps, less safe than it had been even under the Japanese. It was many months before all prisoners-of-war, internees and threatened people in the East Indies could be got at, and the operation of extracting them under the disturbed conditions was an exceptionally delicate one. The British Army (the 5th Indian Division included) did a magnificent job in those troubled, and then lawless, islands.

I have said that the Military Government did not perturb the local people and that they quickly got down to work, and, where possible, amusement, but I do not mean they were healthy and carefree. Among the prisoners-of-war and internees, there were some Asiatics to be found, who had either been fighting with the British Forces or had been put behind wire for pro-Allied sympathies. On release, they were in no better condition than the Europeans, who had shared their captivity. Their number was not great, however, compared with the multitude of the missing. Many thousands of locally domiciled families in Singapore had lost members, who had been taken away, or forced by the Japanese to leave, and who might be dead or alive. At least one hundred thousand persons were said to be seeking relatives, and the burden of this on the minds of the people was not light. At any time, it would have been heavy to bear, but it was particularly hard coming, as it did, on top of other sufferings consequent upon the occupation. The B.M.A. tried earnestly to help and set up a Missing Persons Bureau in an effort to relieve the distress of uncertainty.

The Bishop of Singapore was one of the internees who was most brutally treated, nevertheless, at the Thanksgiving Service he said: "Those of us who were interned suffered much—very much—but perhaps some of those outside infinitely more." Astonishing words not lightly spoken, the truth of which could be gauged by any who cared to enquire. There were degrees of suffering both inside and outside the camps and the worst of one was as bad as the worst of the other, though one would expect that, on a strict average, those outside gained. Even at that, the overall effect on the local inhabitants was sufficient to darken most lives for a long time.

They did not emerge from the nightmare into a very easy life, and influences at work in various directions added difficulties, which, even in their darkest hours, were never contemplated. The first problems for most were, probably, lack of money, and the various implications of the word 'collaboration'. Enough has been said about money to indicate the shape of that problem, but collaboration was not a simple matter of having, or not having. Doubtless, a man with a clean conscience was on good ground, but how was he to know that what appeared clear to him would appear likewise to a Military Government, and if, through the whisperings of mischief makers, he became suspect, it might be uncomfortable.

His fears would be less real than imaginary, but, with the mental attitude of fear and uncertainty, built up over the previous years, they would be nonetheless disturbing, and, in addition, the private acts of vengeance going on all around might easily involve him. Taking the case of a government servant, who had worked directly under the Japanese, it is easy to imagine how he would be fearful lest that should be held against him, and, indeed, one of the first acts was to pass all such through a security screen. The Supreme Commander's policy was lenient in the extreme, but the people had no previous experience of British ideas on the subject, or knowledge of the complicated legal arguments involved and the rigid proof required. Some alleged collaborators were brought to trial, and, as a result, there were both acquittals and sentences, including sentences of death, but, on the whole, activity regarding collaboration proved to be much less than some feared and others hoped.

I wish I could record that, on the other hand, many rewards were made for bravery or devotion to duty during the enemy occupation, but, in my opinion, the few decorations granted left many a very worthy deed unrecognised. Some show was made of decorating sixteen Guerilla leaders with the 1939-45 and Burma Stars, when they paraded in front of the Municipal Building on January 6th, 1946, and saluted the Supremo with closed fist, in communist style. Three were Malays and the rest Chinese. Such few civilian awards as there were came much later, and were quite insufficient to make the people generally feel that virtue had been rewarded.

When the pressing money problem had been solved for most and the fear of retaliation, both public and private, had diminished, the people's biggest worries were food, clothes, housing and transport. All of them remained major difficulties for a long time. In the first few weeks, there was a slight drop in the prices of essential commodities, but they rose again, and the fixing of maximum prices under the Price Control Proclamation did not greatly assist the ordinary consumer, for retailers, almost universally, ignored the official rates, charging often three times as much. The Press published from time to time details of expected shipments of food, cigarettes and other goods, so that people continually expected the position to improve in the immediate future. The information about those expected shipments probably came from official sources, and were given entirely in good faith, but other factors outside the control of the Malayan Authorities must have diverted the supplies—possibly to more needy areas—for the abundance did not materialise and disappointment grew.

In a very short time after liberation, the same conditions prevailed in Singapore, as were common in many parts of the world. The average person found that his pay was unable to buy him clothes or transport, or to provide him with good housing, so he spent most of it on food, and such entertainment as he could get. Much of the food, necessary for anything beyond mere existence, had to be purchased at exorbitant prices, but even so, with no other buying, he had possibly some balance. Too much money, too few reasonably-priced goods, the now-old story. At least that was how the authorities chose to look at it, and the old remedy, a savings campaign, was started. For the lowest-paid men, there was no balance after food had been bought, there was not enough to buy food in reasonable quantity at the prices demanded. There was no remedy for it, as adequate supplies could not be obtained, though no stone was left unturned to get them. The lowly paid thought that the remedy lay for them in higher wages.

The Authorities knew that the black-marketeers increased their prices with every rise in wages, and that the legitimate cost of everything depending on labour went up as well. With the Army as the main supplier, and individual market gardeners and fishermen doing the rest, it was scarcely a question of more equal distribution of profits, and it was, certainly, in the circumstances, impossible to introduce overall rationing and control.

Hungry men, many of whom were illiterate, could not be expected to reason closely on economics, or, after so long in the dark, to be very familiar with world conditions. Perhaps they would have struck work of their own accord, perhaps not, but others, better fed and with a wider knowledge, saw to it that they did. As early as October 21st, the Docks suffered from a strike of 7,000 workers who stayed away for a mixture of economic and political reasons. That strike, like many subsequent ones in Singapore, took place before any demands had been made, though it eventually came to light that the strikers wanted more wages, objected to loading ammunition for the forces in Java, and wished to demonstrate their sympathy with the independence movements in the N.E.I. and Indo-China. A few days later, the Traction Company (the public transport company) had a strike among its employees, which all the rickshaw and tri-shaw men joined in sympathy, thus paralysing the city's transport, such as it was. The last week of October also saw strikes among workers in the utility services, and left few of the larger employers of labour unaffected. In all cases, there were instances of men being forcibly prevented from working, and indeed it was obvious, in some sections at least, that the great majority of the workers were on strike to satisfy a very few extremists.

The Administration was anxious that there should be properly registered Trade Unions and machinery for negotiation, but strikes, commencing six weeks after reoccupation, had left little time for anything to take shape. On October 25th, 20,000 labourers met in a mass meeting to form the Singapore General Labour Union, and, presumably, it was formed, but, in my experience, it was not a compact disciplined body. Every now and then, a small group would form itself into a so-called Union, and make demands, irrespective of what the General Labour Union did. It was often extremely difficult or impossible to know with whom to deal; in other words, the whole position was confused and uncertain, and agitators from inside and outside the workers' ranks made trouble where they could.

From October 1945 onward for a considerable period, Singapore was never long free from strikes. The last fortnight of December that year saw a particularly bad one, when almost all the employees on the utility services ceased work without making any formal demands. Workers at the main hospital were also out, and some 1,000 men from a big engineering firm downed tools. Although that general strike passed with the year, it was obvious that things were not happy and both sides began preparing for the next one.

About then, the B.M.A. decided to issue extra rations to heavy labour, a move which was welcome to the recipients, but not to those who were left out. The definition of heavy labour did not satisfy everyone, and caused endless internal difficulties in departments employing a mixture of so-called heavy and light labour. Nothing better could be done, as supplies were not available to allow the extra rations to all. It is questionable whether that attempt to help improved or aggravated the general labour situation. Anyway, it did not call a halt to strikes, and the end of January 1946 brought a serious situation.

The general strike, which took place on January 29th was almost certainly instigated by a relatively few political agitators. As it was apparent that great efforts had been made to ensure that it would be a test of strength, the situation was very ominous. The Army, however, was ready and in a mood not to be trifled with, so that, after two days, the strike suddenly collapsed. A few days later, the chairman of the Singapore General Labour Union was reported by the *Straits Times* to have criticised the Administration, during a Press interview, on a number of heads, most of which appeared to be political rather than Trade Union. The fusion of political and labour interests had gone a long way, or perhaps it would be more accurate to say that the pushing of political interests through labour unrest was well advanced.

In the next move, politics were undisguised. The Singapore City Committee of the Malayan Communist Party requested permission to hold a procession and a mass rally on February 15th. Requests were also made that this day should be a holiday for workers. Now February 15th, 1942, was the day Singapore surrendered to the Japanese, and, although the Communist Party's requests were couched in terms intended to convey the impression that liberation was being celebrated, it was obvious that something very different was in the minds of the promoters. Both requests were refused on the grounds that the day, which was ill-chosen, might be misconstrued, and that a further interruption in work following so quickly on Chinese New Year would be against the interests of the town.

As the day approached, there were indications that the Communist Party was not going to give in easily, and the Authorities expected that an attempt would be made to carry out the Party's programme, at least in a modified form. The Army and Police took many precautions. The headquarters of the Party and the General Labour Union were raided on the preceding day, and arrests were made. On February 15th, Army and Police patrols went out in great numbers, ready for any emergency.

The precautions were welcomed by almost all, for the atmosphere of the town had become tense. On the whole, the day passed quietly and most of the workers reported for duty, but there was one clash in the Bras Basah Road area. A procession tried to form, and when the Police interfered the demonstrators, who carried banners and sticks, attacked them. Shots were fired, killing one Chinese and wounding several. The Supreme Commander ordered an immediate enquiry, which found that the Police action was justified, nevertheless, a great song and dance was made, in some quarters, about the alleged brutality of the Administration. The majority of people thought strong action was long overdue.

The condition of the town and countryside may be judged by the fact that the Supreme Allied Commander found it necessary to issue, early in February, a Proclamation making the carrying of arms punishable by death. Armed assault and robbery had become so common that no other course was possible, if gangsters were to be prevented from holding the public at the pistol point. When the Proclamation was issued, the courts acted on it, and a number of death sentences were passed. The situation in Singapore took a turn for the better, anyhow temporarily, but crime was far from being wiped out.

The Guerilla Force, which had been receiving pay from British Army Funds, was disbanded towards the end of 1945, and early in the new year, what was probably the last official ceremony in connection with the movement, was held. The body of Colonel Lim Boh Seng was buried with honours on a hillock overlooking the McRitchie Reservoir. Colonel Lim was the most outstanding local leader of the Malayan People's Anti-Japanese Army. He escaped to India when the Japanese occupied Malaya, and subsequently re-entered the country by submarine. Within and outside Malaya he was continuously engaged in organising and assisting the guerilla activities. Eventually he was caught by the Kempei-tai in 1944 and tortured to death at Batu Gajah. By agreement with Chiang Kai-Shek's government, he was posthumously promoted to the rank of Major-General, and, undoubtedly, his name will be long honoured as an exceptional leader.

It was now the time of reckoning for the torturers of Major General Lim and many thousands of others, and the trials of Japanese war criminals, in the Supreme Court Building and elsewhere, attracted considerable attention. Foremost in interest was the trial of twenty-one members of the Singapore Kempei-tai, which commenced on March 18th and lasted for some considerable time. Two of the accused were Chinese, who had joined the Kempei-tai, which was, of course, open to traitors. The prisoners were accused of committing atrocities against Singapore civilians, including those who had been taken from the internment camp on October 10th, 1943, and of whom fifteen had died as the result of torture.

On entering the court and looking at the prisoners, one felt that a trial was scarcely necessary. Extreme brutality, utter depravity and callousness were plainly displayed on most faces, combined with that something, which made you feel that the owners were, or could be, murderers. Throughout the proceedings, the faces remained almost expressionless, except for that of Lt.-Colonel Sumida, the leader of the gang, who frequently produced a sickly, contemptuous smile. As the sentences were pronounced, there was the same lack of expression, but, here and there, one could see a man swallow heavily, in indication that he was not entirely unmoved. On the face of it, many must have thought the bunch got off lightly, with only seven sentences of death. A few were acquitted, and the rest imprisoned for various terms. When the seven men condemned to death were hanged in July, they went to their death with songs and a 'banzai' to their emperor.

There were at least two notables, who arrived in Singapore during March, Lord Killearn and Pandit Nehru. The former was sent by the Foreign Office on, as far as one could guess, a variety of missions, of which the most publicised was food. The latter came, I expect, on his own initiative, to see what was going on in another Asiatic country, which might, in the future, interest him more than it had in the past. He was assisted during his visit, in all ways, by the Administration, and entertained officially by both Indians and Chinese.

During that March, signs were abundant that the return to Civil Government was imminent. A Governor had been named for Singapore and another for the Peninsula, and it was also revealed that there would be, in addition, a Governor-General. There was an inclination both by the Administration and the public to shelve big issues, until the new regime commenced, but, nevertheless, everyone was extremely busy. The B.M.A., which had been initiated with the idea that it would function under very different conditions, had long since found itself a military organisation in little but name, and its resources had been heavily taxed in trying to deal with all the paperwork accompanying the processes of civil administration. Its officers knew that the return of civil government would not mean any break for them, because the great majority would merely take off their uniforms and carry on. It would, however, mean a gradual increase in the number of shoulders to carry the burden, as the officials, who had been interned, would be slowly filtering back from leave.

The return of the pre-war European population had already started, and almost every day more old acquaintances were treading the familiar places. To them, military government in Singapore, was out of place, and they joined the increasing number, who thought that the sooner it died, the better. Everything, they thought, would be all right once civil government was restored, It was true that the Military Government did restrict activities for some, especially those affected by the moratorium on debts and land transactions, which had been proclaimed at the outset, and those who suffered from the limitations of the courts, but, on the whole, the average person scarcely felt the difference, though, vaguely, he did not like the idea.

When the time came for the Army to hand over the functions of civil government, which it had assumed in an emergency, it could look back on a difficult task well done. The Island had been brought through a very dangerous period, to a point where normal administration could hope to operate. While there had been many ominous situations, none had been allowed to get out of control. Major attacks on law and order had been squashed, the people had been fed, at least adequately to preserve life and improve health, amenities such as water, light and power had been supplied with little restriction, and, apart from a minor outbreak of infantile paralysis, the public health had not been seriously threatened. There was, at times, a tendency to distinguish between the Army and the B.M.A., but there was no distinction. The B.M.A. was as much a part of the Army as any other unit, and it was not the only army unit which took over civil functions. Others were very much in the picture, the 'Q' organisation on supplies and transport, various regiments on police work, and the Royal Engineers on the utility services—to mention a few. The Navy worked on harbours and rivers, and the Royal Air Force transported men and materials to assist. On one occasion, the military ruling of Singapore was described by the Deputy Chief Civil Affairs Officer as a combined operation, and it was nothing short of that.

When Major-General Hone relinquished his command of the Civil Affairs Service (Malaya) on April 1st, 1946, he could justifiably consider that his Administration had tackled the immediate aftermath of liberation with no small measure of success. The journey over the hill had been accomplished and a choice of paths lay before.

CIVIL GOVERNMENT

THE territories generally known as Malaya were, prior to the Japanese occupation, governed in a complex and cumbersome manner. Three distinct kinds of administration existed within the area. Under direct British rule, the Crown Colony of the Straits Settlements consisted of the islands of Singapore and Penang close to the Malayan coast, the mainland territories of Province Wellesley and Malacca, Labuan Island off North Borneo, Christmas Island and the Cocos-Keeling Islands to the south of Sumatra. Though not strictly in Malaya, Labuan Island, Christmas Island and the Cocos-Keeling Islands formed part of the Colony, which was preponderantly Malayan. On the peninsular proper, there were four native States, which, by a degree of amalgamation, formed the Federated Malay States, and five others, the Unfederated States, which had not come into the Federation. In each State of both types, there was a Sultan, who retained sovereignty, although, by agreements with Great Britain, each was bound to accept British advice on all matters excepting those of the Mohammedan religion and Malay custom. The King had no jurisdiction in any of the Malay States.

A certain amount of co-ordination over the whole area had been achieved by making the Governor of the Straits Settlements also High Commissioner for the States, where he was represented, in each Federated State, by a British Resident, and in each Unfederated State, by an Adviser. As the Colony, the Federation and every State had a legislative body, action was necessary by eleven legislatures before uniformity could be obtained throughout the Colony and States on many matters.

A complicated system such as that had obvious disadvantages to the territory as a whole, and it was considered by the British Government that, on reoccupation, there would be a favourable opportunity of putting the administration on more practical lines. With that in view, Sir Harold MacMichael was sent to Malaya shortly after liberation to conclude new Agreements with the various Sultans. The negotiations did not appear to take long, and, well before the end of 1945, all the Sultans had signed documents giving the King full jurisdiction in the States and providing for the establishing of a Malayan Union incorporating the Federated and Unfederated States, Province Wellesley, Malacca and the Island of Penang. About the same time, Singapore, Christmas Island and the Cocos Keeling Islands were constituted as the Colony of Singapore, by Act of Parliament. The remaining part of the Straits Settlements, Labuan Island, was intended to be included in a new North Borneo Colony.

The re-arrangement called for two Governors, where there had previously been one. A Governor was named for the Malayan Union, and another for Singapore, and, further, in order to co-ordinate and direct policies in the two areas and in North Borneo, a new post of Governor-General was created. At first, it all seemed logical enough to the ordinary person, but, not long after the scheme had been promulgated at the end of January 1946, objections began to be voiced, not only by local people and interested persons in England, but also by some of the Sultans themselves, who appeared to regret their earlier compliance. The protests grew rapidly and it is quite possible that, given more time to mature, they would have prevented Civil Government returning in the form it did.

As it was, the two months between the publication of the proposals and the arrival of the Governors afforded little opportunity to modify the proposals, or even fully comprehend their implications.

The former Colonial Secretary of Hong Kong, Mr. F. C. Gimson,[11] was the Governor-Designate of the Colony of Singapore. He left England by air towards the end of March in time, as it was doubtless hoped, to be installed as Governor on the morning of April 1st. Delays to aircraft threatened his schedule, and kept the Military Administration on tenter hooks. In the end, he was two days late, but the inauguration of Civil Government was not delayed for the want of a Governor. Mr. P.A.B. McKerron, C.M.G., was sworn in as Officer Administering the Government, on Monday morning, April 1st, 1946.

Contrary to long-standing custom, the ceremony took place in the Municipal Board Room instead of the Council Chamber of the old Government Offices. The audience was different too, especially the official section of it, for there were no white colonial uniforms. Jungle-green and khaki took their place, most of the B.M.A. Officers having merely shed their military insignia. Outside the building, guns fired a salute and troops paraded but there was little excitement, as, for many, it was just one more of those shows Singapore had become so used to. All the same, Singapore was again under civil administration, and there must have been many, who braced themselves to make best use of all the possibilities that implied. The cry for postliminy died.

Two days later, at a similar ceremony, Mr. Gimson was installed as Governor and Commander-in-Chief. He had

---

[11] Now Sir Franklin Gimson.

arrived in a flying-boat the evening before, and spent the night on a cruiser in the harbour, in order to follow the tradition that a Governor of the Island always arrives from the sea.

Simultaneously with Singapore, the new Malayan Union dispensed with its Military Administration, by installing Sir Edward Gent as Governor. On May 22nd both Governors attended at the Municipal Building for the installation of the Governor-General, the Right Honourable Mr. Malcolm MacDonald, P.C. Unique in Malayan history, the occasion was graced by a Governor-General, two Governors, a Special Commissioner for South East Asia, a Supreme Allied Commander and a host of other distinguished people, and, yet, the day was scarcely a success.

Everyone agreed that, if there was to be a Governor General, Mr. MacDonald was an excellent choice, but every one did not agree that the reorganisation, which created the post, was desirable, and some decided that it was to the Governor-General their objections should be brought home. The Sultans stayed away from the ceremony, and the Municipal Commissioners, in an address of welcome, stressed that the breaking up of the Straits Settlements was a backward and undemocratic step. On the whole, it was not an auspicious beginning, although I hesitate to agree with the *News Review*, which declared that "his installation was as flat as the local beer".

When the White Paper on Malayan Union appeared, its reception by the Press was mixed. Very naturally, the Malay papers showed the most concern, because the Malays, apart from anything they might gain, appeared to lose most by the change. The paper *Utusan Melayu* suggested there was a sacrifice of Malay rights and that the Sultans had made "a descent from the throne to the pulpit", on account of their surrender of sovereignty and retention of little more than religious power. With more matured consideration, criticism of one or more features of the plan became general to all sections of the Press. It was said, among other things, that the Sultans had been forced or hurried into signing the Agreements, that the people had not been properly consulted, that Singapore could not be divorced from the rest of Malaya and that the Administration, for the whole area, would be top-heavy. It soon became apparent that the British Government would have to think again, and, indeed, it showed no hesitation in doing so, once the general feeling had been clearly demonstrated by mass protest meetings and sustained agitation. The Governor General and the Governor of the Union, assisted by some advisers, held prolonged talks at Kuala Lumpur with the Sultans and representative Malay organisations. A Parliamentary Delegation from Great Britain also had something to say, and so the Malayan Union was well and truly in the melting-pot. Out of those talks, a new plan emerged some six months later, which proposed a Federation instead of the Union. By the end of 1946, the Federation plan had received approval from the British Cabinet in principle, but opposition to it had already sprung up. The opposition included, among other things, an objection to the separation of Singapore from the rest of Malaya, a feature which the new plan shared with the old.

After the inauguration of Civil Government, the appearance of military predominance in Singapore slowly faded, and the uniformed population perceptibly dwindled. Many buildings were vacated by the Services, European civilians arrived in large numbers, and some civilian transport became noticeable in the streets, sandwiched between convoys of military trucks. The

Army's task had not been finished, but the back of it had probably been broken, when the Supremo left on May 30th. In addition to occupying and administering the country, the Services had been engaged in building up the Island into an effective base, and it was this latter work which had been largely responsible for the presence of great numbers of men and much military transport on the Island.

Before leaving S.E.A.C., the Supreme Allied Commander held another parade, and presented a Japanese gun and a Union Jack to the people of Singapore. In return for all he had done, Singapore selected Grove Road, at that time mostly occupied by the extension of Kallang Airfield, and renamed it Mountbatten Road. When the five Allied flags disappeared from the top of the Cathay Building, an epoch in Singapore's history had passed.

The last military parade I saw on the Padang was the King's Birthday Parade in June. In pre-war Singapore, it had been a great event in the annual calendar, and, doubtless, in 1946 it was a very fine parade, but somehow the atmosphere seemed to me very different to what it had been. Many times I had sweated in that annual parade to help make a Singapore holiday, and I had felt thrilled and proud to do so, as Company after Company of the local Volunteers vied with each other in smartness. This time, there were no Volunteers, and, in consequence, a lessened local interest. It emphasised the passing of the old days, when an enthusiastic handful of patriotic men had fondly believed that they were making a valuable contribution to empire security by sacrificing their leisure and it had come to—what?

What remained of those men was now back in Singapore, but Singapore was different. At his installation,

Admiral the Lord Louis Mountbatten
Decorates a Malayan Guerilla

the Governor General said: "Indeed, Malaya was most
famous round the world for that happy state of affairs
which contrasts so favourably with the situation in some

places. That spirit of friendship amongst all the people of these territories is perhaps the most precious treasure of these rich lands." That was how it had been, and, even in 1946, the friendship among various races was very marked, but differences between classes and ideologies were raising their ugly heads, and many interests started pulling against each other.

Prominent among the complaints, being aired in public, was that of the civilians (mostly returned ex-internees) against the Services. The former were bitter at so many civilian premises being requisitioned, they resented the apparent monopolisation of transport, and they blamed the loss of furniture and the increased cost of a good many things on the presence of the Forces. Having formerly been a civilian in Singapore, I heard, possibly more than most Army Officers, the forthright opinions of civilians. Frequently they said to me: "When is this b— Army getting out?" "When are we going to finish paying for the Army's occupation?" "The b— Army took my furniture," "If we could only get rid of this khaki swarm we might do something," and so on. The Forces had their own point of view. They maintained that if it hadn't been for them 'those civilian fellows' would still be sweating for the Jap. They (the Forces) didn't ask to be sent to Singapore, and didn't want to stay any longer than they could help. They didn't use any civilian vehicles, it was untrue that there had been any large scale moving of furniture, and their presence had little or nothing to do with prices, as they lived almost entirely on Army resources. They resented what they considered the inhospitality and hostility of the civilians, and thought, in view of what they had done and the way they assisted when any civilian undertaking was in difficulty, that the buildings and amenities, which they used, should not have been grudged. The truth was that the position was inevitable, and the men at the top of affairs on both sides were trying their utmost to make its consequences as little unpleasant as possible. Nevertheless, the controversy raged for a long time and bitterly, as the main bone of contention, accommodation, could not be quickly dissolved. Nevertheless, great efforts were being made to relieve the situation. The Army built temporary accommodation for some units at lightning speed, and transferred others to tented camps. That was an earnest show of its desire to help, for only in extreme circumstances were troops required to live under canvas, in the unsuitable Malayan climate. Progress on those lines allowed a fair number of premises to be de-requisitioned each month, but the problem was so large that time was needed. There were also difficulties of materials and costs, and, in connection with the latter, it was later reported that the Army's Chief Engineer had threatened to cease building, because local contractors were asking up to five times too much.

Clubs, which played a big part in the pre-war life of the European community, were the subject of early agitations. Although the Servicemen desperately needed the recreational facilities they afforded, the G.O.C., Major-General Cox, most helpfully arranged to hand them back, so that the Cricket Club and the Swimming Club reverted to civil control on July 1st, and the Tanglin Club followed not long after. The clubs had benefited with furniture and fittings during the period under requisition, and it is good to relate that the new civilian committees, on re-opening, extended certain facilities to service men. Once more, as in pre-war times, the best relations were to be found on the sports grounds.

The anti-military feeling extended backwards to the defunct B.M.A. There seemed to be a conspiracy among returned civilian officials to forget that such a body had ever existed, or, if forced to remember, to heap scorn upon it. Some of the ex-internees were inclined to blame the B.M.A. for the fact that Singapore was not up to pre-war standard. Naturally, perhaps, they found it difficult to appreciate the dreadful condition in which the town had been discovered after the collapse of Japan, and they did not fully understand the immense world shortages, which prevented them having everything to hand. As a simple example, it shocked some to find the bill-boards plastered with notices urging people to save electricity, gas and water and to defer buying, where previously the same boards had advocated using electricity or buying endless goods. At best, there had been, on release from internment, a big gap in world knowledge in the mind of the internee and a period of leave had not in all cases, filled that up. That often made it difficult for an ex-internee and another to talk the same language. I knew some men whom I considered the experience had deepened and broadened, but on others, who appeared to think of it as a capital asset, the results were not always so good. Those who accepted internment, believing it to be for the good of Malaya, deserved well of the country, but somehow one did not expect them to make it a platform. In the first flush of their return, something rather like that happened. An Ex-Prisoner-of-War and Internees Association was formed, which, I believe, had the object of promoting their interests, though it was difficult to see what common interests could be promoted without laying claim to benefits based on their incarceration.

As an unfortunate result, the civil community, at first, tended to be separated into two camps, one consisting of the ex-P.O.W.s and Internees, and the other of those who were not so distinguished. I was present at a meeting where a name was proposed for office, and immediately it was asked: "Is he an ex-internee?" the inference being that, if so, he was all right. Comradeship springing from adversity is one thing, sectarian bias another. In fairness, I must add that quite a few, who had suffered behind wire, wished only to forget it.

Within the ranks of the ex-internees all was not happy either. That was not the fault of those who had been interned, but came about through a generous gesture by the Colonial Office. The Colonial Office decided that all Government and Municipal employees, who had been prisoners-of-war or internees, should receive not only a period of full pay leave, but also their accrued salaries for the period of their internment (less anything they or their dependants might, meantime, have received). The repercussions of that were many. Firstly, it separated the Government and Municipal servants from commercial and other non-Government employees, as the latter received, or did not receive, recognition in accordance with the ideas of their employers. In many cases, very little, if anything, can have been given, because in some quarters financial recognition was not considered necessary or desirable, and, in others, funds would not permit. Secondly, as most of the internees were Europeans, it laid the way open for the accusation that Europeans were being treated preferentially in Government service. The *Straits Times* in a leader on June 11th, which was headed "The Internment Bounty", said: "The Tragedy of it is that this most excessive discrimination between the Government servant inside and outside the internment camp has wiped out the goodwill that had been engendered in the people of Malaya by the knowledge that by far the greater part of the European official personnel of the country went through the Japanese occupation with them as internees or prisoners-of-war." Thirdly, the Colonial Office had acted in the matter on behalf of the Municipality, before the latter was reconstituted under Civil Government. Municipal Officers, when informed of the decision, were allowed to draw the accrued pay immediately, or leave such portion of it as they wished to be drawn later. Some took it all, some took part, and some took none at the time. When the Municipality again came into being, it was at first disinclined to take any responsibility for the decision and some officers began to fear that they had indeed been foolish. It was a fantastic situation, which was only corrected for the ex-internees some seven months later, when Mr. Rayman returned to the Presidency.

In the article from the *Straits Times* quoted above, the following sentence also appeared. "Whatever the difference between life inside and outside the barbed wire, it certainly was not as great as the difference between three and a half years full salary and three months rehabilitation pay." That is also what the local subordinate staffs thought, for they organised and agitated for similar payments. The agitation went on for a long time but had little success and the alleged discriminate treatment still rankles.

Whatever the rights and wrongs of the matter, the controversy did not add to the general harmony, which was threatened and broken in a number of other ways. Crime continued rampant, indeed it seemed to grow in volume. It took every form that the ingenuity of many races could devise, and frequently the culprits were armed. The situation was so bad that, one day in July, the *Singapore Free Press* appeared with this; "GUNLESS DAY IN SINGAPORE-only one simple robbery was committed in Singapore throughout the whole of yesterday." The most frequent crime was theft, in one form or another.

Organised gangs pickpocketed in buses, cars and lorries were held up and robbed, blackmail and extortion were common, and all kinds of premises, banks, churches, warehouses, depots and residences, were burgled. One house was reported to have been broken into thirteen times. The warehouses or godowns at the docks were particularly attractive, and, when entry to the area was made more difficult from the land, the thieves, undaunted, used sampans to approach from the sea. Thefts of cars and lorries did not abate, in spite of numerous precautions, and many a vehicle, which had been difficult to obtain, disappeared with surprising ease. Gun-running and, particularly on the mainland, smuggling became favourite sports. Guns were obtainable in Sumatra for very little, as the Japs had dispersed them widely, and, no doubt, they fetched a splendid price in Singapore. On the other hand, smuggling ordinary goods to Singapore was not very profitable, unless they were scarce, for on account of the free port status of the town, only a few things like spirits and tobacco were subject to customs duty. On the Peninsula, the position was different, and evading the customs was worthwhile. The very horrible forms of crime, which sprang from revenge and private feud may have lessened somewhat, but did not, by any means, disappear, for, with arms available and police inadequate, the paying off of an old debt was relatively simple. The whole position was made much more difficult for the Authorities by the widespread intimidation of potential witnesses, who, fearing their own safety, could not be persuaded to put their knowledge at police disposal. The Police and certain sections of the Army worked hard against lawlessness, but, without normal assistance from the public, it was an uphill task. Arrests were made, arms dumps found, and little wars fought, but crime, on a big scale, continued.

To strengthen the arm of the law, additional legislation was passed from time to time. Power to inflict the death sentence for carrying arms has already been mentioned, as a measure introduced by Proclamation during the Military Administration. Proclamations issued during that period remained law after the return of Civil Government, until repealed, and this particular Proclamation was, and continued to be, needed as much as ever. In addition, during the summer of 1946, power was obtained to declare certain areas as "Protected Places", in which sentries could shoot any unauthorised persons after dark, who did not respond to a challenge. That power was later extended to cover certain sea areas near the docks. In the autumn of 1946, a curfew was placed on lorries during night hours, because thieves used those vehicles extensively to carry away looted goods, and, further, to impede car thefts, powers were sought to control or examine any businesses, which dealt in second-hand vehicle parts. Although it scarcely affected Singapore, it will help to complete the picture to mention that, in the spring of 1947, it was made illegal to wear unauthorised uniforms. The ban became necessary, on account of large scale gangster activities by uniformed bands in the Malay States, which indicated that the subversive elements had organised more intensively and became bolder.

In Singapore, modern police methods, hitherto unnecessary there, were invoked, and, although they had successes, the struggle went on. By February 1947, the fight was so far from won that the influential Singapore Association advocated the strengthening of the Police by a new European force of 'G' men on lines similar to the Federal Bureau in Washington, U.S.A. The significance of

252

the suggestion can only be assessed, when it is realised that action on those lines would be directly contrary to the trend of affairs in recent decades, which, in deference to popular opinion and in accordance with Government policy, had been to replace gradually the European personnel in the public services by local recruits. Only under great provocation would any responsible Malayan body publicly advise even a temporary reversal of that policy.

In the last few paragraphs, it has been my intention to show briefly some of the difficulties which Singapore had to face, and which were a part of the legacy left by the Japanese. They also form a part of the background against which the future of the Colony must be viewed. I have probably understated the situation, and a better idea of it can be obtained from the following extract from the leader in the *Singapore Sunday Times* of February 9th, 1947:

> "*Singapore and the Malayan Union are tired of lawlessness, tired of strikes, tired of the black-market and the black marketeers, tired of the rackets and racketeers, tired of anything and everything that to-day is hindering its progress toward sane and peaceful living.*

> "*The limit has been reached of public tolerance of the bandits and murder gangs, the ineffectualness of authority, and strike after strike in which illegal union after illegal union has thrown common sense and sweet reasonableness to the winds. It has more than had its fill of intimidation and corruption, especially of the kind practised by Singapore's transport workers and a system which allows our Jap prisoners to demand openly cigarettes and money for the performance of simple public services...*"

The above quotation indicates that strikes played a big part in the Singapore scene. That was only too true, and the old resident must have sighed for the days before the war, when strikes were almost unknown. I think I am correct in saying that, during my sixteen years experience of Singapore prior to 1942, there was only one strike among the Municipality's 8,000, or so, employees and very few in other public services. There was a great difference after the liberation, large strikes were the rule rather than the exception, and, with every allowance made for just claims and a changing world, they were mostly inexplicable, and, in the form they took, unjustified. A strike in Singapore was, by home standards, a curious thing, in which one always suspected intimidation. The men stopped work, but in little else did they seem to act in unison. An employer got demands from various sources, from individuals and from bodies, calling themselves unions, of which he has never heard. It was often exceedingly difficult to know with whom to deal, or who really represented the men, and, as likely as not, every deputation purporting to speak for the employees was different.

Trade Unionism in Singapore had not crystallised into a workable form, and, I believe, it is yet uncertain whether this western growth can successfully be grafted on to an oriental people. In Singapore, it was undoubtedly heavily weighted with political aims, and it showed no great desire to learn from the advisers, whom Government had so painstakingly provided. During 1946 and 1947, continual strikes crippled the essential services, the docks, the public transport, and almost everything else that the people relied on for the necessities of life.

The waves of crime and labour unrest may have passed over the heads of a few people, but there was no one on the island, who was unaffected by the shortage of food stuffs and textiles. Since the liberation the ration of rice, which is the basic food, had always been small, but, on May 20th, 1946, it was reduced from three katties[12] a week to two and a quarter for men, and for women from two and a half to one and a half. In August of the same year, it was reduced again to one and a quarter and three-quarters respectively. When it is realised that an overwhelming majority of the population normally ate little else, and that ten katties a head, a week, was a reasonable pre-war consumption, the hardship involved may be gauged. In December, the ration was raised slightly to an average of one and a half katties and again in February 1947 to two and three quarters for men and two for women. Even that small improvement was not maintained throughout the year. Food shortages, in much of the world, had become common enough in 1947 to arouse little surprise, but one or two factors made the Malayan shortage different from the European one. In oriental countries, rice forms a much larger part of the diet than any single food in the West, and, consequently, when it was reduced to a very meagre quantity, the resulting hunger was correspondingly great. The effect on the rice-eating peoples was, perhaps, aggravated by the knowledge that those, who lived on a western diet in their midst, were amply fed. Being near to Australia, New Zealand and other sources of western food, Singapore was relatively well supplied with meat, butter, cheese and other European eatables. A third point is that Malaya was capable of growing much more padi than it did, but had always preferred to use its energies on the more profitable rubber crop, and could not change over quickly. Where increased production was possible by small

---

[12] 1 Kati=1.5 lbs.

farmers, the Government endeavoured to stimulate it with an offer of cloth—itself in very short supply—in return for padi, cloth being much more sought after than money. Large scale production requires lengthy preparation, but, as a result of post-war experience, Malaya is likely to pay greater attention to the little grain in future.

The other great shortage was ordinary living accommodation. In my experience, Singapore had always been short of houses except, perhaps, during the artificial contraction, caused by the slump in the early 1930s. At that time, economic stringency had forced two families to live where one had lived before. In Singapore, that might mean that two families occupied a single room, or that ten families occupied a house previously occupied by five. In better times, one family to a room, or five to a house, was still not good. The Municipal Health Officer's report for the year 1939 contained the following:

"Of the 17,966 mothers visited by our Staff Nurses, 14,700 were living in cubicles or single rooms, i.e. 81.9 per cent as against 80.55 per cent last year."

It will be noticed that, before the war, the bad position was deteriorating.

A snap census taken in 1939, revealed the population density, in one block of buildings, to be 1,335 persons to the acre. Other blocks gave figures ranging from 500 to 900 persons to the acre, figures, which can be understood better, when it is remembered that the 'Housing Manual', issued by the Ministry of Health in England in 1944, suggested 120 persons an acre for central areas of large towns. That is not all the story, for Singapore's houses are mostly two or three story buildings, which, of course, means less house space for each person-assuming the same number to the acre—than would be the case with higher buildings.

Those were the conditions in 1939, but in 1946, they were much worse. Many houses, by then, had become uninhabitable, and few, if any, new ones had been built. In addition, the local population had increased, and a number of residences had been requisitioned for military purposes. The position was atrociously bad, and the problem acute.

After studying the question, during 1944 in London, I had, with a view to speed, recommended the erection of prefabricated houses in large numbers immediately after reoccupation, and the partial dispersal of the surplus population in satellite communities over the Island. The reader will remember that an officer was appointed to the Malayan Planning Unit to implement those proposals, and that he arrived in Singapore towards the end of 1945. On December 13th of that year, the B.M.A. disclosed the scheme to the public through the *Straits Times*, but in spite of the outcry for houses, the Civil Government appeared to abandon the proposals in the summer of 1946, and the officer concerned was sent back to England, no houses having been erected:

For the first year after the Civil Authorities had returned, that is up to April 1st, 1947, it is doubtful if any houses had been erected by public or private enterprise, although at least one cinema had been built, and there were plans for the early construction of others and of great skyscraping commercial buildings. In those circumstances, it is not surprising that people built their own illegal shanties in all sorts of places. Squatters multiplied and defied the authorities by putting up unauthorised buildings, more quickly than officials could have them pulled down. The buildings were constructed with bits of wood, sheet metal, attap, or any other cheap or scrap material obtainable. In the tropics, such buildings suffice after a fashion, affording a roof and a place to put belongings, but the great danger, in the longer view, is to health, for they readily become sources of disease and infection. Again as with food, housing was not a want unique to Singapore, but the lack of accommodation added considerably to the worries of the liberated people, and must take a prominent position in any picture of the disillusionment.

Much crime and many strikes, combined with food, clothing and housing shortages, would seem adequate to scatter peace and happiness, but there was at least one other matter which caused widespread discontent. It was the question of back pay, which has already been referred to. "Back pay" meant pay for the three and a half years of the Japanese occupation. The seed for this agitation was sown when the Government and Municipal servants, who had been interned, received after their liberation, salaries for the period of their internment. Those payments may have been made because there was a legal obligation to do so, or again, they may have been a gesture of sympathy and consideration for people, who had suffered much. They can scarcely have been in the nature of a reward, because they were made to interned Asiatics, who cannot have merited more than many of their fellow countrymen, who, by chance, escaped internment, though doing the same job with the same faithfulness.

Apart from natural sympathy, there would appear, on the face of it, to have been a legal obligation, as the public servants had not had their service terminated by any notice, although, in the case of the Municipality, a ruling was obtained that that body had ceased to exist at the fall of Singapore. The ruling was, at first, acted upon, and, for some purposes, the period of the occupation was declared as not counting in any way. That seemingly harsh ruling was reversed later, with what effect I do not know, but I imagine that, in the meantime, it had done harm and caused hardship.

I do not think that the various claimants, who agitated and appealed for back pay, thought much about the legal side of it. They argued simply that the Europeans had had it, and they should have it too. Apart from internment, there was another difference, if not a great one. Those at liberty had received Japanese pay in most cases, which had, let us say, provided current living expenses, but, if there had been any savings, these were rendered valueless in common with all Jap currency. Equally, I suppose, it could be argued that the internees had their living found, and at the end of the period both were in the same boat. Six months later, the position was very different, the internees had had four years real pay (six months leave-pay included), and the others had had six months salary, for six months' hard work.

Whether or not their claims were justified, the Government and Municipal subordinate staffs asked for back pay. Many others joined in the request, including the Volunteers, the Civil Defence, the Dalforce (a military force organised by Colonel J. Dalley during the Malayan battles), the doctors and dentists in the public service, the Perak Hydro-Electric employees and the employees of the Batu Arang Colliery. The last two were not Government employees, and their demand indicated a spreading of the claim to non-Government bodies. The spring of 1947 saw tentative, and then so-called final, offers by the Government. The claimants were far from satisfied.

It appeared that if the full demands were not met, there would be a deep-seated grievance for a long time, but if, on the other hand, they were met, the costs to the Government of Singapore and the Malayan Union or Federation would be colossal. The bill for back pay to internees cannot have been small, and, on top of that, the two Governments shared—the rightness of which will scarcely be questioned by anyone—a payment of $750,000 to cover debts incurred in the internment camps for extra food and medicines. Much money will be needed over many years for the work of rehabilitation, and a share of war damage claims may add to the burden.[13] The task of balancing post-war budgets is increased by the loss of the opium revenue. Opium brought much revenue before the war, but its sale has been prohibited since the liberation, in accordance with a policy dating back to the time of the League of Nations. The Budget proposals for 1947, as presented by the Financial Secretary, Singapore, on December 5th, 1946, included a sum of $15 millions, which it was estimated would be received from income tax. Since about 1920, Singapore had had no income tax, although a temporary war tax, on the same lines, had been in force just prior to the Japanese war. The proposal to introduce income tax in 1947 amounted to bringing in a new and permanent form of taxation, to set off against increased expenditure and the loss of opium revenue. The estimated return from it amounted to one quarter of the total revenue of the Colony, yet opposition to it, from the unofficial members of the Advisory Council and from numerous organisations on the Island, was so strong that the proposal was dropped, and the Budget revised in a stop-gap way. During 1947, Singapore was still without income tax, but the threat of its introduction in the future

---

[13] By the end of 1949, few people had received anything for all their possessions lost in 1942.

remained.[14] Part of the argument against income tax was the difficulty of collecting it fairly from a polyglot community, which keeps its books after many fashions, when it bothers to keep books at all.

Singapore was not heavily taxed, by United Kingdom standards. There were taxes on liquor, tobacco, petroleum and entertainment, but, in 1947, it was still possible to buy cigarettes at about two-fifths the price prevailing in Britain. By the same standards, a number of other things were cheap, but not the cost of living as a whole. That was very high, for both the European and the Asiatic, though by comparison with 1941, it had probably increased more for the latter than for the former. Government and Municipality started off by paying the same salaries as in 1941, and it was some time before an insistent clamour, from both senior and subordinate staffs, achieved the grant of a cost-of-living allowance, at first of a trifling sum, but later increased. Still, conditions in the public service did not appear to be attractive, and there were a number of resignations. A Member of Parliament was reported, towards the end of 1946, as having addressed the Colonial Secretary on the subject, saying that the pay and other conditions of the Civil Service had led to a spirit of extreme discontent, and he had been told by correspondents, that only pension rights had kept them from resigning.

On the first anniversary of the Surrender Ceremony in Singapore, the *Straits Times* leading article was headed: "Rejoice we cannot" and the following sentence appeared below: "To-day after twelve months that have brought little

---

[14] Income tax was subsequently introduced on a small scale in comparison with United Kingdom standards.

relief or happiness to anyone who has to support a family in this city we reach the anniversary of that day."

The *Singapore Free Press*, in summing up the year after liberation, said among other things:

"The British Military Administration was handicapped by shortages both of material and staff, but they rarely lacked initiative in taking decisions, even wrong decisions, and when the local people of Singapore saw that the return of the British did not mean an automatic return to times of unlimited plenty they quickly began to help themselves… Then came the return of Civil Government. As in the case of Burma, the handover to civil government came too soon to Singapore. However energetic and well-intentioned a Government might be, it is impossible to govern without staff and most of the staff were on recuperation leave in U.K. The immediate result was a slowing down in the administration. Officers still in uniform from B.M.A. days waiting either for reliefs or Colonial Office contracts found they could no longer take action as necessity arose. Instead they wrote long minutes and passed-them-on-to-you-please and waited for the answer over cups of coffee in the G.H. Cafe.

"Gradually as more and more trained staff returned there has been a slight speed up in the administration…"

Earlier in this book, I gave it as my opinion that the ex-internees imagined themselves to be more fit than they were. Subsequent records confirmed that, for there was much recurrence of illnesses contracted in captivity, and outbreaks of others that sprang from it. Men returned to conditions of very hard work, great strain and relative discomfort, and not all could stand up to it. The Government appreciated the necessity for ample recuperation leave and did the best it could, but the need of an extended holiday was not confined to European ex-internees, and the problem of giving the subordinate staffs a chance to recuperate must have caused much head-scratching, without producing a scheme, which was entirely satisfactory to all concerned. The loyal, hard-working locally-engaged employees considered, not without cause, that they got the rough end of the stick most ways, but the situation was extremely difficult and goodwill alone could not solve it.

The difficulties and discontents, which Singapore and its Government were heirs to, have been set down in the preceding paragraphs with a view to contrasting the post-war conditions with the harmony, which had prevailed before the Jap disturbed it. They may easily colour the canvas for a long time to come. The aftermath of war is seldom pretty to an observer, but for those, who know and love a country like Malaya, it is particularly sad to see a falling from standards, however archaic some of those standards may have been. I am not one of those who believe it is possible, or even desirable, to go back to what now seems the pre-war heaven, and, indeed, I was annoyed in Singapore at the frequency of the expressed wish "Let's get back to where we were". However, in common with most people, I like any change to be for the better, and I find it hard to think of the change which has come to Singapore as an improvement. The *Straits Times* of March 12th, 1947, seems to be convinced that it is not. These words are taken from its leader:

"...and post-war Singapore is such a horrible place, to live in anyway, that one factory more or less won't make any difference..."

Giving the context would not alter the implications of that quotation.

In spite of many dark spots, the picture and the prospects are not all black. There is still a surprising amount of racial harmony, there are still regard and deep affection between many individual employers and employees, there are legitimate aspirations legitimately pursued, there is wealth and there is sunshine. Rubber, the greatest source of wealth, is there in abundance, for the estates suffered relatively little under the occupation. Tin is there also, though, for a while, the lack of dredgers and other machinery held up production. Industrial companies are mostly doing exceedingly well, and the country (considering Malaya as one country which must be done for many purposes) does not lack other potential sources of wealth such as pineapple and padi cultivation and timber. I have no doubt that private grievances, petty jealousies and individual feuds will die out, and I am sure that, given stability, hardship and want will be reduced almost to the negligible proportions of the "good old days". Only two things seem to me to be in doubt, the political stability and the happiness of the people. The political future is complicated by many factors, and happiness, among the people, will not necessarily depend on prosperity alone.

The modern town of Singapore was founded by Sir Stamford Raffles in 1819, who purchased the island from the then Sultan of Johore. In 1887, a statue of the founder was erected on the Singapore Esplanade. The statue was moved, in 1919, to a position in Empress Place, in front of the Victoria Memorial Hall and Theatre, near to the spot, where it is considered that Raffles first landed. To mark the occasion of this removal a bronze tablet was placed on the statue with the following inscription:

1819-1919

This Tablet to the memory of Sir Stamford Raffles to whose foresight and genius Singapore owes its existence and prosperity was unveiled on February 6th, 1919, the 100th anniversary of the foundation of the Settlement.

Shortly after capturing Singapore, the Japanese had the statue removed to the Museum, and there it remained unharmed during the enemy occupation. It was considered that replacing the statue was a necessary adjunct to the re-establishment of Civil Government, and that a significant ceremony should accompany the re-erection. Raffles was an officer of the East India Company, and the commercial community, always jealous of its status, felt that Raffles belonged to them, and that his presence on the familiar pedestal would demonstrate the predominant commercial interests of the port.

In the summer of 1946, on the anniversary of Raffles' birthday, July 6th, the statue was replaced, with due ceremony and speech-making. The Governor did the unveiling, and all communities and interests were represented. Under the shadow of its founder, Singapore felt its importance, as a great commercial metropolis and shipping centre, was no longer eclipsed.

The tumult and shouting of a kind died, and it was time for certain Captains and other temporary officers to depart. In mid-August two sweating, grinning and skin-deep pleasant Nips carried my air-bag, haversack and suit-case on to a troop ship bound for home. The blistering sun poured down upon "a land which seemed always afternoon", but wasn't, and, as the great ship pulled away from the dockside, I covered my ears to shut out the canned music, so that my last view of Malaya's green islands and opal sea should saturate my senses and remain forever.

SPECULATION

I BELIEVE that the difficulties and troubles which a country undergoes frequently appear to an observer at a distance to be greater than the man on the spot considers them. That is because the man at a distance gets much of his information from newspapers and from people, who, although they know both the pleasant and the unpleasant, tend to stress the latter on account of its sensational value. Happiness and contentment are not news in the popular sense, even in a world where they are rare. Certainly for a long period after the return of Civil Government, newspapers from Malaya, and many people who had recently been there, drew a gloomy picture of the country. The picture has not improved with time.

The Malayan Union was the outcome of Agreements with the Sultans, which were negotiated by Sir Harold MacMichael immediately after the liberation of the country. Subsequent events showed clearly that those Agreements were made too hurriedly and without a sufficient number of people being consulted. The Malayan Union still existed in 1947, but, since the spring of 1946, it had been recognised that some modifications would be necessary, and deliberations towards that end went on during the following year. That year, it almost looked as if —assuming such a thing was possible—too many people were being consulted and too much time being taken in introducing an alternative to the detested Malayan Union.

As a first step towards an acceptable arrangement, the Governor-General, the Governor of the Malayan Union, the Sultans and some Malay representatives got round a table to thrash the matter out. By November 1946, a new plan had been prepared, which had the approval of the nine Sultans and an influential and representative body known as the United Malays National Organisation. This plan proposed a Malayan Federation to replace the Union and differed from the Union scheme in some important points and in some details. Particularly, it restored to the Sultans sovereignty in the internal affairs of the Malay States. It retained the idea of a strong central government, and, in common with the first plan, made provision for inhabitants with certain qualifications to obtain Malayan citizenship. The citizenship idea was new to Malaya and possibly unique in the world. It was devised to meet the peculiar circumstances of a country, in which the majority of the population consisted of alien races. It was not intended to supersede, nor to be a substitute for, nationality. As proposed it was additional to nationality, and might be acquired by peoples of other nationalities provided they had certain language and residence qualifications, and were prepared to make a declaration of permanent settlement in the country and take a citizenship oath.

The Malayan Federation proposals were, at the end of 1946, agreed to by the British Cabinet in all essential features, but it was declared, at the same time, that there would be no question of reaching any final decisions on the matters involved until all the interested communities in Malaya had had full and free opportunity of expressing their views. No doubt this provision was considered necessary, because only British and Malays were participants in drafting the Federation scheme. It had always been a guiding principle that the special position of the Malays should be safeguarded.

The Federation scheme provided for a Federal Executive Council and a Federal Legislative Council. Also, in each State, a State Executive Council and a Council of State with legislative powers, and, in each of the two Settlements (Penang and Malacca), a Settlement Council with legislative powers. In all, two Federal Councils, eighteen State Councils and two Settlement Councils. Twelve of these Councils were to be legislative bodies, making one more than existed in the same area before. Their powers would be different to those of the pre-war Councils, but the criticism which was made, that the proposals went back to the pre-1942 constitution, was not without some foundation.

Notable points in the plan were, that it did not exclude the possibility of other territories joining the Federation later, and that, while future elections were envisaged when they became practicable, the initial Members of the Councils would be appointed. The title of 'Governor' set up by the Malayan Union Act was to be replaced by that of 'High Commissioner'. The Malay Rulers were to undertake to accept the advice of the High Commissioner in all matters of government of the Federation except in matters concerning the Muslem Religion and the Custom of the Malays. The King was to have complete control of defence and external affairs.

In order to give effect to the undertaking to consult all interested communities, a Consultative Committee was set up immediately, under the Chairmanship of Mr. H. R. Cheeseman. That Committee offered to consider the opinions of all interested individuals, communities, bodies and groups, and, I imagine, all Mr. Cheeseman's outstanding ability and tact were called upon in implementing the offer.

The Federation proposals received immediate support from the United Malays National Organisation, whose representatives assisted in drafting them. Their acceptance, as a beginning, was also advocated by the *Straits Times*, the leading English newspaper in Malaya, and a few other representative bodies, here and there, may have approved them as they stood, or with minor qualifications. Those who approved, however, seemed much less numerous and less energetic than the opposition. The typewriter, used on the final draft, can scarcely have ceased to click, before opposition began to appear. The Malay Nationalist Party was first in the field with down right denunciation, thus splitting the Malay view. Shortly afterwards, a new body was formed which called itself the Pan-Malayan Council of Joint Action claiming to have as members, and to speak for, a large number of associations and groups of all nationalities in Malaya. The Council of Joint Action not only expressed outright objection to the proposals, but also boycotted the Consultative Committee. Various Chambers of Commerce and racial parties throughout the country declared opposition to the plan as a whole, or to certain parts of it. In the main, the objections appeared to be on the grounds that it was pre-1942 in conception and retrograde, that it was undemocratic and contrary to the Atlantic Charter and that Singapore should not be excluded from the Federation.

It was in connection with the last objection that the matter primarily affected Singapore. Although the Federation plan did not exclude the possibility of Singapore, and other territories, being incorporated later, that was not sufficient to satisfy many people. In the other parts of the old Straits Settlements and in Singapore itself, there was a strong reluctance to break the former ties between Penang, Malacca and Singapore. The Singapore

Association proposed far-reaching alterations to the plan, in addition to the immediate inclusion of the Island. It proposed that free trade should be adopted throughout the Federation and that the Federation (which should include Singapore) should form part of a Dominion of South-East Asia.

A word is necessary about the free trade suggestion. Singapore has always been a free port and, in consequence, has flourished exceedingly. It has always strongly opposed any attempts to alter its free port status, and so, appreciating that inclusion in the Federation would be unsatisfactory, so long as the two areas maintained different tariff policies, the Singapore Association naturally preferred that the Federation should make the change— that the tail should wag the dog. Tariffs on the mainland and free trade in Singapore was always an awkward arrangement. Prior to 1942, the Federated Malay States and each Unfederated State had their own customs, and a journey from one end of the country to the other involved passing through some half dozen custom barriers. If all the States on the Peninsula were federated, under the new plan, and Singapore excluded, one barrier would replace many, but that barrier would likely be more exacting than any single one of the previous lot, and behind it from the Singapore point of view would be Penang and Malacca, which previously had not been separated. Neither would it please everyone on the mainland, especially the people of South Johore, for whom Singapore had always been a shopping centre, because, instead of dealing with Johore State Customs for exports and imports, they would have to deal with a Federal organisation centred in Kuala Lumpur.

Strange as it might seem, it was not at all certain that the Peninsula wanted Singapore to be included. For more than a decade before the war, the tendency had been for

271

everything to be centralised in Singapore to the detriment of the Malay States, and, no doubt, many felt that, if the Federation included Singapore, the process would be continued and accelerated. Other big issues might also depend on whether or not Singapore ever came into the fold.

The Singapore Association also recommended the rejection of the citizenship idea, on the grounds that it might confer status on a number of people who would not have corresponding responsibilities. In its place, State and Settlement franchise was suggested, to be introduced in accordance with the ideas of each area. Criticism of the Federation plan, from other sources, was also directed against the failure to provide for immediate elections, and, on account of that failure, it was dubbed by some undemocratic.

All objections and proposals were doubtlessly considered by the Consultative Committee, but when its recommendations appeared in the spring of 1947, they contained nothing which might alter the plan fundamentally. The main recommendations were that the Federal Councils should be increased in size and that some modifications should be made to the residence and language qualifications for citizenship. The matter was again with the British Government for consideration during the following months and the approved constitution was published in a Command Paper in July. It was substantially the same as that originally proposed in 1946, modified slightly by the findings of the Consultative Committee. The Federation came into being on February 1st, 1948.

A first step towards introducing more democratic forms of Government had been taken when unofficial majorities were appointed to the Singapore and Union

Advisory Councils by the B.M.A., shortly after the liberation. The Advisory Councils were interim bodies, to be replaced, at latest, when the proposed constitutions crystallised. At least one body, the Singapore Ratepayers' Association, seemed to question the wisdom of that advance, for, in December 1946, its Committee expressed the opinion that it would be unwise for the Singapore Government to give up its official majority in the meantime.

The new right to vote is restricted to certain sections of the community and the system of elections has not yet been greatly tested. Elections for the Singapore Municipal Council were the first to be held followed, in 1948, by elections for the unofficial members of the Singapore Legislative Council. The Federation is likely to be well behind with elections to its Legislative Councils.

Democracy has not gone very far in Malaya up to the moment, and, seemingly, there is a long road to be traversed, before anything like popular government is attained over the whole country. Can it come about gradually and constitutionally is a question which must exercise many minds. On it I propose to speculate a little.

Tremendous political developments have taken place in the South and East of Asia during the last few years. Before the war, India, Ceylon, Burma, Malaya, all of the East Indies, Indo-China, Hong Kong and the Philippines were dependent territories, and only in the last was independence in sight. Now the position is very different. The Philippines have been a republic for some time, much of the East Indies has lately become a republic, with a slender Dutch link, India has been split into two independent countries which, though still members of the Commonwealth, are by no means committed to that connection for all time, Ceylon has self-government and

Burma is independent and outside the Commonwealth. Much blood has been spilt in Indo-China, where the urge to independence is exceedingly strong and everything indicates that, before long, she will be at least as independent of France as Indonesia is of Holland. Another break from western influence has been caused by the return to China of the International Settlement at Shanghai. In a few years' time, it is most unlikely that western powers will have any control anywhere in this great area, outside Hong Kong, Malaya and North Borneo. How long can control in these territories be maintained and what if it is not?

During the war, there were many rumours that Hong Kong would revert to China. Those rumours may have been quite unfounded, but I feel that its existence as a British colony is only possible because, in the unsettled state of China, the Chinese themselves, or certain influential elements of the Chinese population, wish to have it as a haven near at hand meantime. Unless there is an unlikely reversal of the trend in South East Asia, it is quite possible that Singapore may, sooner or later, find itself similarly an island haven close to a distracted and alien land. If it were to join the Federation, even that might be denied it.

Malaya is now surrounded on all sides by independent countries, India and Burma to the north-west, Indonesia to the west and south, Siam (and possibly before long Indo-China or Viet-Nam) to the north. China and Siberia are not very far away as Asiatic distances go. Among those countries, peoples are to be found with strong crusading qualities, when it comes to spreading political convictions, and it is anyone's guess how long the Malayan peoples can withstand their attacks or approaches. Some brisk action is necessary if it is to be for long.

The total population of Singapore as revealed by the 1947 census is 940,824. In round figures the numbers for the three largest communities are 115,800 Malays, 730,000 Chinese and 69,000 Indians. For the territories now making up the Federation, pre-war estimates were, 2,201,000 Malays, 1,799,000 Chinese and 684,000 Indians. From these figures, it will be seen that the Chinese far outnumber other races in the Colony, but are slightly less numerous than the Malays in the Federation. The Chinese and the Indians together exceed the Malays in the Federation, and over both areas the Chinese are the largest community, amounting to almost half of the total population.

Supposing, for a moment, that each racial community were united within itself, then, if any vital question was put to the vote and everyone had the right to vote, the Chinese could carry the day against all opposition in the Colony. In the Federation, the Malays could have their way if the opposition were split, but not if it were combined, and, in the areas taken together, the Chinese would have a majority over the Malays or Indians, but not over both. Should everyone in the country gain the right to vote, it is obvious that the Malays would be faced with a difficult problem in what must be considered their own country, but, on the whole, they would be better off if Singapore did not join the Federation.

The situation is much more complex than that, and, in some respects, better for the Malays. Under the present qualifications for citizenship, a far greater proportion of the Malays than of any other community gain the status, and their voting power on the Peninsula should far exceed that of the Chinese and Indians. The time might come, however, when that would no longer be the position and their political power (given peaceful conditions) would then depend on what legislation had been passed in the meantime, and how other races acquiesced in it. Alas, the Malays are not united, nor, for that matter, are the Chinese or Indians. The country is split, not into two camps, but into many.

The United Malays National Organisation, which supports the Federation, is opposed by the Malay Nationalist Party, and the two parties, in uncertain proportions, share Malay support. The latter is reputed to have communist leanings and has associated itself strongly with representative bodies from non-Malay races. The Chinese are split in their sympathies with the two great parties in China, the Kuomingtang and the Communists, and the Indians are divided into Muslims and Hindoos with all that that means. At least some section of each of these large racial groups is working toward the idea of an independent Malaya.

It is not surprising that, among Malays, there should be found people with that ambition. Under the Japanese, Malaya and Sumatra were administered as one political unit, and now the latter has, by action not divorced from violence, become republican. There are strong grounds for believing that Indonesia is playing a big part in Malay thought and it has been suggested that Indonesia not only trains some Malays for nationalist endeavour, but also sends its own experts to Malaya to further the cause. Many of the so-called Malays are themselves of Indonesian descent, and, apart from odd words and phrases, the two peoples speak the same language. There can be no doubt that an independence party in any eastern country will receive support, at least in some measure, from its neighbours. In January 1947, the Malay Nationalist Youth Corps (the A.P.I.) issued a statement which contained the following:

> "The A.P.I. is the spearhead of the national struggle for the independence and the freedom of Malaya. This struggle for the freedom of Malaya is inseparable from the struggle being waged by our Asian brothers in all Asian countries against imperialism for their national independence."

> "The A.P.I. therefore supports and welcomes the call of Sarat Chandra Bose for help for Viet-Nam in its fight for freedom."

The openly-avowed Chinese Communist Party in Malaya is obviously not in favour of retaining British rule, and it is difficult to imagine that any large section of the Indian community desires to see Britain predominate anywhere east of Suez.

These things will make it difficult for Britain to retain Malaya. The word 'retain' may suggest something beyond what I have in mind, for I imagine Britain would not wish to retain the country against its will, or to the extent of waging a colonial war. The legitimate will of Malaya must, however, for a long time, be particularly difficult to assess on account of its political immaturity, its illiteracy and its alien communities, some of which will no doubt shout loudly and wield influence without having any constitutional right to do so. It is Britain's declared intention to guide the colonies to self-government and to grant that, when they are ready for it. If a colony demands self-government and independence before it is ready, what happens? When is a colony ready? Is it ready when it is financially stable? When it can maintain law and order? When its people have the administrative and technical ability to man its services? By those tests, a number of countries now independent would, perhaps, fail to qualify. It seems to me that, in practice, a country gains independence when it shouts loud enough, makes enough trouble and succeeds in obtaining outside support.

If those things are really the preliminaries to independence, then Malaya is well equipped. In British territory, there is a maximum of free speech, and, in Malaya, there are those who know how to take advantage of that freedom. There are also those who do not hesitate to make use of the fact that the British are a tolerant race, slow to anger. In February 1947, some serious disturbances broke out in the Malay State of Kedah and the situation was so threatening that European women and children were evacuated from the State. On March 8th the London *Times* published an article from its special correspondent from which the following is an extract:

> *"Many Asiatics are contrasting its fear-laden atmosphere of to-day with the comparative security of life and property which prevailed during the Japanese régime. It is not possible for the British Administration to employ the summary (although effective) methods of the Japanese, but there is a widespread desire in the Union for the Government to take a much firmer line in restoring order."*

> *"This desire for strong action is by no means limited to British officials and planters and Asiatic property owners. It is wanted by at least 90 per cent of the Asiatic population, whose store of good will for the returning British administration has been steadily whittled down as much by the latter's failure to restore orderly conditions as by economic stringency."*

The Kedah incident was but a forerunner of the widespread and more serious lawlessness which burst upon the country in July 1948 and which, up to the time of writing, shows little sign of ending. Well-organised guerilla bands of bandits (they were at first called 'communists') have murdered and destroyed all over the Peninsula (Singapore has been immune)[15] since that date and all law-abiding people in isolated areas live in constant danger under terrific strain. Whether this vile campaign results from the lack of strong Government action earlier, whether it is a logical sequel of guerilla activity encouraged during the war, whether it is communist inspired or a part of the new found Asian nationalism, or a combination of all these, matters little. If it shows signs of coming out on top, there are plenty of people in Malaya, now sitting on the fence, who will flock to its banners. Should it succeed, and its triumph mean the end of British control, then nothing but chaos lies before the country for as long as can be foreseen. The withdrawal of Britain would be followed by endless and bloody warfare between the races and ideologies.

I think it true to say that the vast majority of the more responsible opinion among all communities in Malaya appreciates that the early withdrawal of Britain would be disastrous, but less responsible, near-sighted and self-interested communities will press for it and make much noise in the process. Eighty per cent of the country's population is almost equally divided between two very different races; one native to the soil and the other possessing most of its wealth and business ability. Surely, it will be only possible for such a country to qualify for self government when those two races have proved over a considerable period that they can work together for the good of the country, irrespective of race, colour, creed or

---

[15] Since this was written there have been a number of attacks in Singapore.

language. A start has been made but there is a long way to travel.

Should the bandits of the jungle or the political brigands gain the upper hand—and there will be plenty of outside help and encouragement for them–then indeed the outlook for Malaya will be black.

Mr. MacDonald was reported to have said, while in Canada at the end of 1946, that he estimated that the nine Malay States and two Settlements were half-way to self-government. One hundred and twenty-seven years of British rule have enabled half the road to be covered. The other half might well have been accomplished in a tenth of the time or less but for the mixed racial composition. As it is, the second half must be particularly difficult whether it be traversed over a long or a short period. The solution lies in Malay-Chinese harmony and co-operation in equal partnership. This is greatly to be desired but, though not impossible, it will make almost superhuman demands on both races. Failing that, Britain must remain or the country be given over to anarchy and ceaseless bloodshed. Perhaps there was some significance in the exclusion of Singapore from the Governor-General's estimate. It may be that in another decade or so, if we take the wrong way, only a few islands will be left to guard British and western interests in Asia, and even those will be precariously situated.

Asia has developed a strong national consciousness and she is determined that Europe and America will appreciate it, even if at times it be at the expense of her own and world interests. To that end she will exert great effort, much of which will be concentrated on eradicating western influence, wherever it is found in Asia. The first Asian Relations Conference was held at Delhi in March 1947 and was attended by representatives from twenty-four Asian countries. Pandit Nehru was Chairman of the Organising Committee, and India played a very large part throughout the Conference. The conference was declared to be non-political, but it is difficult to see how politics could have been avoided at such a conference, in the circumstances of the time. They will be equally difficult to avoid in the future, so long as there are dependent countries in Asia. Pandit Nehru was reported to have contributed an article to the *New York Times* not long before the conference in which he said: "the whole system known as colonialism has to go", and that must be in the mind of many Asians to-day. It is also worth noting that, at the conference, there were men from six Soviet republics.

The trend of affairs in Asia justifies much concern. Something like an iron curtain may develop there, behind which a block or blocks, of countries will resist western influence and western trade. Asian countries may ally themselves in all sorts of ways, for a variety of purposes, and divide the globe, even more than it is, into great areas mutually antagonistic, and miles apart in thought and aim.

* * * * *

Twenty odd years ago, I looked at an atlas to discover the exact geographical position of Singapore. I was not alone in my ignorance, for, when I got to Singapore shortly afterwards, I noticed that letters arrived there, addressed in a number of ways. It was not uncommon to pick up an envelope addressed to "Singapore, China", "Singapore, India", or "Singapore, F.M.S.", and at least one guesser tried "Singapore, Pacific Ocean". The correct form was, of course, "Singapore, Straits Settlements," but the average correspondent had other ideas. Now the Straits Settlements have ceased to exist, and I am not at all sure that one can substitute for "Straits Settlements" the word "Malaya" and receive the approval of purists. It is certainly unnecessary to put anything more on a letter than the one word "Singapore", for the Island has now, both literally and figuratively, a place in the sun, and no one is any longer in doubt as to where nature has put it.

In those good old days—I don't apologise for the expression, as it does not exclude the possibility of better days. Singapore was a happy place, clean, healthy, harmonious and prosperous, and—speaking of the Island —it had claims to a certain natural beauty. The people were smiling, friendly and generous and did not appear to think that they were being oppressed or exploited in any way. They were honest too. Nothing seemed to get stolen, though doors and windows, where they existed at all, remained almost permanently open, inviting, and, at most residences, unguarded. Freedom was in the air, if not on the statute-books, and I doubt if any comparable place on earth could have boasted more of it. Anyone, however lowly, did not hesitate to walk across your garden, or sit under your durian tree, without fear of reprimand, or earn it. Your goods and chattels were borrowed extensively throughout the neighbourhood without your knowledge, and always returned. The business community and shopkeepers trusted you and you trusted in return, and neither side was often let down. When anyone betrayed that trust, he became an outlaw. You could depend on man's humanity to man, and you could even be excused for wondering if further progress on the lines of civilisation's text-book had anything much to offer.

In those good old days, the face of nature had not been greatly disturbed outside the town. There were no airfields, no Naval Base and no ribbon development. The narrow, red, restful roads timidly opening the east and west areas of the Island, penetrated luscious foliage to reach secluded spots, and the main road north to the Peninsula, more pretentious with its asphalted surface, but little wider, wound around the spurs of hills, on a track dictated by the limitations of sauntering bullock-carts. There were unfrequented places to explore, nooks and crannies to hide in, wild fruits for the picking, and much that town-tired men could rejoice at. Sea and jungle, the birth rights of every Malayan island, were yet unsold.

The intervening years have brought change. Much of the harmony, the trust, the tolerance and the beauty have gone, and in their place has come a greater degree of world importance and an awakened political consciousness. That inevitable exchange will inevitably seem to some a loss, to others a gain. In the new Singapore, as I went around, it did not appear to me that the people were any better off, and, certainly, they were not happier. In the town, it was difficult to be persuaded that living conditions had improved, in spite of all which I knew had been done. There were, it's true, more paved streets and back lanes, more modern sanitation, and, here and there, good buildings stood where slums had once been. Even those things were not all net gain, for slums and filth had found abiding places further out at the expense of nature. The little red, laterite roads had acquired fringes of ugly and rickety buildings, and bore, on their now black surfaces, a volume of traffic out of all proportion to their design. The road to the mainland had become a wide speedway, over which streams of vehicles rushed each way, day and night, and around which industry and commerce had entrenched. The beauty and the peace of the Island had fallen sacrifice to its trade and military importance.

Loss or gain, inevitable or deliberate, the transformation could not be accepted without moments of nostalgia for the first Singapore I had known. Sentimentally and unashamed, I occasionally sought a spot—there were a few left—which had changed little and where the days that were dead could be resurrected temporarily. One such place was the Government Bungalow at Changi. The approach to it had become repulsive, but once inside the compound, it was easy to forget twenty years. There I could see in miniature most of what was worth seeing in Malaya, and submit to the charm, which had, through the years, held so many captive.

The old-type wooden bungalow, with its red roof of Chinese tiles, was raised well above the ground. A flight of steps gave access through a swing gate to the broad open verandah, running the full width of the building and commanding a view on three sides. Low balustrades skirted the edges and rolled chicks hung from the deep eaves, ready to be lowered against the monsoon which might blow up in the twinkling of an eye. Spider-like fans hung by long iron threads from the ceiling, prepared to circulate the air around easy cane chairs which invited sun-soaked bodies to recline and order a long cold drink to be placed on the little table near-by. Further back were the bedrooms, austere and cool, boasting little more than a bed and an almeirah, but each possessing its own verandah, from where descent could be made to a bathroom on ground level, which, although a shower replaced the time-honoured Shanghai jar and dipper, was still of true Malayan vintage.

The early morning and the evening hours, just before sun down, were the best times to appreciate tropical Singapore and that particular part of it. The bungalow stood on a gentle slope, overlooking the Johore Straits, and at dawn, from the verandah, I could not fail to be overwhelmed by the beauty uncovered and gilt before me, as the sun rose from the sea with its dazzling white and gold of indescribable brilliance. New-born, sunlit and lovely the light-blue sky with minute puffs of snow-white cloud challenged the deep-blue sea with minute specks of snow white foam. Light-green islands in the Straits merged with the dark-green background of the mainland, and that dark-green changed to slate-blue on the more distant hills. Little grey white pockets of mist stuck tenaciously to the valleys, or, if dislodged, wandered with diminishing volume among the taller trees. Dew glistened like a million diamonds on the long blades of lalang in the compound and washed the leaves of the jungle trees on either side to a brighter hue, before it evaporated.

Although neglected for a long time, the compound at my feet was a riot of colour. Ordinary Malayan flowers and trees produced that colour, and, all the year round, the almost seasonless climate had a store of bloom ready to replenish any loss. Pink and mauve bougainvillea pressed against the verandah in enormous clusters, yellow alamanda, pink hibiscus and blue jacaranda lined the overgrown paths, red and yellow cannas and white and pink-mauve orchids, once carefully planted, had lost their red-earth beds and nestled down amid the rank, green grass with heightened effect. Pink honolulu and the diurnal, deep-purple morning glory hung from any and every convenient branch. Scattered about the compound at random, a drooping cassia wept yellow tears, a flamboyant flame-of-the-forest made a tent of scarlet fire, a great spathodia opened its flame-red trumpets to the sky, and a coconut palm pursued its useful life in isolated starkness. Other palms were there too, a royal palm looking truly regal, a sealing wax palm glorying in its red and spineless stems, and a traveller's palm, so exotic with its open fan that newcomers refused to believe that it was nature's unaided handiwork. High in the air, belying the stillness of the morning, feathery casuarinas waved gently in a breeze, which brought to the nostrils the smells of sea-salt, heavily-perfumed frangipanni and delicately-scented tembusu. Although birds were everywhere and the air full of song, my eye refused for long to leave the golden orioles, whose exquisite colouring added the last touch to an unforgettable experience.

The hot day gone, the sun declined with all the splendour of a tropical sunset. The compound and the sea lost their colours, or lent them to the sky for the last minutes of daylight. The heavens were filled with rapidly changing colours—blue, green, yellow, flame and a deep, deep red. It took but a few moments to paint immeasurable areas and again wipe out the pigments. The sun left Singapore for another twelve hours, and, in the ten-minute twilight, there was just time to see the flying-fox and the sea-hawk overhead, the Chinese junk with brown sails spread to the evening breeze of the Straits and the Malay fishermen paddling out to their night on the keylongs. When I walked back, in gathering darkness, from the swimming pagar to the bungalow, the warm air was filled with the shrill calls of cicadas, and, on the verandah ceiling, chechaks chirped in love or in anger. Around the old building, which had moulded itself into a perfect setting, Malays, Chinese and Indians squatted in little family gatherings, and engaged, with different languages, in endless streams of laughing talk.

Those sights and sounds were the things, which, in the past, captured the loyalties and affections of people from many lands, who must always hope that, in a changing and uncertain world, the green Island will regain the beauty, humour and harmony it once knew.

~

Oswald Wellington Gilmour

ABOUT THE AUTHOR

Oswald Wellington Gilmour (1900–1978) was born in the town of Ballymena, County Antrim, (now) Northern Ireland on the 3rd June 1900. Before the war, he worked in Singapore, and in 1940, he was given a command post in the Civil Defense Organization and was one of the last to leave the invaded city during the Japanese invasion of 1942. After a series of adventures, he reached Ceylon (Sri Lanka)—a journey described in his book, *Singapore to Freedom* (1943).

Returning to England in 1942, he joined the Malaysian Planning Unit set up by the War Office to plan for the reoccupation. By September, 1945, he was back in Singapore directing its engineering services. He stayed on for a time as Acting Municipal Engineer under civil government, writing about his experiences in this book (*With Freedom to Singapore* (1950)).

Colonel Gilmour—a rank he received for his war-time work—eventually returned to the United Kingdom to take up an engineering appointment on the constructional side of a large postwar town project. He died in the town of Harlow, Essex, United Kingdom on the 19th August 1978.

Dust Jacket of the 1950 first edition of
With Freedom to Singapore *(rear)*

Dust Jacket of the 1950 first edition of
With Freedom to Singapore *(spine/front)*